D0775453

THE
HEALING
SPIRIT

THE HEALING SPIRIT

Explorations in Religion and Psychotherapy

Paul R. Fleischman, M.D.

BONNE CHANCE PRESS

BONNE CHANCE PRESS EDITION, 1994

Published in the United States by

Bonne Chance Press
209 River Bluff Road
Cleveland, SC 29635

Copyright © 1989 by Paul R. Fleischman
All rights reserved. No part of this book may be reproduced,
in any form, without written permission from the publisher,
unless by a reviewer who wishes to quote brief passages.

Originally published as The Healing Zone: Religious Issues
in Psychotherapy by Paragon House in 1989
Published under present title in a paperback edition
by Paragon House in 1990

Library of Congress Cataloging-in-Publication Data

Fleischman, Paul R.
[Healing zone]
The healing spirit: explorations in religion and
psychotherapy / Paul R. Fleischman.—2nd paperback ed.
p. cm.
Previously published as: The healing zone. 1989.
Includes bibliographical references.
ISBN 1-55778-334-90 : $13.95
1. Psychology, Religious. 2. Psychotherapy—Religious
aspects. I. Title.
[BL53.F46 1990]
291.1'75—dc20   90-35390
CIP

Manufactured in the United States of America
10 9 8 7 6 5 4 3 2

To Susan

"Early in the day it was whispered that we should sail in a boat, only thou and I, and never a soul in the world would know of this pilgrimage to no country and to no end."

—Rabindranath Tagore,
Gitanjali, poem no. 42.

And to Forrest

"When I bring to you colored toys my child, I understand why there is such a play of colors on clouds, on water, and why flowers are painted in tints . . ."

—Rabindranath Tagore,
Gitanjali, poem no. 62.

Contents

Acknowledgments

The Department of Psychiatry at Yale University School of Medicine gave me shelter. Drs. Stanley Jackson and George Mahl, former teachers and senior colleagues who guided me into my profession years ago, also read and vigorously commented on earlier drafts of this book. Dr. Jim Phillips has kept me tuned to the humanness and indeterminacy of psychiatry, to the breadth of relevant literature, and to the fecundity of professional friendship. The seminar on Psychiatry and Religion and its participants provided me many occasions and conversations.

Dr. Stephen Dashef provided helpful commentary on earlier drafts, and contributed a case study to Chapter X.

Ira Sharkey exemplified friendship with his thoughtful encouragement.

I am indebted to Makarand Dave for deepening my exposure to religious literature, and for providing a mooring on the new shore. The late Juan Mascaró reached out with his message; he and Kathleen Mascaró faithfully welcomed me home so many decades later; his reverence for words remains my example. Koshi Ichida provided timeless friendship, deep insight beyond words. To S.N. Goenkaji I am profoundly indebted for living transmission of universal truth.

To many others, whom the confidentiality of my work prevents me from naming, I am indebted, for using me so well, and for working with me in vital truth.

Susan Fleischman provided endlessly receptive listening and perfect pitch for the ring of authenticity in the human story.

Karen Thatcher provided impeccable technical assistance.

Preface

How can religion be the origin of healing, soothing, care-taking forces, and at the same time the source of cruel, violent, destructive hatreds? How does religion, this vast, history-forging zone, appear in the lives of individuals who are seen through the close-up lens of psychotherapy? Psychologically speaking, is religion one or many, diverse arenas, inappropriately categorized under one word?

These questions are close to the core of my life and work. To study them, I have balanced myself with the tripod of individual experience,[1] of studying and teaching the literature on psychiatry and religion in conjunction with my seminar on their interface in the School of Medicine at Yale University, and of practicing clinical psychiatry. My interest in this area has stirred up its own response. Patients have come to me, or have been referred to me, in the expectation that I might be particularly helpful in shedding light on their religious backgrounds, their current affiliations, disaffiliations, beliefs, or despairs. Of course, for many people, psychotherapy is not primarily concerned with this arena, but my caseload has tilted in the direction of religious issues, giving me greater opportunity to study them. But whether religion is clearly labelled or not, I have sought for the zone, the node, the point of origin, the moment of bifurcation where the uniform impulse we call religion emerges and takes its various saintly or demoniac forms. Hypothesizing, searching for, perceiving, and understanding this choice point has touched my clinical work significantly, changing what I hear, how I think, and what I say or do to help people. This activity occurs within the matrix of standardizable, communicable, and broad-based psychodynamic psychotherapy. Many patients can be treated without an overt discussion of religious issues—I have nothing to say about rules, certainties, schools of thought, shortcuts, or cures. On the contrary, I mean only to highlight another of the questions about human life, concurrent with the psychological treatment of individual illness. My study is to observe and understand how the threads of religious issues are woven into the fabrics of suffering, healing, and health, and not to explain away or reduce one aspect of life to another.

Introduction

Religion can be approached and understood as one aspect of personality. At the psychological level, religion can be defined as an encompassing sense of life's dimensions, meanings, purposes, and ordering forces, coupled to the sense of one's own particular locus within that totality. "Religion is an experience of existence in totality . . . and the exemplary solution of every existential crisis."[1] This is the conclusion of Mircea Eliade, the great historian of comparative religion. From this viewpoint, religion is not merely an institutional affiliation, but it is a structural aspect of personality. It differs from our philosophical self in that it seeks to *discover* meanings, not to create them; and it differs from our scientific self in that it seeks to discover *meanings,* not causal forces. Seen from the standpoint of psychology, religion refers to those overt and covert aspects of personality in which there is a questioning drive, a quest, to relate meaningfully the particular to the whole. When William James sought for the common psychological base to all the varieties of religious experience, he wrote: "Religion is man's total reaction upon life . . . the completest of all our answers to the question, 'What is the character of this universe in which we dwell?' "[2]

With James's question in mind, we understand that each person has some religious life, and psychotherapy is replete with religious issues. Of course, religion can also be understood from the theological, liturgical, political, economic, anthropological, sociological, and other points of view that cannot immediately facilitate individual psychotherapy. Conversely, a dynamic psychotherapist cannot settle for the face value of statements; institutional, denominational, liturgical, and sectarian statements may dynamically contain other issues, while comments from other realms of life may encompass religious concerns. I hope to demonstrate both religious themes in apparently secular material, and psychological dimensions in doctrinal positions. This can be done only by going to a fundamental psychological level that asks, what, essentially, is religion? It has been my observation that both non-religious material and denominational statements may come early in therapy, but that true religious issues, as I have come to understand them, tend to belong to the later, deeper stages of long-term individual psychotherapy. Not every patient will, or needs to, get there. But every psychotherapy that is embracing, exploratory, and personality transforming (as opposed to limited, specific, and situationally helpful) will probe this religious substratum. By elucidating the core building blocks of religion, I will be able to open up a channel to religious concerns widespread in the ordinary, everyday, private struggles that bring patients to therapy.

I will describe ten religious issues, ten elements of religious psychology, that are heard during the practice of psychotherapy. Each element is both psychological and religious; that is, each can be understood from a standpoint that validates both perspectives. It is the combination of these ten elements, I believe, that forms the active, complex, compound of religion. I intend to create a matrix of understanding and action for clinicians that is neither blithely sanctifying nor cynically reductionistic. I hope to be complete, so that every major religious phenomenon that engages our work as psychotherapists is contained in these ten issues. While I intend the whole of religious psychology to be present, the ten themes do overlap, blend, or articulate like body parts. Rather than forming tight, exclusive compartments, these themes move easily and fluidly into each other, to create a functioning psychological anatomy.

Each issue represents a need, a problem, a dilemma in human life that requires a solution; and the listening psychotherapist, who in his or her own life has to deal with the same issue, must avoid both poles of imposition and reduction. This aspect of the psychotherapeutic task consists of listening to, confronting, clarifying, and interpreting origins, internal relations with other aspects of the self, and interpersonal aspects of religious issues. This must be done without imposing one's own questions and solutions or reducing this realm of the patient's life to some other, and thereby disqualifying or eliminating it from further therapeutic exploration. Each theme, as it actually emerges in an ongoing psychotherapy, can be heard as an idiosyncratic, personal, developmental aspect of a universal human problem, which in any one instance may be integrated with, or split off from, healthy or sick modes of being a person.

In the case examples that I will describe, I will compress and linearize, so that lengthy, multifaceted human stories and psychotherapies can be used to illuminate particular issues. I will lop off many of the branches encountered in the work to expose the trunk. All of the examples come from adult outpatient psychotherapy. The cases are all true, in the sense that their human essence is something I heard and participated in during the practice of psychotherapy. The cases are fiction in the sense that the particular person I describe does not and has

3

never existed. Since the themes I am writing about are scientific discoveries—general rules about religious psychology that have been abstracted from aggregated data—they recur repeatedly in many human stories. I haven't written about a religious issue that isn't common to many psychotherapies. The case examples are true fictions, in which real issues that confront many patients are presented as occurrences in the lives of a composite image. Patients may recognize their own words in the mouth of someone entirely different from themselves, and people I have never met may also hear their own words and find moments of their own lives apparently described. No one real person is presented in any case, but every detail is true. Each one of us, I hope, is revealed.

The way we meet our religious needs may facilitate, pervert, or actualize our lives. I hope to elucidate how religion, which Jung called the "zone of world-destroying and world-creating fire,"³ can be both healing and destructive. I will describe religion as a circle with ten segments forming a whole and containing: witnessed significance, lawful order, affirming acceptance, a calling, membership, release, a worldview, human love, sacrifice, and meaningful death.

◇ 1 ◇

Witnessed Significance

... I was seen and known, heart and soul, and in the same way knew those who circled me ...

A graduate student became increasingly frantic over his inability to complete his long-delayed dissertation. He read voluminously, wrote hundreds of pages of notes that he soon felt to be useless, stuck himself in front of his typewriter like a slave and slave driver, obsessed, desperate, exhausted, unable to eat. His dissertation advisor referred him to me. He described a crescendo of travels, writing, brief romances, and confusion wherever he turned. He was clinically depressed: tearful, sleepless, underweight, distraught. The only clarity to his life was his motive force: he felt an absolute necessity to transcend what he perceived to be his parents' grey, meaningless, impotent anonymity in the blue-collar neighborhood of a small, Southern industrial city, by writing a world-transforming work that would make him famous. This breathless longing for quick, irrevocable fame was an internal fire consuming him.

His parents had belonged to a small, Southern Christian sect. Their church was a wooden building "on the wrong side of the tracks." When he went to school, he felt the Baptists, the Episcopalians, the members of real churches were real people—rich or poor, they sang with one voice, spoke about this tangible world. But his parents' little church seemed to him to be a madhouse in a blind alley. There, semiliterate, frustrated laborers went to services *daily,* working themselves into a lather of excitement to relieve their drab, failed lives. Every day of the week, the preacher exhorted preparation for the day of judgment. The only salvation was public protestation of faith and public repentance. The willing congregation would sing and yell in a chaotic frenzy of passion and desperation. Some would race about over the backs of pews, defying gravity and safety for salvation; others would fall to the floor, thrashing, spouting gibberish, talking in tongues. The task of every individual in that church was to give up his own will, to surrender, and repent. The graduate student had never been able to do that or believe that. In disgust, in fear, with pride and guilt, he stood apart from his parents, their church, their image of God; he felt planted, rooted, stuck in himself.

By the age of twelve, on the pretext of superior Bible study classes, a pretext his parents couldn't challenge, he had joined the Episcopal Church, leaving his family behind, and launched himself on his literate, verbal, scholarly career. High school teachers fathered along his independent, thoughtful mind. By the time he reached college he was a modern atheist scholar, brilliant in seminars, the center of attention with his cynical derision. He started graduate school with fanfares and fellowships and arrogance, then stalled and came to a standstill.

The initial focus for psychotherapy was to ease his grandiose strivings. He domineered in every colloquium, aggressively challenged every guest lecturer. He pushed his way onto panels at professional conferences, and elicited praise from his senior department members. But, in fact, he doubted that anyone was listening. He felt alone in a fraudulent universe in which everyone prayed and no one responded. He felt a false reception everywhere—in the pious smile of his parents' congregation that he felt only wanted to break, tame, humble, and destroy his mind, and in the quick accolades of academia, where his "tongue" was applauded, but he was lonely, from the wrong side of the tracks, unknown as a person.

He came to therapy sessions late, argued about the fee, wrote long letters to me to avoid full expression of himself during the sessions themselves, tested and checked his therapist's care and attention. After a number of months he began to weep.

Patients will talk about the need to be seen, known, responded to, confirmed, appreciated, cared for, mirrored, recognized, identified. This need is prototypically fulfilled by parents, and by the nurturing strata of society—grandparents, teachers, doctors, priests. It corresponds to the needs written about as "early infantile narcissism" in psychoanalytical writing.[1] The need is universal. Depending upon the vicissitudes in any one individual's life, fulfillment may be sought in aching and raging desperation, or in calm and confident relatedness, but the need is more than a childhood deficiency helped by soothing or holding. I call this need: witnessed significance.

The need for each individual to feel a sense of witnessed significance for his or her life has traditionally been noticed and responded to by religion. This is the essence of the Psalms: "Hear my prayer, O Lord, and let my cry come unto thee."[2] So, many Psalms begin as number 101 does. Psalm 141 is even more poignant and instructive: "I cried unto the Lord with my voice . . . I make my supplication . . . I poured out my complaint before him . . . When my spirit was overwhelmed within me, then Thou knewest my path . . . I looked on my right hand, and beheld, but there was no man that would know me: refuge failed me; no man cared for my soul . . . I cried unto thee, O Lord: I said, thou art my refuge . . . Attend unto my cry . . . bring my soul out of prison . . ."[3] In this chilling outpouring, we can hear the ancient author cry from an eternal pain. No man would know him; no man would care for his real self, his soul. He yearns for, postulates, relates to a transcendent being, who, in this Psalm, is not a God of justice, or revenge, or creation, but a God of listening. He is praying to a God who will attend. Only such a God can end the psalmist's sense of being in the prison of unreality that encloses the person who feels unknown, uncared for, and unheard.

The Bhagavad Gita—an ancient Sanskrit text of enduring popularity and importance in India, widely called "The Hindu Bible,"—assures its devotees: "I am the Father of this universe . . . thy friend, thy shelter . . . and the Master who watches in silence."[4] The Koran reiterates recurrently: "He knows the thoughts within the breasts. God is all-hearing, all-seeing, God keeps a watchful count over everything . . ."[5] Jesus preached: "Ask, and it shall be given you; seek, and ye shall find . . . till heaven and earth pass, one jot or one tithe shall in no wise pass . . . There is nothing covered that shall not be revealed . . . Every idle word that men speak, they shall give account thereof in the day of judgment."[6]

The scriptures reassure us that we are being watched, seen, known, taken seriously, and cared for. They break open the clouds of loneliness to reveal the heaven of constant attention. In religions that offer no father in heaven, there may be a belief that the Guru can know his disciples' hearts, or read their thoughts. Psychoanalysis has been considered by some of its critics to be a religion,[7] and, whether that is accurate or not, it surely contains this one religious element: the years of spontaneous confession available through free association to an attentive listener provide the sense that one's inner life is of interest, importance, and significance.

Religious ritual and magic are different from each other in critical ways: ritual is symbolic and expressive; magic is inaccurately instrumental, superstitious. Yet both owe part of their pervasiveness and importance to the drive for witnessed

8

significance. Both enable participants to transcend the incomprehensible impersonality of the universe and to feel infinitely important eyes turned upon them. In magic the participants feel the levers and wedges, the gods and their realms, attend to them, obey them. The goal may be partly to have power and control, but it is also to be noticed, known, and taken into account.

In rituals that are not intended to coerce God or the gods, but to artfully evoke profound emotions and experiences, there is a sense of mutual witness among the participants, or witness by a free, higher eye. Not a hut in India, not a hogan in Arizona, not a camp on the Sahara, but the people within evoke and feel the watchful presence of someone who will monitor their thoughts, and guide their hands and eyes so that they do something of great importance correctly—to see that they do not live alone.

This need for witnessed significance may deteriorate into a fusion with an imaginary, omniscient, anthropomorphic delusion. Psychotic individuals and many religious sects imagine themselves to be under the continuous scrutiny of a "wise old man in the sky." The graduate student mentioned in the example above grew up in a world where this delusion was the norm.

At a slightly less concrete level, the need for witnessed significance may exist in the form of grandiose self-importance, coupled to a desperate drive for acclaim. Here significance is attained not by recognition from a concerned human-in-the-sky, but by standing away from, above and beyond the rest of humanity, who are expected to witness this rise above the common lot with admiration and awe. This perversion of the need for witnessed significance typifies manic and narcissistic self-inflation. The individual imagines himself or herself at the focal point of all humanity. The graduate student was verging on this state.

A sense of witnessed significance can also be obtained by submersion into the human mass, which is then elevated to a

9

transcendent scale of importance. Charismatic religious movements and Fascism share these psychological tools of group rallies and marches and public protestations of faith, which are meant to replace feelings of insignificance and impersonality. This form of search for witnessed significance may well explain the emotional power of the modern media, with their aspects of worldwide witness. We can also look here for at least one explanation of why out-groups, political and religious minorities, and neglected social fragments frequently turn to religious fanaticism to satisfy one of their fundamental needs. The fantasy of being the favored intimates of a divine eye provides the very ingredient that their normal lives lack. Their sense of loneliness and neglect can be reversed by the special attention and focal importance of religious imagery. Similar are the isolated murderers who stalk famous politicians and other celebrities, seeking notoriety at any cost. They may also be desperate to balance the essential human equation of witnessed significance. To these isolates, being placed on television before the eyes of millions is worth more than life itself.

The psychiatrist will frequently see patients who seem driven by the need for attention. In one instance, a man will move from woman to woman, through several girlfriends or divorces, constantly hurt and angered that his female friends never seem to care enough. In another instance, a woman will trip up, irritate, or offend her husband continuously, making herself the lightning rod for his frustration and anger. Others will seek out attention from doctors, tests, and hospitals. Others will threaten suicide, rush away dramatically, only to return and threaten again and again. Of the multiple variations of wishes, fears, hopes, experiences, and dreams that may contribute to these dilemmas, one is the wish to hold center stage to watchful eyes. The need for witnessed significance may be sought through infantile dependence on the expression of approval and affirmation of a particular other person. Here a spouse or a physician is expected to play the role that the God of the Psalms, Koran, or Bhagavad Gita plays for His respective devotees. A distortion of the need for witnessed significance can contribute to pathological masochism and dependence. When authentic significance seems unattainable to the broken soul, the illusion of significance may come from another person, or even from a fantasy person.

At its extreme, this dependent mode of the search for witnessed significance deteriorates into the heightened self-reference of psychosis. Then a mixture of delight and terror accompanies the imagined creation of a world in which one person is at the center, and every event is a sign that points towards the self. ". . . The suspicion or possibility of relevance soon proceeds to the 'idea of reference,' perhaps the cardinal characteristic of psychotic experience . . . Everything experienced is measured as to its possible relevance for the individual."[8]

But this need for witnessed significance, whose developmental nucleus we can feel in the preschooler's urgent demand on his mother and father: "Watch me!" is also a precursor for art, literature, honest communication, and trusting confidence. It is not merely a psychotic, grandiose, narcissistic, exhibitionistic, or dependent urging, but it provides the impetus for deep, rich, and full human communication. It lies beneath the poetry of the Psalms and all those artful symbols of the soul in which one heart is bared to others, or to heaven. It is the drive behind social communication at the level of ultimate meanings.

A moving example of both the need for witnessed significance in a robustly healthy soul, and the catalytic role this need can play in the generation of culture, can be found at a seminal juncture in the history of psychiatry. Here we can see knowledge, ideas, values, moving into new spaces opened up by lines of force extending from this need. Heinrich Zimmer, the preeminent student of India in the twentieth-century Western world, wrote:

> Now, after his long collaboration with Richard Wilhelm on Chinese wisdom, Jung was ready to take over similar stuff from Indic scholars . . . I introduced myself with a lecture on types of Yoga . . . from that time on I had lectures every year . . . [at many Jung clubs throughout Europe] . . . the good fortune to have Jung among those who were interested in the things I had to offer constituted one of the principal elements in the next six years which I permitted myself to spend on the continent in spite of ever-increasing pressure and peril from the Nazi regime . . . in the concentration camp which Germany was to become in this period. You cannot just talk to the stars or to the silence of the night. You have to fancy some listener, or, better yet, to know of somebody whose mere existence stimulates you to talk and lends wings to your thoughts, whose nature sets a measure to your undertaking . . . the mere existence of Jung . . . the mere fact that nature allowed this unique mountainous example of the human species to come into existence was, and is, one of the major blessings of my spiritual and my very earthly life, one of those gifts of life, not to be imagined or prayed for, but showered upon you as a secret compensation by a generous Providence.[9]

In response to his new audience, Zimmer stopped addressing his writing to German technical Sanskrit scholars and wrote instead to a worldwide audience.[10] Through Zimmer, Jung learned about mandalas and the concept of the Self, two Indian ideas that he turned into cornerstones of his analytical psychology.[11]

The need for witnessed significance may lead to productive, creative, quests for the right colleagues, the right scholarly or literary audience. It may also be the force that impels autobiography. Of course, autobiography is by no means limited to spiritual confessions, but this specific genre exposes not only the drive to witnessed significance, but it also reveals one of the creative, religious fruits of the drive. Consider St. Augustine's

Confessions,[12] or Gandhi's *The Story of My Experiments With Truth*.[13] In these and other autobiographies of great religious figures, we can find one of the hallmarks of their lifework: the ability to invest apparently insignificant and personal details of their lives with a sense of universal significance, to feel every ordinary moment swell with the discovery of the universal goals of love and reason.[14] As does a psychotic, these religious autobiographers and great founders see meaningfully pregnant signs everywhere—but unlike the psychotic, they see also that the same signs are intended for all humankind.

Gandhi's famous "conversion" is an example.[15] He was thrown off a train in South Africa a few days after his arrival there in the 1890s, because he insisted on sitting in the "white" compartment, even though he was a "coolie," the South African designation for an Indian. That he was an English-trained lawyer made no difference to the trainman. Gandhi describes sitting totally alone, in the dark and cold, surrounded by his bags, at the unknown train station. Up to that moment he had been hesitant and self-doubting—his life and abilities seemed of no significance. He wasn't true to his Indian heritage; he was an imitation Englishman. He was a role-less, identity-less isolate. But when a racist had the arrogance to treat him as insignificant, a chord deep in him rebelled. Gandhi understood his plight, as a victim of discrimination, to be one common to his people. Suddenly, his own feelings stood for those of millions. In the pit of helpless, despairing, impotent insignificance, he discovered his significance. His personal feelings weren't the idiosyncratic reactions of one "imitation" Englishman; they were the wellspring of his people's liberty. He decided he was the only one who could address racial injustice in South Africa. He not only fought, but he publicized his fight, making public opinion his witness and his tool. He commanded attention on the world stage he strode for more than forty years not only because of his legal brilliance and his moral stature, but also because of the torrent of writing and attention-focusing, symbolic actions with which he insisted and intruded his significance before the eyes of the world.

Just as his plight of insignificance had been his peoples', now his every act stood for the history of a large segment of humankind. Eventually, when he became the leader of the Indian Independence movement, he would feel the eyes of the world upon his every step and gesture (as when he took his Salt March), and on every sip and bite (in his numerous life-or-death fasts). His capacity to turn ordinary motions, like picking up a pinch of salt on a beach, into dramas of freedom was a central feature of his charisma and represented the penultimate elaboration of the drive to witnessed significance. On one level, we can imagine he was compulsively undoing the humiliation of being totally abandoned, outcast, alone, and insignificant. But on another level, we can observe a religious talent skillfully wielding one of religion's ancient and universal tools: the transformation of anonymous lives into lives of participation in acts of public, historical, and religious significance. What Gandhi did, a mass then did. He and then they were seen and counted. Each small sacrifice was part of the ultimate one. He provided this sacrament for himself and a nation.

The yearning for witnessed significance can mature in ordinary lives into the quest for deeper self-knowledge followed by mutuality of knowing, "mutual recognition,"[16] and for courageous self-expression. The powers of art in general, and of words in particular, spring from this need and its resolution. Through words we can elevate what is innermost and disperse it before the eyes of an infinite chain of witnesses.

The creation of a logos through community represents the culmination of this need.[17] The seminal confirmation of reality available through words is at the core of the "talking cure"—Freud's term for psychoanalysis—and also the Biblical assertion, "In the beginning was the Word."[18] Being known and knowing are essential human needs. The need for knowing to matter, to have meaning, to have presence and resonance in the creation, is one of the building blocks of religious life. "He wants to be heard by the nameless, unconceived, inconceivable other, by whom he wants to be understood in his having understood."[19] In this way human life is led to the revelation of the heart.

The graduate student mentioned above was blocked in his work both by psychopathological grandiosity and void-like isolation. Because of his agitated depression, which was severe enough to require antidepressant medication, and his grandiose qualities, I had to constantly keep in mind the possibility of a biologically based mood disorder—in other words, his grandiosity may have been a manic pole of a bipolar mood disorder. He certainly had a narcissistic character disorder when I met him—unable to maintain or nurture friendships or intimacies, sexually frustrated, slaking his interpersonal needs in fantasies of future fame and acclaim, while devaluing everyone around him, giving vent to temper tantrums, and occasionally stealing because he felt he was poor and deserved more. I had to hold tightly to therapeutic boundaries, insisting recurrently on the integrity of time limits and fees. I had to rebalance myself continuously to confront his smug contempt in the transference and to nurture his wounded, skeptical, frightened self.

Along with the biological treatment of his depression and the psychological treatment of his narcissism, there was another aspect to the therapy. I imagined I saw in his striving for literary and intellectual genius a core of health, a drive for witnessed significance that was elevating, constructive, and sparing.

He had grown up in a home of chronic depression and fundamentalism. His demoralized father, easing himself down in front of the T.V., barely noticed him, and had reduced his advice to his son to: "Obey the foreman, and pray to God." What little attention his mother could spare for her children went towards his sister, with her church-sanctioned dates and boyfriends. He had felt trapped incognito in a hidden pocket beneath the universe. His blocked dissertation topic was little more than an understandable, yet unshapable, adolescent diatribe against fundamentalism.

To work with his sense of witnessed significance, I had to take several steps. Initially, I had to hear what he was talking about. I had to separate his concern for witnessed significance from the narcissistic issues with which he entangled it. As my own thoughts became relatively clear in this often murky area, I attempted to translate back to him this distinction and its importance.

For example, as a result of my interpretations, he had come to see that underneath some of his academic drive was his need to achieve recognition in order to compensate for the neglect he had felt at home. But he heard my interpretations in his own way, and he soon began to doubt the validity of all of his career ambitions. He discussed whether he might not find more security, and money and status too, by going to law school. He thought pursuit of a law degree would be less driven by his exhibitionism. I neither agreed nor disagreed. I felt he was giving a reductionistic and self-punitive distortion to my words, but instead of analyzing that, I urged him to discuss more and explore further what underlay his desire to write. As he unravelled motives, memories, and images, I clarified that these seemed of varying significance. Some were based on fantasies of retaliatory dominance over his parents and their congregation. Some were grandiose compensation for his sense of helplessness and insignificance. Others sprang from a sense of justice. Still others, it seemed to me, expressed his yearning to use his newly congealing adult powers to speak forcefully to other intellectuals about what he knew and felt.

He was unable to respond verbally to my clarifications. He kept shifting his putative career plans as he attempted to decipher which side I was on and to please me by obeying.

Apparently moving away from witnessed significance, I commented that his yearning to use me as an approving father made him lose sight of his own goals. He replied directly with a flood of excited gratitude. Never before had he felt someone listen to him so attentively, care about him so overtly. Through therapy, with its mixture of nurturant attention and confrontation of the contempt he generalized out from his parents onto everyone, he began to feel that somebody cared, saw, noticed, and was there to respond to him. While we discussed *him*, not his work, he reshaped his thesis into a topic that met scholarly as well as personal needs. He picked an area of the utmost social concern, of vital importance for future generations. Over two years, he wrote a dissertation that he accepted as very good, passable, though "not the best thing to come out of the department." The hallmark of his dissertation was his continued, strident, relevance. Though I had hammered away at his caustic grandiosity, I was careful to see his current work not as a pocket of residual narcissism, but as a talent, an expression of an empowering search for witnessed significance, with real consequences. He was now clearly capable of separating grandiose strivings on the one hand, and self-depreciating retreat from career goals on the other hand, from a powerfully motivated, socially effective drive to witnessed significance.

By reflecting to him the difference between his prospective need for witnessed significance and his retrospective narcissistic compensations, I had helped him reshape his dissertation and his career. Now, a similar tangle was emerging in his personal life.

A dynamic throughout the therapy was the way he used me to regulate his self-esteem. Sometimes I was set up as a positive mirror in which he could see himself as he wished to be seen; sometimes he elicited, with the depth of his disingenuous revelations, an emotional warmth; and sometimes his caustic derision demanded my energetic confrontations and interpretations about his devaluing defenses. But this psycho-therapeutic work on his narcissism did not free him from the social isolation he had created as his stronghold against the hurt and rejection he anticipated from others.

I continued to feel that the intensity of his childhood religious immersion must have had formative influence on his fears and defenses. He was surprised by my interest in his religious life. He had long ago learned that his background was greeted with incomprehension by the Northeast intellectuals he was struggling so hard to join. The insistence of my questions validated the suppressed reality of his past.

It was not easy for him to admit that the wound he sustained from his fundamentalist background was more than the exposure to repressive dogma and rigid black-and-white thinking. He felt much more deeply traumatized by the fact that he had never had an experience of God's grace. And he felt ashamed to admit to such a yearning. He immediately began to reassure me that he knew there was no such thing. Instead of colluding with this apparently rational position, I asked him how he felt about his failure to be worthy of grace. That is, I listened to the hurt, which was genuine and contemporary, rather than affirming with or arguing against theology. He was bitter, bitter against God, against the phonies who attested to grace. He was furious at himself for his failure. He felt excluded from the eye of the universe. To acknowledge this was relieving to him. He marvelled that I seemed to know so much about religion. (In fact, I had said nothing about religion.) He who had felt incomprehensibly excluded from divine attention, de-lighted in my validating questions, and he idealized me as a unique psychiatrist.

For the first time, he found a girlfriend. He read out loud to her from the Gospels. He said he didn't believe in them, just found them beautiful. He wanted to let her know about this part of himself. I think he wanted also to continue exposing the issue that he had felt put him at the center of my attention.

When the relationship with the girlfriend drifted apart after a month or so, he became disappointed with me.

I reflected that he could use me to appreciate, but not share, his religious life. Inside of him was a carnival, a passion play of imagery embedded in years of development in the florid life of his parents' church. I told him that what he believed or didn't believe wasn't my concern, but I did think that he couldn't just excise that part of himself, or encyst it with my help in therapy. This world in him had to be clarified and, in some manner, expressed. In order to grow, he required more than rectification for the hurts of neglect and failure. He needed to bring into a human arena the harmonies and cacophonies of his struggle with grace. Although he claimed to believe no longer in such a phenomenon, he continued to feel the necessity to be known and understood in not merely a soothing, but a substantial, generative way. He wanted to be swept up and used by the world.

In response to my comments, he joined a liberal campus church, where he felt his personal struggle could be acknowledged and appreciated, rather than repressed as heretical willfulness. Rather than butting his will against an invisible, fundamentalist God, or against a self-erected icon of unobtainable, unique greatness, he could actively overcome his worst fear: meaningless anonymity. Child of depressed parents who paid no attention, socially isolated brother of a socially successful sister, heretic among believers, member of a weird sect rather than a mainstream church, unresponded to and unresponsive to the surrender of grace, he was finding now in therapy a person who responded, in church people who empathized, and in writing a wide range of expression for his intellect. He rejoined Christian meaning, logos. For the first time, he could stand back, relinquish his joust with God, and observe the history, poetry, and music in church. Instead of spending weekends watching television sports, he joined potlucks, several in his apartment. His thieving ceased. But he made no close personal bonds, preserving the therapy as a sphere of unique intimacy and self-revelation. The talks he gave at the church put him up front, where he felt he belonged. When he left town, with his doctorate complete, for his new job, he used both his identity and affiliation with his new church, to hold himself together against this fresh, lonely challenge. He seemed to me guarded, much less though still narcissistic, possibly harboring a bipolar mood disorder (though off all medication for eighteen months), fragile, and in pursuit of a vital, socially committed scholarship that I admired, the importance of which he wanted the world at large to witness. His personal needs were weighty but not consuming, and his mind had been released to cry out not only for himself, but for a collective future. He was on the doorstep of a social life and in the corridor of a spiritual one—lonely, worried, productive, his words and thoughts flowing somewhere at last in the consciousness of humankind. ". . . Incline thine ear unto me . . . my heart is smitten, and withered like grass; so that I forget to eat my bread . . . I watch, and am as a sparrow alone upon the house top . . . this shall be written for the generation to come . . ."[20]

◇ **2** ◇

Lawful Order

... I bowed to the one who opens in dawn, and I lived in harmony with the order, the principles, the laws of the day ...

Patients will talk about the need for a parent, a father, a guide, a source of order, power, or lawfulness. The need is for dependence—upon someone or something, limits or rules, which can be known and counted upon. This need, which is prototypically answered by a father, and by other authorities, forms the nucleus of the Father-in-Heaven, the anthropomorphic, paternalistic image that has been at the center of the religions of the Near East.

Freud thought that the infantile wish/fear for an omnipotent father was the neurotic bedrock of religion ". . . once before one has been in such a state of helplessness. The longing for the father is the root . . . the father nucleus had always lain hidden behind every divine figure . . . when the child grows up and finds that he is destined to remain a child forever . . . he creates for himself the gods . . . now that God was a single person, man's relations to him could recover the intimacy and intensity of a child's relation to a father . . ."[1] The image of a father so dominates the scriptures of the Western religions and the imagery of the tribal and totemistic religions Freud had studied, that it was possible for him to confuse it with the core of religion itself. But we need only glance at non-Western religions to see that religion exists independently of paternal imagery (e.g., Buddhism),[2] or in conjunction with multiple forms of relational imagery for the divine (e.g., Hinduism, where God is variously related to as mother, paramour, grandparent, or child).[3] And it is clearer today, than in Freud's time, that, although Western religions are replete with paternal imagery, they are not limited to concrete adherence to such imagery.

A rabbi felt himself succumbing once again to the rage-filled depression that had already led to divorce, recurrent depression, and had haunted him his whole life with suicidal despair. When he came to therapy he was belligerent, blaming, loud. It was unclear whether he came on his own steam, or under a suggestion, or command, from the older Rabbi to whom he was an assistant. He drove for over an hour, from a neighboring state, to see me. He blamed his foul mood on phone calls from his sister, and on troublemakers in the congregation. He was off-putting, and his externalizing made me wonder whether I could help him, and I told him so. My unpampering directness got his attention, as did my refusal to prescribe him more Darvon for his back pain. Still, he complained about his pain for several months, asking for hypnosis, then relaxation training, before he could talk about himself and his own life.

His father had been a scholar in Europe, who had turned flight to America into financial and social success. But when the future rabbi was four, his bearded, kind father had died. He recalled his stunned despair. He never cried. But he began to have fantasies of dying, of going to heaven. Death seemed a haven. He imagined his mother was unable to bear living. In

his reconstruction of these long-past events during psychotherapy, he remembered giving his mother all his attention, rescu-
ing her from her shaky desperation, but she remained distant.
She sought solace by burying herself in Hebrew lessons, leaving
him home in the care of his only, slightly older, sister. In the
darkness, he observed planets through a telescope that had
belonged to his father. His mother remarried a crude businessman who manufactured zippers—the two of them seemed inac-
cessible. The rabbi portrayed his stepfather as cold,
mechanical, mocking, belligerent, "a Nazi."

Although he claimed to remember clearly his father's
death, he could find, and the therapy could evoke, little more
direct emotion than he remembered to have shown as a child.
Instead, his feelings were directed toward his stepfather, and
then, one by one, to a series of teachers, rabbis, and rabbi-
bosses, all of whom he identified as "usurpers"—false authorities, undeserving of their position, enemies to be fought. The
feeling that dominated his conscious life was not sorrow, but
anger. In fact, once when he had come home from college, he
picked an argument with his by-then aging stepfather, and
almost unleashed his conscious wish to strangle him; but he
had let his mother's horrified intercession prevail. That violent
anger, just below the surface, always seemed coiled to spring
out of him. He controlled it by changing jobs, leaving towns
and people, and by depression. Not anyone could provoke this
anger, only "usurpers": those in perceived authority, who,
when revealed to have foibles or vulnerabilities, would drive
him to disappointment, followed by fury. He yearned, expected, demanded that "adults" (for he felt himself to be "a kid
on a three-wheeler") be as perfect as he remembered his stately,
wise father to have been. His greatest anger was saved for
Judaism, a nest of fraudulent hypocrites, who gave him nothing
but empty formulas to go on. He wanted guiding authorities
and found only weaklings.

But he was very responsive to the idea (insight or interpretation) that his life was an unconscious reproduction of his yearning to be close to an ideal father. This concept was coupled to his resentment of all real, available men as disappointing stepfathers. In his adult life, he was continuously reproducing and reliving the trauma and frustration imposed on his childhood. His religious career represented both a search for the law-giving rabbi-father-teacher, and a need for salvation from a life he was sometimes ready to abandon in exchange for his real father's household in death. He felt constantly tempted to kill himself. He wanted so badly to be close to the one he had lost. Insight helped, but the stunning loss stayed with him—those memories of that tall Jewish Tolstoy, with a quiet authority and pervasive dignity, vanishing, ripped away by a vacuum, to be replaced by two bickering hawkers.

Underlying the image of the Lord as my Shepherd, and the Father who art in heaven, is the need for lawful order. It is the universal human need to inhabit a cosmos, not a chaos,[4] to dwell in a creation, not a mere existence (see also Chapter 7). Lawful order is different from chaos on the one hand, and from arbitrary, frozen regularity and stasis on the other. This fundamental human yearning is for a composite of variability and growth with familiarity and purpose. We want to know that we are not stuck and that there are rules to the unfolding game. Lawful order is the essential human ingredient that with the sweetness of nurturance leavens the bitterness of loss into the bread of presence. Lawful order is evocatively symbolized as a law-giving, protective father, who gives us security, but also demands that we manifest the rules in our actions.

A sense of relative continuity and predictability is essential for people to recognize directions and meanings; but these only constitute the structure or skeleton of life. When the recurrent and reliable realities are seen to arise from a sense of rightness, correctness, goodness immanent in the very nature of things, a religious dimension of life is felt, and a religious need is slaked. The religious sense of lawful order is not just one of social regularity and political reliability, but it is the experience of the intrinsic coherence within the world— that the sap and juice in things is meant to taste good. The sense of a just universe is a slightly anthropomorphic version of this feeling. At its center is the assumption that what is necessary for life is available, that a human being and his or her world are fitted to each other. They have evolved together, so that the unfolding of the world around one in time and space will provide an adequate pavilion for life, understanding, and love. That the world is lawfully ordered is one element of the complex concept known as "faith" (see also Chapter 7). This sense of lawful order is set apart not only from disorder, anarchy, and aribitrariness, but also from rigidity, immobility, and inflexibility. The lawfully ordered world is not arbitrary, quixotic, or malevolent; it can be counted on. It is not masterable, for it derives from the great first causes and origins. But it can be understood, joined, entered into. It has the feeling of a new, not-fully-known yet knowable way station, for a pilgrim travelling between the greater unknowns of birth and death.

The vision of reality expounded by the Buddha did away with the Father in Heaven, but not with lawful order. In fact, one of the hallmarks of Buddha's teaching, with its easily memorized, arithmetic framework (the Fourfold Noble Truth, the Eightfold Noble Path), is its reassuring emphasis that by controlling ourselves we fall in step with the wheel of the universe:

> What we are today comes from our thoughts of yesterday, and our present thoughts build our life of tomorrow: our life is the creation of our mind.
> If a man speaks or acts with an impure mind, suffering follows him as the wheel of the cart follows the beast that draws the cart . . .
> If a man speaks or acts with a pure mind, joy follows him as his own shadow.[5]

Anthropomorphic imagery of the divine is not necessarily ignorant, superstitious, or infantilizing. Its pervasiveness measures its utility and power in expressing features of the urge to lawful order. Because we are human, we can think, feel, intuit, and relate most vividly using the imagery that reflects our own form of being.[6] To imagine that the universe is ordered by an old man in the sky is to descend into fanciful, infantile projection that blocks the sense of the onward and reduces vision to the world of childhood. But anthropomorphic imagery may also be symbolic, suggestive, imaginative, and evocative, leading us onward through all our human modes of relatedness towards the ultimate.

In his "Afterword," appended to *I and Thou* more than forty years after he wrote the main text, Martin Buber deftly captured the wealth and error in anthropomorphism. Initially he had written: "The relation to a human being is the proper metaphor for the relation to God . . ." and now he added: "The ground and meaning of our existence establishes each time a mutality of the kind that can obtain only between persons. The concept of personhood is, of course, utterly incapable of describing the nature of God; but it is permitted and necessary to say that God is *also* a person."[7]

Anthropomorphic imagery in religions serves two functions: it facilitates a retreat into permanent childhood, in which the unknown is given the mask of a face; and, as the most powerful tool of religious imagination, it lifts our glance upward towards the face of the unknown.

The need for lawful order may deteriorate into fanciful illusions that an aged adult male is personally witnessing, extending significance to, and running a classroom-world. It may deteriorate further, into sadism. In sadism, humankind is at its worst, and yet is distinctly human, not animal. Sadism has frequently entered the same door as religion. Sometimes it has sulked in monastic shadows, but all too often it has stepped up to the front and taken command, so that religion and burnings,

26

racks, dungeons, swords, mass conversions, and genocides are entwined around each other through history. Clinically, in individuals, sadism has its particular psychological causes in the way a child is taught to deal with himself, his body, and others. The frequent infusion of sadism into religion, the relative receptivity, or stickiness, for sadism that religious institutions have demonstrated, may well have to do with the yearning for lawful order. When this yearning is made concrete, it provides a channel for sadism and, in itself, foments delight in the awful.

The experience of unlimited power, the destruction of someone else's mind and body, invest the tyrant with the tools of gods, those all-powerful lawgivers beyond law, the arbitrary king-god-despot-father. A fund-raising letter from *Amnesty International* begins: " 'We are God in here' . . . That's what the guards taunted the prisoner with as they applied electric shocks to her body . . . her cries were echoed by the screams of other victims and the laughter of their torturers." This lust to embody the power of life-and-death, in order to avoid feeling subject to it, may well be the most dangerous force in the world, and religions can unleash this force in individuals and groups through identification with the fantasy of omnipotence. Thus, religion can not only be infused with sadism, but can stimulate and evoke it through the imaginative emulation of the perceived cruelty of fate, reenacted by those who out of desperate necessity must believe that horror has been personally entrusted in their hands.

Orthodoxy and fundamentalism are religious forms in which the yearning for lawful order sweeps aside and dominates other features of religious life. These religious forms express a desperate need for lawful order in an unambiguous, imagination-blunting way. Frequently, this need to impose clarity at any cost comes from a fear of disorder and a sense of threat from a person's own instinctual life. To help himself control his own impulses, he domineers over others; if women stimulate him sexually, and he can't control that stimulation, he may command them to veil their faces, and find in scriptural passages of lawful order a rationale for this. When religions pander to outward control rather than psychological harmony, they ignite authoritarianism and injustice: "Men are the managers of the affairs of women/for that God has preferred in bounty/one of them over another, and for that/they have expended of their property./Righteous women are therefore obedient." That quotation from the Koran might well be based on the New Testament lines from St. Paul: "Let the woman learn in silence with all subjection/But I suffer not a woman to teach, nor to usurp authority over the man, but to be in silence."[8] Through the need for lawful order as expressed in deteriorated forms of orthodoxy and fundamentalism, the seminiferous garden of creation is reduced to the fine points of rulebook and grammar. Truth is no longer a matter of quest and dedication but is given, defined, exegetical. In confronting the anxiety of change, some people prefer to sacrifice their human complexity in order to establish certainty and security—and religions can cater to this retreat through orthodoxy and fundamentalism. These religious forms are always present, but they are on the rise today.

Another perversion of the need for lawful order is "machinism," the religion of the machine. In the scientific worldview, the lawful order of the world reveals a mechanistic integration, but the meaning of the whole is left to curiosity, discovery, wonder, and reverence (I will comment more on this in Chapter 7). Machinism is a fragment of science elevated into a description not only of how the pieces fit together, but into an explanation of the essence of the whole. This becomes the engineering model of self and life. A cold, dead world is seen by a skeptical eye; discharge of function replaces fulfillment of meaning; the universe is understood and related to as lawful, orderly, hollow. This deteriorated form of a psychological universal can be seen in obsessive-compulsive characters, in which the yearning to establish a lawful order overtakes and obliterates other psychological needs. Machinism is not an expression of the presence of unfolding life in the universe, but causes the ultimate questions to rise up suddenly out of denial like horrible ghosts. And these horrible, sudden evocations of what humans could well spend their lives answering, in turn feed the quick, desperate closure of fundamentalism. Bad science spirals into bad religion. A denial of the mysteries feeds a didactic version of them.

Lawful order is one of the guiding forces behind monasticism, religious orders, and religious communities. Within walls, or within psychological boundaries, the confusions, anxieties, and doubts that perplex man can be confined and managed. At every point in human history, ancient or modern, of the East or the West, we find religious fortresses or gardens, where both self and the world can be more regularized, disciplined, and simplified. The religious retreat may constitute a garden where the flowers of the human heart can spring up and flourish in the atmosphere they require; or it may provide a desperate avoidance of the call to life, and a mere slinking in the shadows of someone else's power, authority, and control. When civil discord and anarchy trouble the individual, religious yearnings may require specially selected and protected environments.

The need for lawful order is the spark that flames into the character discipline essential to adult function. When it grows, it turns inward as well as outward. It inspires the capacity to know, order, and rule the self. It lends control to one's needs, impulses, goals, and relations. In this way the lawful order of the universe is microcosmically contained in the ordered person. This correlation between internal integration and a sense of harmonious external order was well known to the founders of religions, especially the most ancient.

Vedantic philosophy, the oldest, richest, and still dominant form of Hindu thought, is based on the identity of the individual soul with the source of the universe. It follows, then, for the practitioner of Vedanta, that by deeply and fully ordering and knowing oneself, one attains spiritual unity with the world as well.[9] In Indian culture, this has become less a philosophy, and more an orientation to life, permeating the civilization. "Joy supreme comes to the Yogi whose heart is still, whose passions are peace, who is pure from sin, who is one with Brahman, with God . . . He sees himself in the heart of all beings and he sees all beings in his heart."[10] (I will comment further on this sense of unity in Chapters 5 and 7.)

Tolstoy interpreted the New Testament in a similar manner. He stressed the importance of deciphering and then living by the truth within:

> The sole meaning of life is to serve humanity by contributing to the establishment of the kingdom of God . . . that is, to contribute to the establishment of the greatest possible union between all beings—a union possible only in truth . . . by the recognition and profession of the truth by every man "the kingdom of God cometh not with outward show; neither shall they say, Lo here! or Lo there! for behold, the kingdom of God is within you" (Luke 17:20–21).[11]

The need for lawful order matures outward as well, into empiricism, knowing, and the desire to understand the rules that guide the universe and society. The need for lawful order grows into morality, the sense of right and wrong, and evolves into ethics, the identification with the pains and aspirations of other living beings, all similar to oneself, and governed by the same hopes and fears. The quintessential tone of the Old Testament evokes this: "Let us hear the conclusion of the whole matter: Fear God, and keep his commandments."[12] Conversely, the deepest human fear is to face the anarchies of personal madness or civil breakdown. That is why the urge for lawful order stands at the bifurcation leading either to imposed tyrannous rules, or to harmonies of inquiry, self-knowledge, and compassionate identification.

In tyranny, a fundamental despair over the possibility of lawful order in the universe leads to an attempt to master it, to become the law, to dispense fate, to externalize pain rather than be subject to it. But when lawful order matures, the laws of the living organism of the universe are understood and counted on to extend through every boundary, to reach everywhere; or to originate everywhere. The same unfolding rules regulate my heart and the stars. There is only one place. There is no person-like being who sees everything with a giant eye; but each event billows upward out of non-being with a sovereignty that marks out the paths of electrons as well as the orbits of galaxies. The simple comfort of a law-giving father can be relinquished, when lawful order brings awareness and comprehensibility to an otherwise improbable and pell-mell world. Dispassionate, accurate observation of reality reveals an infinitely layered and exponentially complex order everywhere. The sense of lawful order is the sense that there is something behind it all, that there is something to it all. "An invisible and subtle essence is the Spirit of the whole universe. That is reality. That is the truth. THOU ART THAT."[13]

The rabbi needed little encouragement to grasp the idea that he was compulsively seeking a substitute father who would live up to his childish ideals, and that he was enraged with the real people who failed to do so. He understood that he felt cheated by life and the arbitrary, incomprehensible destruction of his father. He realized that the chaos of a four-year-old's absolute, bitter, furious, denial continued to live on in his late adulthood. He understood, but felt unchanged.

In a wry, undercutting, and affectionate way, the rabbi began referring to me, a good ten years his junior, as "Daddy." This was his psychoanalytic in-joke. Then he put me to a test: after a summer vacation in Europe, he filled several sessions with punctiliously detailed descriptions of houses, streets, and people associated with his father's origins. If I had showed the slightest insensitivity to these meandering and tangential details, he told me later, I would have revealed my inability to understand him. He was rebuilding a new father on earth, a mosaic of the facts, history, and geography of his real father, with the emotional responses of his therapist.

He asked me to give a talk at his synagogue. I said I would think it over, but, as the request seemed like a deviation from usual therapeutic boundaries and helpful therapeutic relationship, I prepared to say I couldn't. Inside myself, I found myself backpeddling, ready to use a made-up scheduling conflict as an excuse. Why? So I told him I would, and did, talking about William James and Freud. In our next session, he told me how pleased he had been to show me off to members of his congregation and thanked me, in a way that made me feel warm, foolish, and on target. I don't like to disappoint people, but I know I have to; but I also don't have to hide or deny valid uses of *me*, just because they are so concretely helpful.

At home, on the piano, the rabbi played music that his father had composed. As he felt less deprived, his short fuse lengthened. He built professional and congregational relationships. He was able finally to trust and cooperate with a holistic family practitioner and a physical therapist, and thereby get substantial relief from back pain without perpetuating his addiction to Darvon. He became more appreciative of and expressive toward his wife. He could understand and regulate, though not always prevent, what had previously been incomprehensible and unpredictable surges of rage. For example, at a gathering of rabbis, he fumed over what to others was merely an abstract theological point, but he managed to restrain the mocking, caustic tirade he wanted to deliver. His delicate mood balance remained contingent on his feelings about me.

I imagined that his religion, with its neurotic origins in the untimely death of his father and the need for and intolerance of substitutes, would fade. He was adjusting himself to what he did not have, and what he had or could find. Since his image of God was developed by his narcissistic needs, I expected it to evaporate as he learned to decipher and meet his needs in social reality. Instead, his image of God took a turn towards life.

He refurbished what had previously been merely compliant behavioral forms into a routine of morning prayer and enthusiastic calendrical ritual, which ordered the days and the weeks and also his inner life. As part of his new self-discipline, he took up cycling with a group of men from his congregation and lost weight. Instead of complaining about disagreeable aspects of Jewish theology, he co-founded a professional association that represented his positions. In the past he had told me: "An assistant Rabbi is really just an impotent stud for a hen yard of widows." Now, instead of complaining about the old ladies who drained him, he looked forward to pastoral activity as a source of satisfaction for his need to care and be cared for. In short, he used religion to become more regulated and productive, though he remained vulnerable and guarded.

What I witnessed was not the elimination of religious involvement when its Freudian neurotic sources were drained, but a reorientation of a well-developed religious life, away from self-referential obsessions, towards social, intellectual, liturgical, and communal practices. Old, partly developed fragments of this widely learned man began to reveal themselves. Other motives that had underlain his religious profession surfaced. His memory of the past, previously constricted by the dominant emotions of deprivation and anger, unbound fresher and more variable memories.

He now recalled, as he had been unable to do at first, that not all male authorities he had encountered seemed to be usurpers. In fact he *had* once found an inspiring father substitute: a Hebrew teacher who had moved him, through example, beyond mere knowledge of the language into love of it—the history and usage of each word, its poetic resonance.

His contempt for the ritual of services as "a magic show" could not be softened by any memories of a meaningful mentor. But, as he described it: "I'm beginning to believe people when they tell me it was a good service. I've always discounted that kind of compliment as another empty ritual. But I could see some people were really moved this Saturday. I could *see* it. It's probably always been true . . ."

I think that my attention to lawful order as an issue in this man's life carried the therapy beyond where it would have otherwise come to rest. The rabbi came quickly to understand that he was searching for a father substitute, and that he experienced me in that role. He utilized me for a corrective emotional experience of a stable, available, enduring father. When he had lost his father, he had lost not only a parent; his faith in life itself was assaulted. That is why he suffered not only from interpersonal problems resulting from his damaged parenting, but also from suicidal despair. The child's basic hope had been smashed. He now felt that failed father substitutes were usurpers, and that the universe was malevolent.

Clarification and interpretation were not important features of my work on lawful order with him. In this way, lawful order differs from witnessed significance. The important aspect of lawful order is not an insight, but a full manifestation in the mode of relatedness. This religious issue does not require labelling, but self-confident actualization by the therapist.

At the primitive level, this work is no other than boundary setting and monitoring, and is a part of all good therapy. My work with the rabbi began with this focus before I had thought about lawful order. He wanted hypnosis and individual therapy; he wanted addicting drugs for back pain; he blamed others instead of seeking insight or understanding. By containing his verbal assaults and delineating what therapy was and wasn't, I was ordering our mutual world, which was necessary for therapy to function at all.

At a subtler though still non-specific level, a therapist conveys the sense of lawful order directly to every patient as a teaching. This happens through our conviction in the meaningfulness of both pathology and health. The activity of studying and exploring mishap, pain, and confusion expresses a confidence in natural law at the psychological level. The steadiness of the therapeutic attempt to understand is itself therapeutic. That neurosis or perversion are not chaotic errors, but products of cause and effect, is the greatest contribution of the Freudian revolution. It is a healing set conveyed by the mere commencement of insight-oriented psychotherapy. The rabbi experienced his own depression and temper as mercurial manifestations of the same willful and inscrutable universe that killed his father. When he came through psychotherapy to understand his depression as a child's reactive despair, and his temper as a boy's frustrated rage, he was prepared to look for more order and meaning where previously he had only squinted with incomprehension.

Specific, intentional focus on the rabbi's damaged sense of lawful order only began when he compelled me to study a conflict he had induced in me. That was when he asked me to speak at the synagogue. Ostensibly, this was another one of his attempts to manipulate the boundaries of therapy. Was he psychopathic, was he borderline—surely I would have kept to cautious psychotheraputic traditions if I had thought so. What I imagined, instead, was that he was feeling a tension I also felt. Though he lived in a neighboring state, my professional interest in psychiatry, religion, and his profession had us living in overlapping spheres. It was through this overlap that he had been referred to me. At some point, during or after therapy, this professional conjunction was likely to produce some contact outside the therapy. Then why not have it happen during and as part of therapy? Boundaries enable therapy, but rigidities are defenses that shatter in life's complexities. I had confidence in our basic work, in him and in me.

His request contained a desire to manipulate me as he could not manipulate his stepfather, the usurper. It was an exhibitionist use of me as a self-esteem–enhancing self-object; it was a transference (and, on my part, countertransference) acting out of his need for a responsive, good father. It was also a moment in which his painful sense of universal disarray could be met. His fear that I was another destructive usurper and that he was a potentially murderous stepchild could be encountered and eased. A therapist is also a symbol of the human capacities in the patient, too. Flexibility is the most complex order. In an absurd world, there are still helpful people. Because such a crossing of paths seemed destined anyway, the fact that I, the previously staunch upholder of every boundary guideline, could comfortably meet particular conditions in thoughtful ways, helped the rabbi increase his own self-trust, because his distrust of himself was based on a fear of his own deportment.

Lawful order in a person is the felt engagement in the process of organic adaptability, an animal responsiveness. It is the psychological proprioception of life's own ability to meet and mold circumstance, flex within it, ease around it, and emerge enhanced and eager. This dyadic dance that the rabbi induced and to which I responded, reassured him that he was fit. He was not abandoned or feared; he was appropriate, reliable, viable. He thanked me for my helping him feel like another adult. He took a turn towards building professional and congregational relationships after this interactionally facilitated internal discovery of lawful order. Not just outside, but inside, he was part of the good world.

What happened, specifically, to his image of the divine? Here he was guarded. Toward the end of therapy was the only time he directly talked to me about his experiences with God. During a depression many years previously, he had felt drawn towards suicide—the abandonment and loneliness of his early loss augmented by back pain and the isolation of bed rest. One sleepless night, he got up to take the whole bottle of pills, two of which had not enabled him to fall asleep. Holding the bottle, he felt God's presence and prayed, and felt he was being saved, being told he was meant to live, was being called to continue his work as a rabbi. Yet this experience had happened years ago. He held it in his heart as a treasured and secret touchstone. Yet he also doubted it. And he felt taken advantage of by it, since, as the years had unwound, he had found in his sacred calling only the same old routine job. Now, he had no new experiences that he interpreted to be direct interactions with God. But he *told* me about this event from the past. My impression was that he was revalidating it.

He kidded me now that I was like the Torah and he was a typical congregation member: once a week the sacred book was paraded around, he reached out and touched it and felt better. This need for concrete, substitute authority persisted, and shortened his therapy. He felt impelled to stop at this point, which to me seemed like a half-way house, because there was, in his joke and in his psyche, no internalized Torah, no reliable inner law and order free of a need for external talismans. But he was on the one hand vastly relieved in mood and energetically freed in behavior, and on the other hand, urgent in his desire to stop. I think he was afraid that the Torah might fall and be desecrated, or that he might rip it up in a fit. He stopped and delayed paying his last bill. Was he holding on to me, getting back at me? He had found some justice, some kindness, some free fatherly giving beyond the call of role, like a real father. The world had begun to taste sweet for him, so that he too could take his place in the land of milk and honey. But this justice in the world of men still could not make up to him for what he felt to be an unatonable injustice by a Creator who kills tall bearded fathers and leaves four-year-old boys alone to hunt for strength, security, and love in a wilderness world.

$\diamond$ **3** $\diamond$

Affirming Acceptance

... I knew myself, saw myself, and held in one embrace
human faults, limits, and successes ...

A prominent violinist was apprehended by the police in a
backyard at 10:00 P.M., after they had received a complaint
about a Peeping Tom. Because he was a well-placed citizen of
a neighboring town, and had no previous arrest record, he was
released with the understanding that he would seek therapy.

He was oppressed by guilt. His arrest had only called
attention to a larger issue. He was haunted by a sense that he
was bad, a failure, despite his having achieved eminence in his
career. His success seemed like a thin veneer over a deep trough
of inadequacies: loneliness, divorce, dissension with his second
wife, and troubled kids. He suffered from a sense of fraudulence
and imminent exposure. Yet he was productive, and lively. He
pursued a difficult career with creativity, energy, and objective
success. He was exuberant, loud, with a gypsy presentation of
jovial banter, silver belt-buckles, and beret.

He recalled his unhappy childhood. His father was a binge
alcoholic, a gentle, soft-spoken Irishman who moved from job

to job, never said a harsh word, and was always kind to his youngest son. His father deteriorated into a bum, shaking with D.T.s in seedy rooming houses, pleading with his visiting son to go out and get him just one more bottle just once. He died young of cirrhosis. The violinist's mother became a devout Catholic. She went to church mornings and evenings, dragging him along. His older brother rebelled totally, left home, and followed his father into alcoholism. His mother's friends, and the priests she selected for friendship, singled out the future violinist, insisting, pleading, threatening that he should be a model choir boy to avoid his father's fate. But defiance surged over surrender. He focused on the violin, where he had precocious talent. Clearly a superior student, he was a continuous discipline problem in his school. He wasn't going to let any nun tell him what to do, and the more they rapped his knuckles with rulers, the more he determined to defy their rules. He talked out of turn and made faces behind the nun's back, disrupting classroom decorum. Nonetheless, he absorbed with inner awe the parochial school teachings about how the saints had turned themselves over to God's will. One description had sunk in deeply, and he repeated it several times to me in therapy. A martyr had refused to recant and let himself be fried alive on a large iron, oiled and heated over a fire, rather than say a word against his God.

On the one hand the adolescent violinist defied the church; and on the other, he felt himself to be a budding saint of the spirit. His artistic pursuits isolated him from his tough peers. With his "smart mouth," he would provoke fights in the playground or on street corners, and, though large and powerful, he would lose, quit fighting, let himself get pounded, but not surrender, give in, or say "uncle." He emulated the church's most sanctified teachings, but turned them against the church. He was a Catholic martyr of the "atheistic church." He told me several times how his face was pushed again and again into the concrete of a Brooklyn sidewalk. He said that when he was beaten up in the schoolyard by a gang of kids, he could see two nuns looking the other way.

He would walk home alone from late night violin practice. He liked the solitude, the dark streets. To him the sun of the day was frightening, and the night seemed safer, more secure. He saw people through lighted windows. Once he saw a girl undressing. He looked for that again.

Despite quick career success, early marriage, and the trappings of maturity, his life remained a struggle every day against guilt and despair. He felt in his heart that he was a sinner against God, although his mind told him he was an atheist. He felt unable to create inner peace or happiness, despite following the prescribed routes. Hopelessness shadowed his restless, frantic, driven accomplishments. Sometimes, when his discomfort in himself reached a peak, he would, against his will and better judgment, prowl backyards, looking for lighted windows.

Patients will talk about the need to be accepted and accepting, integrated and whole. This is a need to feel integral and unified: one will, one mind, one direction, one set of drives and impulses in one personality and one body. It is a need to be all of oneself, and only oneself. One must be able to call upon all of oneself to meet the vicissitudes of life, yet one must be able to see one's limits. There is a need to feel responsible, an active agent of choice, a point of origins. Yet there is a need to feel absolved, pardoned, having done enough, tried enough, succeeded enough, and when finished, to feel done and complete. With this feeling, one is solid in solitude, self-filling and entire, without need for external reinforcement and acclaim. Yet one can also be comfortable in proximity with other selves, enriched and not threatened or lessened by continuity with them. This need is usually referred to as "wholeness," but to highlight its dynamic, tensile quality, I call it "affirming acceptance." Affirmation includes the thrust upward and outward of the life force, the driving forward. Acceptance balances affirmation with relinquishment: the realization that each life is essentially incompletable, transitory, a spark from a fire, a message across a synapse.

Religious institutions have developed psychological methods of dispensing a sense of affirmation and acceptance as part of their binocular vision that simultaneously points to secret failings and places them in pardoning perspective. If religions simply affirmed, then the individual participant would know, in the privacy of his heart, that a chaotic, selfish, libidinous creature had been certified as a full member of the fold. The individual might then feel accepted and hopeless—hopeless because the divine and its spokesmen were fools blind to his real nature and to the nature of those around him. Yet, if religions simply pointed the unmasking finger at the sexual and aggressive chaos potential within each person, without offering solutions, guidance, salvation or redemption, they would compound anarchy with a sneer of justifiable nihilism. Sensing this dilemma, religious founders and religious institutions developed modes of baring the confused, avaricious, inchoate urges of the beast, and then incorporating, channeling, giving direction and blessing to the uncoiled energies of the human animal. A core of the elaborate complex we call religion is the holding together in one directed person of the diverse urges that churn human character. Affirming acceptance is the ligature of religion. This psychological tool must be unblinking and probing, yet soothing and guiding. The many voices in the chorus of the person are witnessed, ordered, then unified, through this universally found feature of religious life.

The attempt to meet the psychological need for affirming acceptance is often the most prominent aspect of organized religion, though its methods and successes vary. Nothing juts out further from Temple, Church, and Mosque than the themes of guilt and absolution, sin and atonement. Religions tell us that we have been bad, partial, weak, and less than we can be and should have been. Yet over, and against, and with us is Another, who calls up more from our hearts, absolves the past, and commands a more complete response to the future. You have sinned, yet you can be saved; repent, be reborn whole and new. That is religions' cant, clarion, and refrain.

The Book of Job of the Old Testament gives a classic account of this:

> Then Job answered the Lord, and said, "Behold, I am vile . . ."
> Then answered the Lord unto Job out of the whirlwind, and said, "Gird up thy loins now like a man: I will demand of thee, and declare thou unto me . . ."
> Then Job answered the Lord, and said "Wherefore I abhor myself, and repent in dust and ashes . . ."
> And the Lord said ". . . him will I accept . . ." . . . The Lord gave Job twice as much as before . . . for he had fourteen thousand sheep, and six thousand camels . . .[1]

The more Job insists he is vile and abhorrent, the more the Lord affirms him. While there are many interpretations of this story, it is clear that an affirmation of meaning in life's horrors is intended, and that this affirmation is available only to those who keep the faith, by, among other things, seeing themselves as vile. When Job refrains from anger and blame, atheism or defiance, but blames only himself, the Lord of this story restores him to a material well-being that confirms and publicly sanctions his spiritual triumph. Through unshakable faith, this story seems to say, all other deformations of ourselves (Job's sores and diseases) can be healed, undone, reborn.

The Koran and the New Testament echo Job. They are aggressive in pointing to human sinfulness, yet proclaim that a rebirth into an embracing all-accepting state is a reliable possibility, and a certainty for the faithful:

43

The sending down of the Koran is from God, the All-mighty, the All-Knowing, Forgiver of sins, Accepter of penitence, Terrible in retribution . . . "Our Lord, thou embracest every thing in mercy . . ."[2]

Repent: for the kingdom of heaven is at hand . . . And if thy right eye offend thee, pluck it out . . . He that heareth my word, and believeth on him that sent me, hath everlasting life . . .[3]

In these quotations, we can hear an archaic, enduring tension between a need to cringe and cripple oneself to find acceptance and an absolving sanction of each human soul.

Martin Buber describes a Hasidic legend about affirming acceptance.[4] A disciple decides to embark on a fast to demonstrate his level of devotion, discipline, and sincerity. He endures the hunger and weakness and pain until the very last day. By this time the desire to eat is overwhelming. He begins to rationalize his problem: his whole fast was just an exercise in arrogance, in willfullness and pride. It would be better if he failed, and were humbled—humility is a greater religious attribute than the worldly success of a fast. As he prepares to take his first bite and destroy his fast, he vacillates again: he has come so far, endured so much, why ruin it now? Where is his sense of devotion? But then another counter-doubt sets in: see how pridefully he has become bound up in his own petty accomplishment. Eat, and be humble. Just then the clock strikes. He has done it! The fast is over; he was successful. He runs to his Rabbi with delight and tells his story. His spiritual leader says only, "Patchwork." Buber adds his commentary. In the disciple's inner dialogue, *neither* side was correct. His error was to undertake action before his heart was unified and whole. His logic was keen, but his spiritual life was still "patchwork." Not any one particular act or thought, but a whole-cloth life is what is wanted.

The Hasidic position, however, is a significant jump away

from Job, the Koran, and Matthew. The three scriptural passages, open as they may be to a psychological interpretation, certainly contain also a possible, even likely, suggestion of a concretely *Outer Other* to do the absolving, integrating, and accepting. The Hasidic story is clearly about psychological wholeness, personal integration. The Hasidic disciple must deepen and unify his own life; his teacher only holds up road signs, and God is not interfering.

A similar psychological position can be found in Buddhism: ". . . there is no 'sin' in Buddhism, as sin is understood in some religions. The root of all evil is ignorance . . ."[5] This is true, too, in some, but not all schools of Hinduism: ". . . the Kausitaki Upanishad (III, 1) affirms that sins are done away with by possession of true knowledge."[6] In this view, the problem of accepting all that is in the human being and then affirming that complex whole cannot be resolved by a formula of sin, self-abhorrent repentance, and absolution by an Other. Here, human evil is ignorance; wisdom is seeing the unity of all life, and accordingly surrendering, excising, relinquishing personal wants, desires, and motives, until a state of malleable, adaptive, loving equanimity with all beings under all circumstances is reached—no mean task! "Exclusion, the rejection of anything, is sin and self-deception; it is the subjection of the whole to a part, the finite superordinating itself to the infinite."[7] In the Western scriptural view, affirming acceptance is the addition of absolution after the searing fullness of inward turning vision. For the followers of Buddha, affirming acceptance is achieved by withdrawal of one's own claims, one's own self, leaving only an unhindered, unpossessed, undesired, impersonal flow of phenomena. Until such an august enlightenment is reached, however, the practitioner of such a religious path might find him- or herself struggling with a need to accept all the egoistic demands of selfhood (what the Western religions call "sins"). In turn, the practioner struggles further with the need to affirm one's life in the presence of these almost-inevitable human failings ("almost," because the enlightened *can* transcend them). Different religious traditions developed different formulas to dispense to their followers for achieving affirming acceptance. All stress a full, panoramic, unabashed, awareness of the human totality. But some stress external absolution, others stress self-surrender; some stress divine dispensation, others stress human ascent.

The synthesizing and restraining need for affirming acceptance can deteriorate into a split between affirmation and acceptance, or into an exaggeration of either pole. An unbalanced stress on affirmation leads to Dionysian willfulness, entitlement, guiltless sanction for all impulses. The diabolically affirmed religious fanatic can accept the unacceptable in himself and feel sanctioned and justified in any expression of his will. A patient described this state to me. Born into a Fundamentalist family and gifted with eloquence, he travelled as a youthful preacher, filled with an expansive power. He poured forth a self-righteous tirade of moralisms. But when advanced education shattered his fundamentalism, he felt powerless, shut down. For years, despite continued educational success, he felt flat, faltering, until he converted to Marxism. Once again he felt a surge of verbal power (this time literary). He rocketed his career forward with unabashed self-seeking, and he justified his ruthlessness as being his own humble contribution to the Revolution! In a similar yet extended manner, Islamic fundamentalist revolutionaries describe war and torture as extensions of their "wholeness."[8] They justify violence and cruelty as an adherence to spiritual values and otherworldly rewards, in contrast to Western rationalism, materialism, and individualism, which merely treasure the life of this body and this world.

But affirming acceptance can also deteriorate in the other direction, into cringing guilt and moralistic repression of one's own instincts. This happens when the stress is on limitation instead of expansion, relinquishment instead of fulfillment. An unctuous acceptance sought from a powerful Other turns into self-constriction, denial of life's sap, and, worse, masochistic cruelty. The perversions of saintliness dwell here, the hair shirts, the corrals of vows, the mortifications of creativity, love, and freedom that can endure briefly behind monastic walls. Searching for acceptance, devotees may strip themselves of what is ripe in them, to cringe before and curry favor with their image of the divine. They live like naughty but appeasing children before a stern parent. They misinterpret and abuse disciplined asceticism, with its productive possibility of intensely focused energy, and they pervert it into a self-abasement to avoid self-responsibility. Sexuality can be condemned, split off underground, to surface in perverse channels. Anger is condemned, turned off, encysted underground where it endures in molten, explosive form. This self-punitive, moralistic masochism easily erupts in a volcano of violence. Unable to accept themselves, their own impulses, thoughts, and feelings, many frightened souls turn to religion and worship a chimera who they hope will do for them what they cannot do for themselves. They cannot accept themselves, and they want to coerce God to do so through the power of their groveling. Then their religion leads them in a spiral of increasing need for repression of their inner world and an increasing self-abhorrence because of their inner secrets. There is an increasing need for a harsh outer voice to reinforce repression in exchange for a superficial acceptance of those who pay homage with the cauterization of their selfhood.

Religious guilt, apparently a product of extreme humility, always harbors arrogance. It functions to make the sinner the focus of God's eye, the center of His concern. In the mind of the self-proclaimed big sinner, the cosmos revolves around his own dirty little life; all the lightning of heaven flashes to light up his obscure pew. He dramatizes his failure to find affirming acceptance, to make himself the hub of upside-down witnessed significance. William James focused on this description of the fourteenth-century German mystic Henry Suso:

> He wore for a long time a hair shirt and an iron chain, until the blood ran . . . in the undergarment he had strips of leather fixed, into which one hundred and fifty brass nails, pointed and filed sharp, were driven . . . in this he used to sleep every night . . . he continued this tormenting exercise for sixteen years . . . in winter he suffered very much from the frost . . . his feet were full of sores, his legs dropsical, his knees bloody and seared, his loins covered with scars . . . Throughout all these years he never took a bath . . .[9]

James adds: "It is pleasant to know that after his fortieth year, God showed him by a series of visions that he had sufficiently broken down the natural man, and that he might leave these exercises off." Suso had to "break down the natural man . . . the fire of his temperament destroyed . . ." before he could hallucinate affirming acceptance.

The need for affirming acceptance also leads to the florid, pious clichés of liberal weekend religion. There, worship passes around the circle of carefully limited acquaintances. Unable to find affirmation and acceptance of their whole selves, some people seek religions that offer mutual mirroring of surfaces, mutual platitudes of a warmth without fire, family language without family life. This is religion of tranquilization, which soothes anxiety without facing its cause. Station wagons fill the parking lot; faces turn up to be counted in a ritual guaranteed to be quick, easy, painless.

But the need for affirming acceptance is the root of religion's healing force. Religion means "that which binds together," and religion can bind together good and evil in one sphere. (I will discuss other aspects of this root meaning in Chapters 5 and 7.) Religions have elaborate methods for raising the unconscious, the unacceptable impulses, into buffered consciousness. I am thinking of prayer, meditation, confession, myth. Here transgressions, antisocial impulses, are permitted to surface and are rechanneled. In congregational prayer or group meditation, for example, a subtle and canny blending of privacy and publicness can permit the worshipper to open the secrets of his or her heart, in the midst of a crowd of equally opened, yet quiet fellows, and thus be simultaneously sinful, guilty, cleansed, and blessed among a representative collection of all humankind. Such a feeling of membership is not hypo-critical when it stabilizes, sustains, or enables an examination of souls. Similarly, the great myths of religion enable us to suck in our breaths and discuss murder, torture, persecution, prosti-tution, and mutilation in the context of community and hope. What we dare not speak is openly discussed, and, if the tone of voice is right, our inner worlds become vicariously public and inevitably human.

While the Bible has a cast of characters to represent or embody various aspects of each of our own less easily accept-able inner lives—helpless beggars, doubters, women of sin— the voluminous Hindu scriptures contain an encyclopedia of every conceivable fantasy. They elevate into public awareness a panorama of what is otherwise hidden, secret, latent, or reserved for dreams. The Sanskrit scholar, Wendy Doniger O'Flaherty has opened up this vast panorama to the contem-porary reader, exposing through three thousand years of In-dian history ". . . what people think and what people think they think . . .," including such themes as androgyny, male pregnancy, the various mythic meanings of blood, semen, seed as food, beheading, castration, animal sacrifice, phallic mothers, etc.[10]

The need for affirming acceptance grows into the human-izing forces of self-responsibility and interdependence. It en-ables self-disgust, blame, and externalization to be replaced by a flexible monitoring of one's own instincts, coupled to ethical mutuality. This is one possible interpretation of the concept of original sin: not that we are a collection of hopeless orphans with incorrigible table manners, not that we are serpents, but that the ceaseless surges of lust and self-protective violence in us are inescapable, our burden, our bond, our equality, our glue. It takes a human being to be crucified. This understanding of original sin leads to empathy. It finds mature expression in Freud's vision that we are all of the same cloth as madness. "Let whoever has not sinned cast the first stone."[11] The internalization and full acceptance of human frailty and evil in all of us leads to sorrow.

Sorrow is the cure for the condemnation of either ourselves or others. Sorrow is a form of acceptance. It means the relinquishment of fantasies of escape. It redeems us from shameful or guilty isolation. We sorrowfully accept our own weakness and failings. It redeems those around us from our pejorative, self-righteous judgments. We sorrowfully acknowledge their human lapses and transgressions. It points towards our lifework. The world is not as we want it to be; we are not as we wish we were. Through unabashed self-knowing, we know what must be done. The revelation comes from within. The world takes shape from what is inside us and how we struggle to reshape ourselves. Affirming acceptance is not complete until we have internalized the capacity for sorrow as an active, creative response that is simultaneously stabilizing via the acceptance it brings, and transforming via the power it brings to hold a truer picture of reality within us.

Socrates, not known for prayers, prayed, ". . . may my inner and outer life be one."[12] When this occurs, sex and aggression are socialized and constructive. The ripening of affirming acceptance is closely coupled to the experience of release (see Chapter 6). We can affirm the forces of life in us, and accept ourselves as we are, when we know that we can bear, in rank and file, the obligation to create the new out of what has been given.

The violinist was caught in a static, two-sided rebellion that pushed against itself and bulged up into voyeurism. On the one hand, he was revolted by his father's and older brother's spiritual and human decay via alcoholism, and so he sought succor in his mother's church. He identified with the strength, self-control, and determination of medieval saints who clearly would never yield to the temptation of alcohol. He provoked fights and voluntarily lost, to test and confirm to himself the strength of his will to endure but not to yield. But he rebelled against Catholicism too. His mother, her priest-friends, the nuns at school, were clearly all of lesser stuff—not artists, not warriors of martyrdom. The saint's defiance of Satan now became the atheist's defiance of God and His sycophants. He wouldn't surrender to alcohol, he wouldn't surrender to bullies, he wouldn't surrender to his mother and her religion. But what about his sexual urges? Saints don't have them, or don't yield to them, so clearly they were to be crushed, excised, eliminated. But bohemian, artist, intellectual freethinkers treasure the sexual roots of the romantic worldview. The violinist also experienced women to be treacherous, undermining, cruel—some of the nuns who had tried to break his spirit were barely more than girls. Feeling like this, he avoided real sexuality as an adolescent. In college he maintained one safely, ritually, controlled relationship with a slightly older girl—as long as they met only on Friday night, and never at any other time, he felt sexual and friendly, but independent. When she wanted more from him, he increased his hours of violin practice and ended the relationship.

Before and after her, he had lonely, secret strolls at night, and from time to time, there were women behind windows. As he grew, he continued to live in defiant rebellion: against several wives, in whose shadow he saw his mother and the nuns, and against his colleagues whose presence echoed with the schoolyard bullies—an embattled, lonely, martyred siege. At the same time, he couldn't shake the feeling that he was a condemned sinner, a failed saint, who had heard the call but refused to obey. His compulsive defiance, and his peeping, felt out of control, but he couldn't trust anyone, couldn't turn to anyone for help, because they might expect him to surrender his self-control! His unusual musical talent, and the success and acclaim it provided, kept him rolling on a speedy treadmill of self-esteem that was just adequate enough to preclude motivation for change. He was neither able to relinquish willfulness, nor to accept himself. His apprehension by the police was the necessary intervention to upset the balance.

In therapy, the violinist provided this history of his life and problems, but nothing changed—though under the threat of the law, he managed to keep himself in rein. I pushed him to remember in more detail the early scenes of his peeping. His most moving and vivid memory was of walking home alone one night, feeling gripped by a penetrating, unshakable despair. He couldn't return home. He had nowhere else to go. He climbed a tree in a park, and sat in it, removed from the city, the people below. No one could see him. No one knew or cared that he was there. He didn't have to buy his father a bottle, or refuse to do so. He didn't have to surrender to the rules of the nuns, or refuse to do so. He felt bathed, buried in the tree in the darkness, nonexistent, safe, free, happy. It was November; the tree was bare; he felt he was among the stars. No peeping happened that night, and although he could never make the association any clearer, and although I could never fully complete the connection, he felt sure that the exhilaration of being invisible and yet able to watch others was connected to that one night, with its symbolic death and rebirth in a tree of life.

Logically, the therapy should have led to an analysis of the relation of this event to his search for naked women in windows. Instead, the therapy jumped—I concurred in the jump—to an ongoing discussion of his current sexual problems and frustrations with his second wife. She was a composer, whom he described as blonde, Scandinavian, and beautiful. Though he admired her work and held her in high esteem, he related to her more as a picture than as a person. He had never breathed a word about sex to her, or to anyone. He felt male banter was not for saints; priests couldn't be trusted or believed; wives were dark partners in this sin. He had simple worries, doubts, guilts about masturbation, keeping an erection, pleasing a woman.

The therapy took a medical, counseling tone. I felt we were talking on two levels. The surface was a doctor informing his patient about scientific facts. Then the doctor and the patient discussed how to live with the facts. One level down was a religious issue. A sinner was confessing. On this level, my words to him, couched in terms of biology, affirmed sexuality and integrated it with society. Authorities had apprehended him. Did authorities also condemn him? Doctors sanctioned sexuality—any sexuality? Unlike working with witnessed significance, but similar to work with lawful order, psychotherapy in the realm of affirming acceptance is not a matter of conscious, verbal interpretation. "You're OK, accept yourself," is feeble advice. No one caught in the grip of the sense of sin can follow that advice. What is called for is a sustained, conscious elevation and embrace of the realm of secrets. A self-proclaimed sinner will always hear soothing words as naivete or hypocrisy. But continuous exposure of his or her shames and failings in the presence of a valued, outreaching other—a psychotherapist—exceeds words. A therapist opening the gate to realms of shame does better to walk forward than to point even a neutral labelling finger.

The violinist stopped avoiding his wife, and the mixture of need and dread around sex softened into what sounded like two adolescents tentatively starting out. He movingly described his suggestion that he and his wife go to a Vermont inn for a weekend, and he told me that, though he had been married for years, to two different women, he had never once previously set aside a time and a place for romance. Sex had always been furtive, brief, blind. To talk about such things with his wife, to buy her a lilac bouquet, was for him an incredible breakthrough. That was enough therapy for him. I was doubtful and said so, but it was his choice.

Possibly the treatment terminated abruptly because I had failed to pursue the deeper meanings and connections of his isolation and despair to his antisocial symptom of voyeurism. I had colluded in avoidance. Possibly the treatment ended successfully—with complete cessation of his symptom—because I did not reduce to mere pathology the secret that was deeper, more private, and more precious to him than even his sexual perversion: that he felt he had a personal experience of what it is to stand alone in ultimate despair on bare limbs reaching up into the cold universe, and to choose to live.

I developed an understanding of him that guided my work, but which I had no chance to verbalize. Initially, his needs seemed too urgent; he had to move on, change; there seemed no time for thoughtful but inessential discussion. This urge and speed were characteristic of him. Later, when I felt there was surely time, he felt therapy was over.

I think one function of his voyeurism was to serve as a substitute for suicidal depression. It bound his sense of lonely hopelessness into an excitement, into eros, into life. It enabled him to feel at once aroused, connected, yet removed, in control, safe. But it was a costly compromise salvation. It required him to isolate and compartmentalize his spiritual salvation into an illegal sexual perversion. By coating his despair with excitement, he could affirm life, his own life force. But he couldn't accept this method of affirmation, for which he felt guilty, and which was also illegal. To treat his problem as sexual perversion, I believe, would have been a destructive error. His treatment needed two foci.

First, his despair of *life* had to be unmasked, exposed, cleansed, healed. The issue was affirmation. There was a disease, a pain in him, more shameful than his peeping, and more potentially devastating, should it ever gain the upper hand. He felt his profoundest sin was his hatred of life, and the threat of suicide was far worse than arrest for looking in windows. His slow, breathless, measured, dreamy, reverie out loud to me of his night in the tree only evoked, but never stated, his covert plan. When I listened to and *accepted* this broken bird's desperate fledgling flight—to him I was a mixture of the police and of a true church where the secrets of the soul could be confessed—that acceptance absolved him in his own heart from the sin he had confessed. The confession's power is not mere abreaction, mere exposure and relief. Confession is itself the creation of a new life, a life in which absolute isolation is dispersed by faith, in other people, to understand, empathize, accept. Before therapy, he had obtained an unacceptable affirmation of life via voyeurism. Now, he had the feeling of acceptance, but he lost the old, perverse mode of affirmation.

That's why he rushed onward so fast, not taking time to integrate or work through, but dashing towards the second treatment focus: the need for an older man, a sober father with whom he could discuss the tools, actions, affirmations of manhood. So far, the therapy had provided him acceptance, but it had deprived him of his initial mode of affirmation.

Despite two marriages and several children, he had never emotionally entered the sexual bond. His real love and excitement was for a picture on the other side of glass that had kept him alive time and again in adolescence, like a guardian angel. But now that he relinquished the despair of his outmoded, self-protective isolation, through the intimacy and trust of therapy, he could exchange the old guardian angel for a flesh and blood woman. New self-acceptance catalyzed new modes of affirmation. Real sexual urges could now be integrated into life. He no longer needed to be split into medieval saint and peeping sinner. He could become one whole married artist.

My "non-psychological," literal, medical style of dealing with his sexual questions, problems, shames, sprang from a psychological understanding. If I had utilized interpretation of his sense of inadequacy and impotence, his fear of women, his contempt for his father, his yearning to have me father him, I would only have shamed and repelled this action-oriented, unpsychological, grown-up boy. By choosing to let these undercurrents flow beneath us unlabelled (but not unnoticed), I enabled us to shake hands as two men. I felt no need to persevere towards logical completeness in analysis. Instead, I actively participated in his creation of new modes of sexual expression. He could identify with me, rather than feel pointed at, accused, studied. Similarly, by leaving his story of the tree unconnected explicitly to his voyeurism, by not pushing towards logical or psychological closure, I lost some analyses but gained some therapy. I understood the core issue to be: acceptance of his choice to live, even though that affirmation had necessitated for many years a perverse sexuality.

Though he left therapy so quickly, I did see him again five years later. His voyeurism remained a thing of the past. To me it seems good that not everyone stays for so careful a therapy, and that some bolt back to life. Life behind glass leaves a hunger. This exuberant artist had wasted time and was urgent to live. He had come to accept his body as a vehicle of the spirit, and to talk straightforwardly of love. To accept his generative, romantic flesh, he needed to be affirmed by another who burns by the same light. "It is from one man to another that the heavenly bread of self-being is passed."[13] I'm glad, friend of the night, that I could pass along plain love of day.

◇ **4** ◇

Calling

. . . I did my job, working in the common cause . . .

Patients will talk about their need to find their tasks, their jobs, their work to be done. The need to feel useful, used, relevant, connected, a spoke of the wheel, a voice in the chorus is the need for a calling. This need is the bedrock of human life. A calling provides a foundation for all human activity, and particularly for utilizing one's personal facets or individuating characteristics. Religions have sought to provide a sense of calling for their members, and many souls have sought to fulfill this need in religion.

Jung experienced and wrote about this need. His personal life provided the ground for him to differentiate career and success, from calling. By 1910, at the age of thirty-five, he was already a widely published, world-renowned psychiatrist, and in that year, at the Second International Congress of Psychoanalysis, he was appointed President. But after several years of growing tension, in 1913, Jung broke with Freud. Though Jung initiated this break-up, it clearly created an enormous shock in him. He lost a beloved and awesome mentor, psychoanalyst, and friend. Towards the end of his life he dictated and wrote autobiographical reminiscences, and one chapter, entitled "Confrontation with the Unconscious,"[1] begins: "After the parting of the ways with Freud . . ." In this chapter he describes his reaction: intense, volcanic, idiosyncratic, monumentally creative yet eerie years of self-absorption—a history-making, unparalleled journey through the figures, fantasies, and characters of his dreams, visions, and unconscious. He was impelled to new depths of self-knowledge, a new sense of isolation, autonomy, originality, and uniqueness.

> When I look back upon it all today and consider what happened to me during the period of my work on the fantasies, it seems as though a message had come to me with overwhelming force . . . It was then that I ceased to belong to myself alone, ceased to have a right to do so. From then on, my life belonged to the generality . . . It was then that I dedicated myself to service of the psyche . . . All my works, all my creative activity, has come from those initial fantasies and dreams . . . It has taken me virtually forty-five years to distill within the vessel of my scientific work the things I experienced and wrote down at that time . . . I hit upon this stream of lava, and the heat of its fires reshaped my life.

Jung saw a transformation in himself, from a successful and eminent professional, the appointed heir to Freud, to a "called personality." There was a figure-ground reversal. He no longer felt himself to be a scientist choosing a topic, but felt himself chosen. He then chose to distill over a lifetime what had chosen him as channel, media, spokesman. His own experience was one of both traumatic personal loss, and that of a genius uncovering a new vein of human thought. He generalized from his own experience to what he felt was a psychological truism, in an essay he wrote about twenty years after he experienced his own calling:

Fidelity to the law of one's being is a trust in this law, a loyal persever-
ance and trustful hope; in short, such an attitude as a religious man
should have to God . . . [it] can never develop unless the individual
chooses his own way consciously . . . the overwhelming majority of
mankind chooses not its own way but the conventions. True personality always has vocation, which acts like the law of God from which
there is no escape. Who has vocation hears the voice of the inner man;
he is *called.* Now vocation is not the prerogative of great personalities,
but also belongs to the small ones. But it happens to not a few to be
summoned by the individual voice, whereupon they are at once differentiated from the others and feel themselves confronted by a problem that the others do not know about. It is generally impossible for
a man to explain . . . Not for nothing is it just our own epoch that
calls for the liberating personality, for the one who distinguishes
himself from the inescapable power of collectivity, thus freeing himself . . . and who lights a hopeful watchfire announcing to others that
at least one man has succeeded in escaping from the fateful identity
with the group soul . . . the greatness and the liberating effect of all
genuine personality consists in this, that it subjects itself of free choice
to its vocation . . .[2]

Jung describes the process of calling as having two stages.
Like a minister and a congregation, like an Afro-American
spiritual with a "call and response" chant, there is first a voice
of the inner man, a call to vocation that has the power of a law
of God. This is followed by a choice, a free decision to obey the
call. This description paralleled his own experience, in which,
first a message came to him with overwhelming force; and then
he chose to devote his life to distilling that message.

Jung's writing has the passionate conviction of personal
experience behind it; it conveys the mood of the process. Peter
Matthiessen describes how this passage of Jung's prose revolu-
tionized his own life, and his own pilgrimage to one of the most
remote regions of the world, which he wrote up into an acclaimed literary masterpiece, *The Snow Leopard.*[3] But Jung's
words in "The Development of Personality" also strike a ro-

mantic, almost strident note. They echo in the dark tunnel of German romanticism that includes Nietzsche, and ultimately Hitler. "Our own epoch calls for the liberating personality . . ." Jung wrote those overcharged words in German in 1934.

Erik Erikson's concept of identity shows some similarities and some divergences from the tradition of religious calling. Erikson has widely written about his malleable and penetrating concept; it has been the subject of one book,[4] and the main axle of many. Here is one definition he has given of identity:

> It is a subjective sense as well as an observable quality of personal sameness and continuity, paired with some belief in the sameness and continuity of some shared world image . . . a unique unification of what is irreversibly given—that is, body type, temperament, giftedness and vulnerability, infantile models and acquired ideals—with the open choices provided in roles, occupational possibilities, values offered, mentors met . . . it is characteristic of a developmental period, adolescence and youth . . . [it] depends on three complementarities—namely, the personal coherence of the individual and the role integration in his group; his guiding images and the ideologies of his time; his life history—and the historical moment.[5]

Erikson's concept synthesizes and unifies divergent arenas of life. It captures the blend of inner and outer, task and matrix, person and culture that calling is also about. But Erikson avoids the religious dimension, the sense of higher order or purpose, the sense of destiny and ultimate relatedness that calling implies.

Erikson's most thorough and vigorous application of the identity concept was done in two psycho-historical studies, and, I think not coincidentally, he chose two religious men. In his study of Luther,[6] where he fully demonstrated the psychological explanatory power of the identity concept for the first time, we can hear an unstated resonance with the Protestant concern about vocation or calling. This reformation concern focused on the importance of a direct, unmediated, one-to-one relationship between God and the individual. This direct line to the divine would result in a specific social task for each person to live out, as an expression of God's will acting through him or her. When Erikson studied Luther, he grasped how this religious concern with calling could also function as a psychological method, or tool, for harnessing psychological energy that had been developing in the individual since childhood. Earlier tasks, accomplishments, and skills in a person's life, such as the development of trust, or autonomy, or initiative, could be focused and tempered by the choice of a calling.

When Erikson studied Gandhi,[7] he was interested in events that happened at a later life stage, long after the formation of his subject's identity (in Chapter 1 we looked at elements of Gandhi's identity crisis in another light). Still, the magnetism that Erikson, founder of the identity concept, felt for Gandhi is connected to the fact that Gandhi's entire life wound around a key Hindu concern that has very close ties to a calling: *dharma.*

In his own writing, Gandhi emphasized the importance of the Bhagavad Gita in his life (see also Chapters 1 and 7 for references to the Bhagavad Gita): ". . . to me the Gita became an infallible guide of conduct . . . I turned to this dictionary of conduct for a ready solution of all my troubles and trials."[8] The Bhagavad Gita stresses *dharma,* sanctioned, pious, role-bound action, as the pillar of life. "Do thy duty (dharma), even if it be humble, rather than another's, even if it be great. To die in one's duty is life: to live in another's is death."[9] Erikson's interest in identity, a kin to calling, was one track that led him to study Gandhi, who organized his life around the Bhagavad Gita, the text that stresses dharma. Not just for Gandhi, but from the dawn of Indian civilization, dharma has been one of its ordering forces, one of the cultural foundations upon which millions of lives rest.

Zimmer's explanation of dharma can be read as a commentary on the Bhagavad Gita and on Indian culture:

The correct manner of dealing with every life problem that arises, therefore, is indicated by the laws (dharma) of the caste (varna) to which one belongs, and of the particular stage-of-life (ashrama) that is proper to one's age . . . Caste is regarded as forming an innate part of character. The divine moral order (dharma) by which the social structure is knit together and sustained is the same as that which gives continuity to the lives of the individual . . . One is not free to choose; one belongs to a species . . . one's concern as a judging and acting entity must be only to meet every life problem in a manner befitting the role one plays. He will then bring into manifestation not the temporal accident of his own personality, but the vast, impersonal, cosmic law . . . by the vigorous practice of prescribed virtues one actually can efface oneself . . . thus gaining release from the little boundary of the personality, and gaining absorption in the boundlessness of universal being.[10]

Dharma may be understood as the divine moral order as it applies to the life of every particular person.

Dharma represents the penultimate development of the religious issue I have generally labelled "calling." It applies not just to the chosen, but to everyone. Unlike the Western, Protestant vocation, however, it is not mediated by a personal relationship to God, nor is it concerned with individuality. Just the opposite: it is based on impersonal social principles, and leads to a transcendence of individuality into universality, into "moksha," release from personal existence, the goal of Hinduism and the focus of Indian civilization. Dharma is not chosen, but is a product of one's position at birth. The devoted soul, however, can choose to follow rigorously what his birth position commands for him to do. Thus, fate and choice are both involved, in a manner analogous to Jung's two-step calling.

Dharma, a variation of calling and the central concern of both an entire civilization and of its stellar individuals, has its roots in ancient history. The Rig Veda is the oldest Sanskrit text, probably three thousand years old; it describes how the Primeval Being of the universe was sacrificed and dismembered, and from his various parts arose the specific castes, each with a specific social role (dharma): "His mouth was the brahmin (priest), his arms were made into the nobles . . . from his feet the servants."[11] In this view of creation, social differentiation dawned with time and the world; it is intrinsic and cosmic, and different people are *essentially* different. Like an arm or a foot, there is no individuality, but created specificity of function. This is similar to the views of other tribal, peasant, or feudal societies, where role differentiation is cosmognified with myths of divine origin and rituals of sanctification.[12] One is reminded of the European concept of the divine right of kings.[13]

As Hinduism developed after the Rig Veda, however, the explanation changed. Dharma came to be explained by the law of karma, in which position at birth, caste, and social role are understood not as automatic extensions of the first moment of creation, but as the lawful outcome of the actions of past lives. This explanation permits both choice, and therefore morality, to enter the picture, while it preserves a cosmic sanction for the current social order. One is born into a specific situation, a caste with its fixed dharma, because of what one did or didn't do the last time one existed. Whether one is born a man or a woman, a barber, farmer, or king, reflects the lawful unravelling of the consequences of past choices and actions, in a scheme of just, reliable causality. Thus, dharma came to be viewed both as an outcome of accumulated moral choices compiled over lifetimes, and of an impersonal, universal law-and-order without caprice or randomness. The continuing vigilant preoccupation of Indian culture with the concept of dharma can be felt in its two classic epics, the *Ramayana* and the *Mahabharata*.[14] These ancient works, which continue to live as the sources of storytelling, theatre, cinema, religious teaching, and poetry, extoll dharma extravagantly and repetitively as a law to be followed logically, beyond death itself.

The comfort of dharma, that one's place in life is given, intrinsic, correct, self-generated, socially vital direction, as well as a doorway to the infinite, is immensely soothing to a core human need. It must be one of the elements taken into account for the remarkable stability and continuity of Indian culture. Gandhi wrote that, when illness and fever had brought him to death's door, "I could not get rid of the feeling that the end was near, and so I began to devote all my waking hours to listening to the Gita being read to me . . ."[15]

A prominent American writer has written to me that throughout the years of his adulthood, as he travelled the world, he always kept the Gita with him, and though not religious, he felt comforted, psychologically stabilized, by the book's authoritarian insistence that he stick to his dharma, which, in his case, meant writing. He devoted his late years to formal study of the Gita in Sanskrit.

The conservative social impact of the concept of dharma is also obvious. Unlike the Protestant calling, it is immutable from birth and provides the rationale for the caste system, which includes untouchability. Ironically, Gandhi, devotee of the Gita, which is the Lord's own exposition of dharma, rejected both his own caste dharma, and the entire notion of caste! His eccentric, radical, personal interpretation of dharma, with typical idiosyncratic flair and with a genius's conviction and expressive facility, refurbished dharma in the light of calling.

Gandhi rejected the notion that duty was a matter of caste and birth, and he suffused his reverence for the Gita with Western and Christian notions he absorbed from the works of Plato, Thoreau, Tolstoy, and others, who experienced duty on an internal, psychological, ethical level. For the Western writers and rebels that Gandhi admired, the sense of a calling was as forceful an imperative as is dharma to the legendary heroes of the Indian epics, except that the Western literary men were called by the kind of personal, individual, inner voice that Jung wrote about in "The Development of Personality." I quoted from Tolstoy's *The Kingdom of God Is Within You* in Chapter 2; that book was one of several that inspired Gandhi to name one of his homes in South Africa "Tolstoy Farm," and to correspond with Tolstoy. Gandhi wrote: "Tolstoy's *The Kingdom of God Is Within You* overwhelmed me. It left an abiding impression on me."[16]

Gandhi made the first translation into Gujarati, his native language, of the Socratic dialogues, in which Socrates responds to an inner voice, a divine madness he must obey, which commands him to a life of self-generated wisdom in confrontation with group intimidation and unexamined living.

> . . . God orders me to fulfill the philosopher's mission of searching into myself . . . Men of Athens, I honor and love you; but I shall obey God rather than you . . . This duty of cross-examining other men has been imposed upon me by God; and has been signified to me by oracles, visions, and in every way in which the will of divine power was ever intimated to anyone.[17]

The yearning for a calling, for a task that fulfills the world as it moves forward in one's own life, for a role that interlocks with the roles of all other men and women and with the goals of the creative powers that brought life into the world—this yearning and need is nourished by different traditions in different ways. Gandhi's absorptive brilliance enabled him to draw many sources into a united action. He mingled calling and dharma, reinforcing their similarities, and remolding them to suit his own needs. That is why his personality was so illuminating for Erikson to study, and so comprehensive yet rambling an example for this chapter. Having wandered through the Rig Veda, the Bhagavad Gita, Plato, and Tolstoy to follow him, we can at last observe him listening to the knotty

American countrymen of those whose duty is to rebel, whose social group is among the gadflies of conscience: Thoreau. It was Thoreau's essay "On Civil Disobedience" that provided Gandhi the tool he needed:

> The only obligation which I have a right to assume is to do at any time what I think right . . . For it matters not how small the beginning may seem to be: what is once well done is done forever . . . Under a government which imprisons any unjustly, the true place for a just man is also in prison . . . You must live within yourself . . . I perceive that, when an acorn and a chestnut fall side by side, the one does not remain inert to make way for the other, but both obey their own laws, and spring and grow and flourish as best they can, till one, perchance, overshadows and destroys the other. If a plant cannot live according to its nature, it dies; and so a man.[18]

Civil disobedience and passive resistance spring from the concept of a personal calling. This inner voice with a personal message is a particularized, non-caste dharma. It is the voice of creation in one's own spirit, as the self-nature of plants and people. Of course, the sense of calling is not intrinsically political, nor does it frequently spur to literary triumph, but great lives, like Thoreau and Gandhi, capture its meaning, diversity, and flavor.

A calling is not the prerogative of the great, literary, or civilized. Tribal peoples also place great weight on similar ideas, as do psychotherapists, scientific or pre-scientific. Marie-Louise von Franz, the foremost interpreter of Jung, writes:

> The earliest origins of modern psychotherapy known to history lie in archaic shamanism . . . [The shaman's] gift of moving freely among the powers of the beyond is sometimes a family inheritance but is more often rooted in an individual experience of vocation . . . When called, he sets himself apart, turns contemplative; often he receives his call through a dream experience . . . During his journey to the beyond the initiate receives instruction from the highest divinity . . .[19]

The premier expert on shamanism is Mircea Eliade, and he confirms the role that calling can play in turning an ordinary person into a shaman.

> ... the "call" or "election" ... the syndrome of the mystical vocation ... the future shaman marks himself off progressively by some strange behavior: he seeks solitude, becomes a dreamer, loves to wander in woods or desert ... the acquisition of shamanic gifts presupposes the resolution of the psychic crisis brought on by the first signs of this vocation. The initiation is manifested by—among other things—a new psychic integration ... a long and often difficult initiation centered in the experience of the mystical death and resurrection.[20]

Eliade has collected many vivid examples.[21] It is not surprising that Jungians study this phenomena because one is reminded of Jung's confrontation with the unconscious when reading these accounts of shamanistic initiations, and it is easy to feel that Jung's calling resided in that lineage.

The Native American vision quest so vividly elaborated in descriptions of Plains Indians[22] is a variant on what Eliade sees as a unified though divergent Arctic and Asian culture. It dispersed throughout Oceania and North America, carrying among other things both shamanism and the concern with calling. Among the Plains Indians, the vision quest was not limited to shamans but extended to *all* young men. Erik Erickson is one of many authors to comment on the colorful, frightening, yet ultimately flexible vision quest:

> ... the adolescent Sioux would go out and seek dreams, or rather visions, while there was still time to decide on a life plan. Unarmed, and naked, except for loincloth and moccasins, he would go out into the prairie, exposing himself to sun, danger, and hunger, and tell the deity of his essential humility and need of guidance. This would come, on the fourth day, in the form of a vision which, as afterwards interpreted by a special committee of dream experts, would encourage him to do specially well the ordinary things such as hunting, warring

... or to bring slight innovations into the institutions of his tribe, inventing a song, a dance ... the higher powers were assumed to have given him a convincing sign that they wished him to plan or change his life's course in a certain way.[23]

Thus, every male member of the tribe felt called by the gods to unique participation, particular purpose, and special protection; in short, divine sanction for the thumbprint of his life upon the untouched plain of the world. Through the institution of the vision quest, a calling became part of the life of every Plains Indian male.

It is not surprising that white Americans also had powerful religious visions that, among other things, confirmed that they had been called to serve divine will. The whites, who settled the continent of people who developed the vision quest, themselves became founders of religions. Joseph Smith wrote:

While I was thus in the act of calling upon God, I discovered a light appearing in my room . . . a personage appeared at my bedside . . . he called me by name, and said unto me that he was a messenger sent from the presence of God to me . . . that God had a work for me to do; and that my name should be had for good and evil among all nations . . .[24]

A chill may come over us as we read this description of the initial upwelling into the world of the forces and inspirations that were to become the worldwide, charismatic Church of Jesus Christ of the Latter Day Saints. Springing out of the Protestant tradition, harking back to the oracular revelations of the ancient Mediterranean civilizations, and with the most riveting, convincing depictions of lights and visions, Joseph Smith conveys the flaming power of a life that feels called to generative action by the creator of the universe. Like Mohammed of Arabia, an unlettered rustic was called to transform human history.

One individual's sense of calling can be an anvil on which

the lives of millions are forged. That happened when Joseph Smith founded the "Mormons." The world-destroying, world-creating zone of religious feeling in humans can erupt, or be launched from, a single individual's sense of calling. Thus, calling is both an individual psychological phenomenon and a formative, historical one. Martin Buber has captured the feeling of both focus and breadth that underlies this phenomenon:

> Here the You appeared to man out of a deeper mystery, addressed him out of the dark, and he responded with his life. Here the word has become life . . . it stands before posterity in order to teach it how one lives in the spirit, in the countenance of the You . . . There, on the threshold, the response, the spirit is kindled in him again and again, for there he recognized true necessity: fate. That I discovered the deed that intends me . . . reveals the mystery to me. He that forgets all being-caused, and decides from his depths, and steps bare before the countenance—this free human being encounters fate . . . it is not his limit, but his completion, freedom and fate embrace each other to form meaning . . . grace itself. Confidence flows to all the people from the men of spirit. Every great culture that embraces more than one people rests upon some original encounter.
>
> Free is the man who wills . . . He believes in destiny and also that it needs him . . . it waits for him. He must proceed toward it without knowing where it waits for him. He must go forth with his whole being . . . He must sacrifice his little will, to his great will to find destiny. Now he no longer interferes, nor does he merely allow things to happen. He listens to that which grows . . . in order to actualize it in the manner in which it, needing him, wants to be actualized by him—with human spirit and human deed, with human life and human death.[25]

Buber describes again the two-step process that we heard about from Jung, and in the concept of dharma. On the threshold of the ultimate relationship, the individual stands before God and meets his own fate. But fate is not dead, static machinery, or thick, impeding walls. God's fate requires human will for completion. The individual must will to complete the fate God has delivered to him. The individual must strive to listen, to decipher, and then to decide from his own depth to go forth with his whole being and actualize destiny by the process of his living and dying. A free man therefore wills fate.

When I read Martin Buber's mountainous, unalloyed prose, I imagine I am hearing the very same spirit of those who created the Old Testament. It is not an inheritor of, or a translator for, but a reincarnation of those such as Job and Isaiah. This voice is transfixing. It speaks to a state of religious knowledge, of a direct encounter with ultimate reality, that is universal and found in the bedrock of all religious traditions. Juan Mascaró, the great Sanskrit scholar, has pointed to the uncanny similarity of the descriptions of this knowledge—knowledge that one has been called to one's own destiny, life and death, from the voice at the heart of creation—that exist in Isaiah and in the ancient Hindu Upanishads.

> The sun shall no more thy light by day, neither for brightness shall the moon give light unto thee: but the Lord shall be unto thee an everlasting light . . . (Isaiah).[26]

> There the sun shines not, nor the moon, nor the stars; lightnings shine not there and much less earthly fire. From his light all these give light, and his radiance illuminates all creation (Upanishads).[27]

These descriptions are of a state of inward-directedness so profound that one slips through the inmost veil, and the inner becomes the outer. The light of the mind becomes the light of the world; one's inner counsel becomes the voice of the Lord. Nevertheless, these two visions of the moment of calling, for all their similarity, differ profoundly. Martin Buber and Isaiah are writing about history, unique events happening in meaningful linear time, destiny. Doubt-free swinging forth into the world with one's whole being becomes a calling that can transform itself into a mission. Effective and responsible action can become extrapolated into messianic self-confidence. The called individual has a historical mission to act as God's vessel and messenger in the world. This Old Testament spirit is also the spirit of Joseph Smith and of the Koran.

The Upanishads, however, are referring to an a-historical, timeless eternity of unending immediacy. They do not call to action, but to knowledge and vision. In fact, the Upanishads have never triggered a charismatic or messianic sense of historical mission. Martin Buber wrote *I and Thou* in Germany in 1923, and I hear in it the same grandiloquent, Wagnerian quality I heard in Jung's "The Development of Personality." This worship of the called man who believes destiny needs him spawned not only evocative psychology such as Jung's, and landmark prose such as Buber's, but it also spawned Hitler's vision of his own role. If a man going forth with his whole being, listening to his own inner voice, interpreting "God" to himself, by himself, *is* destiny, what checks upon arrogance and self-aggrandizement exist?

The bombastic, operatic, world-destroying romanticization of the concept of calling that was spawned in early twentieth-century German culture failed to place *calling* in the context of other religious elements. (See, for example, Chapter 8.) Such romanticization was also based upon one of the fundamental aspects of Western religious heritage that Martin Buber captures concisely:

> Every person born into this world represents something new, something that never existed before, something original and unique. "It is the duty of every person in Israel to know and consider that he is unique in the world, that there has never been anyone like him, for if there had been someone like him, there would have been no need for him to be in the world . . ." Every man's foremost task is the actualization of his unique, unprecedented and never-returning potentialities . . .[28]

West and East, overlapping historically and culturally, yet so different in so many ways, diverge diametrically on the concept of calling. Buber's language in this quotation is an almost word-for-word opposite to the concept of dharma, as Zimmer described it (see above). In dharma, uniqueness is seen as a form of separation from the divine, and the general, universal, eternal, and impersonal are thought to lead to ultimate reality. In Buber's prototypic Western view of calling, individuality and uniqueness generate a world-creating or world-destroying sense of historical necessity. In the dharma of the Gita, or the universal light of the Upanishads, the Self that is identical in everyone and everything evokes an impersonal integration with a cyclic, non-historical now. Both Western and Eastern views, however, do share a blessing and a danger that are intrinsic to all forms of calling.

The sense of calling, in its various forms, can be thought of as facing in two directions. On one face, calling provides the possibility of expanded, harmonious participation. It gives the individual a place within the whole that integrates him with the outposts and colonies while he remains hardworking at home. It focuses the person on his own particular challenge, his weight to lift, his responsibility to live up to, but it also provides a boundary, a limit beyond which the person need not go. A calling commands accomplishment in one sphere, here where one stands, yet facilitates a relaxation of personal mastery in other spheres, where other callings take over, permitting harmonious, integrated, social action. This face of calling points towards responsibility coupled to mutual interdependence.

Another face that can appear on the sense of calling is that of excised, superior dominance. The need for a calling can deteriorate into self-important, unbridled self-righteousness, or abstracted self-absorption. Rather than being at the hub of participation, it can cause a fantasy of exemption from the human condition. The exemption can be historical and messianic, or a-historical and aloof. The lonely murderer, like Dostoyevsky's character Raskolnikov in *Crime and Punishment*,[29] or the excited, pathetic martyr in a Shi'ite suicide squad,[30] justifies his destructiveness by feeling *called* to it. Gandhi described how so much of his daily inspiration came from the Bhagavad Gita, but his assassin was inspired to shoot him by studying the same text.[31] The manic psychotic, and the paranoid schizophrenic, often feel called to insane acts. In the wards of a state mental hospital I have met many people who felt called—to preach incomprehensible word-salad messages, to masturbate all day for months at a time while "making love to Jesus Christ," to drag their children across the country while following an elusive, chaotic, private, divinity who always proffers but never delivers a sense of greatness to compensate for insanity and failure.

The widespread injunction to go and preach, and to publish the gospel among all nations, and to convert the heathen, so common to diverse scriptual literature, can easily serve as an inducement to, or a justification of, a sense of privileged position as messenger and monitor, rather than member of humanity. A patient I saw gave an interesting illustration of this.

An articulate and intelligent clergyman, he quickly rose to national prominence. Then, just as quickly, he began to lose jobs. His trail was marked by personal conflicts at work, despite his genial warmth, interpersonal skill, and wonderfully humanistic values. He rationalized the conflicts as a result of his calling: to hold mankind and himself up to the highest moral standing. Wherever he went, he thundered with the law. In therapy he discovered that his calling as moral standard-bearer to his denomination had an adolescent precursor.

While he was still a teenager, living alone with his alcoholic mother, he exercised his impressive intelligence and determination to force his plight on the attention of a court. He got his custody changed from his mother to his father—his parents having been divorced some years earlier. The legal victory over his mother was an exhilarating triumph—the court exonerated him in his contempt for her!—but he felt terribly guilty. Over and over he found himself repeating that old scenario: challenging congregation members and board members to live up to *his* standards or be replaced. At the same time he punished himself for his guilt about what he had done, by damaging his own career. I had to focus him on the question: was his true calling, as an inspired leader of good faith, being contaminated by a compulsion to place himself repeatedly in the role of the remarkable and exempted child?

A calling has objective and subjective aspects. Objectively, it has to do with the world one builds and engages during one's lifetime; and, subjectively, it has to do with how one experiences, feels, and relates. There is no exact division between a calling and a fulfilling, uncalled career and family life, just as there is no exact measure to separate a calling from a strident, self-proclaimed guruship. Several vignettes will serve to clarify the flexible relationship between job and calling.

A Lutheran minister who sought therapy for the depression that followed his divorce had a dream in which a cross on the wall shook, fell, and broke. As his therapy progressed, he talked about how his calling to the ministry now seemed like a uniform he had donned as a young man to avoid his sexual confusion, and the uncertainty of a career as a historian, which he really wished to be. His *calling* wasn't a calling.

A painter came into therapy because of impotence. He was filled with self-contempt, and despite unusual economic success for an artist, he felt his career was a second-rate choice, meant for effete losers. His father was a very aggressive and successful corporate businessman. In therapy, he saw that his self-hate and impotence had a different constellation of origins than his art, which had arisen and grown with continuous delight and commitment despite many obstacles. He had kept his calling couped as a career, due to his neurotic self-disparagement and his ignorance of the depth of his inspiration. When he terminated therapy, his career was en route to feeling like a calling.

An economist who directed a think-tank and was the

author of six books in his field came to therapy because of the depression that followed his second divorce. He was a suave diplomat at work; then he came home alone to his apartment and watched T.V., alienated from wives, children, without true colleagues or friends. His work, despite his success, was as empty as his personal life. He retired early to pursue his hobbies of women and antiquing. Career prominence has nothing to do with calling.

In the absence of something akin to calling, the work of life can deteriorate into utilitarianism, without inner and outer meaning. Work then becomes occupation. Accomplishment and creation then become merely narcissistic expansion, or survival-oriented functionalism. A calling enables the fulfillment of the need to feel used. In his *Report to Greco,* Nikos Kazantzakis captures this feeling in the inscription:

Three kinds of souls, three prayers:
(1) I am a bow in your hands, Lord. Draw me, lest I rot.
(2) Do not overdraw me, Lord. I shall break.
(3) Overdraw me, Lord, and who cares if I break![32]

Kazantzakis comments further: "Happy the youth who believes that it is his duty to remake the world . . . woe to whoever commences his life without lunacy . . . What, then, is our duty? It is carefully to distinguish the historic moment in which we live and to consciously assign our small energies to a specific battlefield . . . immortality means to divine and join immortal rhythms." Kazantzakis's passion illuminates the distinction between the secular tone of identity and the religious dimension of a calling. An identity must sweep up into its midst and sew together biological givens of talent and temperament, with historical givens of conditions, opportunities, occasions, and constraints. Its threads are economic necessities and pragmatic realities.

A calling must stand on that developmental foundation,

but it points beyond and higher. In Kazantzakis's words: "A silkworm turns his entire life into making silk, and dies. A man turns flesh into spirit."

The need for a calling can spur orchestrated, attuned participation, what Erikson called "craftsmanship" and "cogwheeling."[33] A calling focuses life within the awareness of interdigitation. Robert Jay Lifton's simple, secular definition of adulthood captures this flavor: ". . . adulthood is a state of maximum absorption in everyday tasks, subsumed to transcendent cultural principles."[34] Aggression can be harnessed into hard work in the common cause. Professionalism and the development of precise skills can become delineated devotion rather than narrowness. One's own work can fall into place on a spectrum of broad appreciation for other tasks and ways.

Most importantly, through a sense of calling, immediacy can beat its point on the anvil of eternity. Like a pinhole for observing the sky, to dampen diffusion of light, so the whole heavens can clearly be seen, a calling is the pinhole through which a person can glimpse the other religious dimensions of life. Without it, there is no history, merely time. Without it, work is the rattling of a dry leaf in the wind. With it, work is the creator shaping the world through our hands. Without it, work is competition against men and women; with it, work moves as a galleon under millions of scintillating ephemeral sails. Worms work to feed themselves; when they are called, they become butterflies. Deeply immersed in the idea of dharma, the Indian poet Tagore wrote:

> I have had my invitation to this world's festival, and thus my life has been blessed. My eyes have seen and ears have heard. It was my part at this feast to play upon my instrument, and I have done all I could.[35]

The theme of calling becomes urgent in our flexibly structured society. The psychotherapist may hear it at the center of some psychotherapies.

A thirty-two year old father of two arrived barefoot, with his hair in a long pony-tail. He worked in a factory, to which he commuted for over an hour from an isolated rural area. He and his wife had been attempting to live with total self-reliance as small farmers, growing vegetables, tapping maple trees for sugar, selling pony rides. Instead of a pastoral idyll, however, they found themselves impoverished, frustrated, confused. "I turned myself into a bear"—he described packing two hundred and twenty pounds onto his six-foot frame, commuting to his factory work and returning exhausted, then flying off the handle at his wife, who was home all day with two toddlers. She had an affair and let him know it. When he had discharged his rage, she told him it was his fault for having neglected her. He wept, agreed with her, and sought therapy.

His father was a distinguished research biologist. His parents had divorced when he was sixteen; his mother was hospitalized with recurrent arthritis; the home fell apart; and his father quickly remarried and distanced himself. He had dropped out of school to live on his own in a defiant, romantic, counter-dependent style. He pumped gas. He wielded a chain saw on a logging crew.

In fact, there was no one he could count on. His father was building a new family and was curt and distant toward his old one. His mother was preoccupied nursing her own wounds. He calibrated his life to counteract his parents'. They were Westchester sophisticates; he moved to the country. They were intellectuals; he became a laborer. They were socially activist Unitarians; he kept to himself and the ecological superiority of poverty. His father drove a red Porsche. To use the minimum resources, to have no car and no home, became his point of pride. One summer he picked apples. With a Homeric twinkle he told me how another young apple picker reached up into the tree, pulling her breasts firm against her chest all day. She had flushed, russet cheeks, blue eyes, and was "all-girl." She loved nature, too. He was by now eighteen, but she was only sixteen.

Her parents were also divorced. His parents had married when their professional degrees were complete. He married now.

The teenage couple rented a dilapidated farmhouse. They turned the soil, bought a pony. He cut and hauled firewood, a lot of it, since the house was drafty. He was strong and thrived on physical labor. She became pregnant. Suddenly, their cash expenses soared. His new life, his touching affection for his young wife, his attempt to find solace in nature, declined into long drives on icy roads, night-shift work, cynicism, anger, depression. A landscape that had seemed an enduring summer turned to winter. The house was cold. The baby cried. The teenage mother doubted herself. He skidded his newly bought used pick-up on a slick curve, crumpling the hood against a maple. They fought to exhaustion, knowing it was wrong but unable to stop. Some years passed with no change. He worked overtime, and a second baby arrived. He wasn't home much (it seemed worse when he was); then she had her affair and he made phone calls and came to my office.

He was testy, guarded, and skeptical as he started therapy, but he was tenacious and strongly motivated. He wanted to know why he alienated his wife, why he had become so impossible and unbearable. Except for a few screen memories, his life before his parents' divorce remained unknown, unrememberable. The shape of his current life seemed to him to be the product of a few recent sweet and bitter choices. I encouraged him to try to see bigger patterns, older forces. He had put the past away, slammed the door shut on the first half of his life. Was there something awful, hidden, he had to forget? No, the worst thing had certainly been his parents' divorce and what followed, and *that* he could remember. Before that, well, he could remember the house, his bike, the yard, the last cornfield and nine acres of rolling hills and oak woods that in those days still remained in his suburban neighborhood, the solitary dairy farm, the smell of the barn, the steaming winter cows . . . but nothing about himself, his own family, and their life together.

In an unusually dramatic series of sessions, he began to associate to a vague memory of an early morning fishing trip with his father . . . and the bear broke down. Sobbing profusely, almost unable to go on, he dragged out of his past not a horror, but an exquisitely sweet panorama of memories about his father's love of nature. Researcher *par excellence,* his father had an unslakable, infectious, boundless enthusiasm for laboratory, microscope, fly rod, field-guide, and trail. Incessantly busy and rarely home, he was a magic carpet of adventure and inspiration for his son when he would sweep in and call out the whole family to watch the moon rise or to help bandage the neighbor dog's leg. His greatest delight was to lead his son through the predawn mist beside a rocky river and go at a battle of wits against browns and brookies, using home-tied flies, and surrounded by the calls of hermit thrush and veery. The bitterness this patient couldn't bear was the loss of his father, and the loss of his own hope to be an equally inspired student and participant in the wonder of life.

The son of the research biologist had his comfortable and secure childhood world shattered during adolescence by his parents' divorce and and breakup of their home. Before that, the world was pregnant with opportunity for him. He would get up early to walk or fish with his father, and his natural curiosity and delight in nature were not only gifts, but a confirmation of his importance. His father's job, it appeared to him, was merely to be alive with curiosity. With his parents' divorce he lost more than the comfort of having two parents under one roof. He lost the behavioral anchor to his identification with his father. On the one hand, that identification was so deeply rooted it was irradicable. On the other hand, he could find no way to express or manifest it. In addition, he was seeing a new side to his father—not just the ebullient naturalist, but the evasive, self-absorbed, interpersonally troubled loner, who could cast aside his family, and leave his child high and dry.

With grief and furious determination, the boy had sprung

forward imitating his father's values, by setting himself up as a countryman, farmer, and eco-purist. His apparent rebellion against suburbia was really an attempt to recapture and align with the best in his father. This was a pose, a role, but not a calling. It used his values, but it didn't use him, his heart, or his intellect. Instead of taking root in the fertile earth, as he hoped, he was changing the oil in his used truck and snapping at his wife. Instead of being called and used to discover, he felt cast aside, rejected.

When in therapy he uncovered the feelings about his father and himself that he had buried under his bear pose fifteen years ago, he began to cast around. He wrote long, hopeful, reparative letters to his father—only to receive cool notes in return. He demanded more variety, more status, more recognition at the factory—and found himself facing job loss.

He told me his problems were societal, not psychological. I told him that he had given me the impression that he would never be happy until he went back to school. But he was thirty-two, had two kids, a house and hadn't completed his junior year of high school! Why couldn't his foreman recognize how inventive he was? Would his father help support him through school? The return letter said, "No." But clearly his position was unsustainable. His exaggerated autonomy and self-reliance made him unable to use himself constructively, socially. Even factory work was a fragile economic stake, since his haughty posing kept him on the verge of dismissal. His refusal to learn anything from anybody was leaving his most fertile field, his mind, unsown. I told him teasingly, but pointedly, that he was a semiliterate who swaggered like a chairman of the department at Columbia (where his father had taught).

He was not easy to talk with. His experience of the unreliability of adults and authorities made him skeptical of me, and only necessity kept him coming back. He defied and tested me. He sat cross legged in the chair, and rubbed factory oil off the sneakers that had appeared over his bare feet onto the cushion covers. He investigated my credentials. When he felt more comfortable, his challenges became more relevant, more personal. He wondered whether I really liked my work. Was I really *fascinated* by it? He expressed dismay that I could charge him money if I in fact loved what I was doing. He informed me that my fan was wired incorrectly, and the snow wasn't shovelled properly. Since I didn't seem very competent in ordinary things, how did I know what I was doing about psychiatry? Did I predict ahead of time that he would cry when he talked about his father?

Some of his more concrete questions I answered. Unlike interactions I have described with patients in Chapters 2 and 3, where I let the boundaries of therapy move, but more like the style I mentioned with the patient in Chapter 1, I stuck to that old, careful, middle ground of asking him why he was asking what he was asking. I felt that his penchant for provocation could easily draw me into an irritated squabble. I thought that his questions were all superficial and misleading forms of a vital, deeper search.

He seemed hypervigilant and paranoid. His jokes sometimes stung. The therapy as yet had no clear direction, and I felt I needed to be cautious. But I had no doubt he held me in admiring affection. I have rarely felt so enlisted by an enthusiastic, if gruff, young captain for a voyage into the unknown. I had no doubt we were exploring together. Curiosity impelled by necessity, steered by skepticism, with results greeted by more curiosity and refocusing—this was an excellent working alliance for two explorers. Only in retrospect did I become aware that the nature of our work was for him a transforming discovery.

Blocking this man's capacity to have ever gone to school, or to go to school now, or even his capacity to get along with his foreman, who saw in him only a smart aleck, was his distrust and his sense of counterfeit nurturance. Even his romanticized and idealized father, after all, hadn't showed he'd given a damn. His bruised mother counseled him in the practice of keeping his distance from other people. A long, circuitous phase of therapy involved his checking me out, provoking me, teaming up with me, journeying into his backwaters and dark oceans with me, and then kicking me like a used tire on an old Chevy to see if I would still hold up.

He took two evening courses at the University extension service. He received straight A's; it was easy, and he let me know it. More courses were just as easy, particularly math, formulas, chemistry, what makes things grow? He sold his country house and moved his family into an apartment in town, to eliminate commuting and be close to classes, and he worked half-time and went to school half-time. Now that they lived in town, his wife could work, but she felt dazed: to whom was she married? Another year, and he was in school full-time, on university loans and loans from relatives. He received advanced standing in an accelerated B.A.-Ph.D. program in catalysis chemistry, which would take him another five years. (The high school degree was clearly irrelevant now.)

Another hurdle had to be passed. He was a wizard in the laboratory, as manually skilled as he was scientifically keen, but undergraduate laboratory courses are also exercises in cooperation. At first, he carried his truculence in with him. When he permitted himself to study with a group of fellow students, who had so far tolerated his less-endearing style in exchange for his brains, he felt a panicky rush of anxiety and brought the problem into our sessions. Who, other than the dependent child-bride he had bonded with and then pushed away, would he let into his life? He would let me in. He had already. He would let these students in. Why? What if the girls were seductive? What if people cheated, used him? I could simply tell him that if he wanted to grow out of the miserable life he was leading, he would have to get along with these students. He wanted to be a scientist, an explorer. He wanted to captain the ship of his sleeping delight into the ocean of the mind. He cooperated.

The last semester we worked together he seemed to me to be a changed person. Instead of scanning his environment for a parental word, he was focused on the development of himself as a scientist. His relationships with his fellow students—some ten years his junior—became quickly offhand, casual. He let his professors know he was a mind to be reckoned with, but he monitored himself for cockiness. He was following a vision, returning to a source, joining a world of people, pursuing a dream. Once again, he cooled to me, letting me know he needed the time to study, cutting sessions back to once a week, then terminating.

Clearly, to understand the change in this man, we have to consider his several levels of identification with his father, his experience of me as a therapist and transference object, his intelligence, his background in and drive for economic well-being. I have not reconstructed the entire story, with its many subplots. I have intended only to clarify that we also have to consider the dimension of calling, in which a particular individual blossoms when filled with juices from the xylem and phloem of life.

The therapeutic process that permits the awakening of a sense of calling in a life of frustration is not a tactic or a technique. It is not a trick of questioning or a specific insight. It is a flavor, an attitude of respect, awe, and toughness. The therapist must respect the apparently foolish and counterproductive pathways in the patient's life so far. Despite their superficial blindness and maladaptation, all of the patient's past actions are to be respected as containing kernels of a search. Respectful exploration of these actions—their motives, meanings, and causes—will uncover within those blunderings some human inspiration. The attitude of awe keeps the patient's future open to the pathways demarcated by an inner light. His future is uncertain. The therapist cannot guide or judge him, cannot predict his next step, but the therapist works with him in expectation of a revelation through action. Toughness holds firm against the flight from awe. While "calling" sounds romantic, even a life of frustration holds some comforts that an unknown future may destroy. Almost no one wants to feel his or her life torn open. No one wants to leave even a drafty country house for the anomie of a city apartment.

At first, it felt easier for the son of the research biologist to disprove my competence or worthiness—and thereby spare himself the danger implicit in our task. Many a time, I, like his foreman, felt ready to throw him out. My only tool (so different from the work with affirming acceptance described in Chapter 3) was to point back at him again and again and counter demand that he explain himself. But the therapist's feistiness can have varying tones. It was my steady gaze upon his unused self, rather than the analysis of neurotic patterns, that frightened, challenged, and thrilled him. It was because of my confidence that I was confronting a robust explorer that I could drive the bear back into the corner where he would break into tears over a life lost and reemerge as a man with a life regained.

Why do I consider this the discovery of a calling, not just a maturation into a profession? The lines aren't hard and fast. In this instance, there were no lights, visions, or gods; there was no self-important rhetoric. But, it seems to me, much more happened than an economic, occupational shift. This man became energized. He felt impelled to his new life. He experienced his drive to become who he was to become, both as a right that no one could take away, and as a duty that he was destined to fulfill. He had an overpowering desire to take on his new world. The change that occurred in him was not just social or instrumental, but his new work integrated and organized his sense of self, sewing together patches of family life, past memory, intellectual skills, self-esteem, sense of work, and sense of play. Most importantly, he experienced these changes in his life as the fulfillment of a radiant world order, the proper and precise fitting of promise and demand with his picture of reality. He felt called, by an inner voice, a relentless, unshakable demand, to bring the beauty and order of nature back into the human world. When he ignored it, he felt he was only an animal, a trapped bear. When he responded to it, despite the very high price, he felt enormous freedom. The two-step process was there: destiny (which at the psychological level may have been his father's infectious curiosity, or his own intellectual and aesthetic response to nature), and willed choice to follow it. For him, as for his father (and many others), study is worship, nature is scripture, experiment is exegesis. He embroidered his courses with extra projects, extra questions, like a child in a garden, like a father with a fly rod and a son casting for rainbow trout. He trusted others and became a member. He relinquished his paranoid distancing, because he had re-experienced in therapy what his father had revealed in flashes from time to time: that you must tell someone about the fish you catch, that seeking the truth is a form of human love.

Two years after we agreed to terminate what felt to be a uniquely successful and gratifying therapy, he called to ask me for the name of a psychiatrist for his wife. School was "wonderful." What makes things grow?

◇ 5 ◇

Membership

*. . . I stirred up dust with my feet, tramping along in the
undivided march of human history . . .*

A Holocaust survivor, who had previously made a good
recovery and adjustment, came into therapy psychotically depressed. He needed medication and crisis management of his
suicidal feelings. The precipitant was his daughter's announce-
ment that she was marrying a non-Jew. He himself had no clear
religious beliefs. But naturally he felt a strong sense of Jewish
identity that he considered to be entirely separate from religion
per se. His only child was irrevocably destroying that. He was
furious, and his depression may have had some passive-aggres-
sive, revengeful overtones, but it was predominantly a true
impasse, a loss imposed on a life built on slender bridges over
chasms of losses. His psychotic delusion was that he would
become a great artist, greater than Michelangelo, but he wept
whenever he mentioned it.

He recovered quickly his clarity, but not his equilibrium,
under medication. He doubted I could understand or help him.
He felt that no one so far removed from the extremity of his

87

own life could help him. In his eyes and mine, the titanic hideousness of the suffering imposed upon him because of his Jewishness gave him an awesomeness and impenetrability to interpretation. He put himself in a position to me—and I accepted it—of a Hebraic Prufrock returned from the dead with terrible, unimpeachable knowledge. He was many years my senior.

He described to me his life as a hunted preteen-age animal in the forests of Nazi-occupied Poland. He, his sister, and another child had escaped a roundup of Jews from his village. They sneaked about the countryside, looking for food. They found a revolver that had one bullet in it. They lived in constant flight and terror for months, ragged, emaciated, empty-handed except for their gun. At last they were caught by Germans. To make their point, the Germans gouged out his sister's eyes while he watched. She was twelve. Through a quirk of attention, a flicker of fate's eyes, he and his friend escaped, with their gun. They debated how to use the gun if recaptured. Should they shoot the enemy or shoot themselves to avoid capture and torture? Two twelve-year-old boys debated: which one had the right to be shot?

He described to me another scene: all the adult men of one town were herded into the synagogue: the doors were bolted, gasoline was poured on the little wooden structure, and the house of God and everyone in it went up in flames while wives and children were made to watch. He told me that he would never go to temple after that, even here, today. He felt all synagogues were traps. Anyway, he didn't believe in that kind of religion.

Only a few years ago, after three decades of successful adult life in America, he had travelled alone to Israel, without his wife and daughter. A memory of a Friday evening in Jerusalem troubled and puzzled him. A tourist, a loner, an outsider, he strolled around the dark streets in the evening. It was warm, windows were open, apartments were lit. Floating over the air in every direction were the sounds of voices, prayer, laughter, chatter, the clink of glasses and plates, the tinkling static of the Jewish Sabbath being celebrated by thousands of families in thousands of buildings—believers, participants, members—while the solitary, wounded, atheist tourist walked alone outside.

Patients will talk about their need for a place inside of, and an orientation to, history. This need to overcome one's individual skin, one's isolation and fragmentariness, to have a group, an affiliation, a community, can be called the need for membership. The need for membership interlocks with a sense of calling. It expresses not only the drive for personal definition but also the matrix within which definition occurs. Through a calling, a person finds his role in the creation; through membership, this role can be actualized and located in coordinates of time and place. This need is to identify *with* others, to identify *them,* and to *be identified* by them. It is not enough to feel a sense of witnessed significance, or lawful order, but a person must feel engaged in the body of the productive human community and human continuity.

Human life is always lived in the media of cultural structures, like marine life in the sea. Membership is what we are immersed in. It means to whom we talk, what language we use, and what colloquial syntax and vocabulary we speak. It determines what thoughts we can think. (No one could think of gravity before Newton; no one can not think of it now.) Our habits, values, thoughts, possessions, our health, food, air, and music are all strung out on lattices of webs reaching from person to person, and for that matter, from person to soil, plant, and animal. Both our physical and our psychical lives are ecological. It is through the webs we spin that we capture bits of reality to consume. The weave of our webs forms our territory, our reality, our lived-in universe. Whom and what we weave out and in is more essentially our "soul" than are the clouds and phantoms of self-consciously religious inner visions.

Not some self-selected, treasured feelings and daydreams, but all we encounter is our "soul." The stars we see are the stars we catch by extending ourselves to watch them. Our realities are not spun alone. They overlap in multilayered depths of intersecting human worlds ". . . until the whole sea becomes an entanglement of watery bodies . . .."[1] We live inside the sweep of history. The large-group vibration is the bass note to our self-determination; it limits, guides, channels what we may be. The Holocaust survivor could convey with his stories the way the world is subjective, local, idiosyncratic, and phenomenological, yet also imposed, external, historical, and absolute.

It is for this reason that Jung wrote: ". . . psychical dangers are much more dangerous than epidemics or earthquakes. Not even the medieval epidemics of bubonic plague or smallpox killed as many people as certain differences of opinion . . ."[2] National Socialist Germany is the penultimate expression of this aspect of human life. The German who gouged out the Holocaust survivor's sister's eyes imposed upon all human minds a fact about what is possible, that is as fundamental as the dependence of biological life upon the sun. In all times and all places the network of contacts in which we are suspended is a critical aspect of who we are. At the height of the Beatles' success, tens of millions of people around the world walked about every day humming and singing to themselves songs that reached them on waves of sound encircling the earth.

Religions always define history. They describe creations and origins. They describe how the world was created in seven days, or how Prajapati was dismembered to form humanity (see Chapter IV, p. 62). Religious myths give a measure to time that places the individual in some meaningful relation to it. For Jews, time flows outward in a line from the crucial moments of the past—eating unleavened bread in the flight from Egypt, lighting candles in the destroyed temple—and individual life is fulfilled as part of the transfer of memory. Christians borrowed this idea of time, and our civilization counts years that have elapsed from the historical presence of Jesus. For Hindus, time is a recurring cycle of aeons, an unending carousel of vast infinite repetition and duration. For Buddhists, history is both an unending, beginningless flux, but it is also a countable number of years distance from proximity with a great healer-savior: Buddha. Religions describe turning points, such as when the angel Gabriel gave Mohammed the order to recite, and the old laws of the Bible were replaced by their final version, the Koran; or when the angel Moroni appeared to the prophet Joseph Smith and instructed him to find the golden plates on which were inscribed the Book of Mormon.

Religious legends and traditions mark and define epiphanies, and other sacred and prototypic moments. Chinese, Japanese, and other Far Eastern Buddhists revere the moment when Bodhidharma with unusual courage, foresight, and determination, spread Zen from India to China and the Far East. Hindus cherish in their memories the time when Vivekananda spoke as an equal, or much more than an equal, to white Westerners, at the World Congress of Religions in Chicago at the very end of the nineteenth century, and in a flash reversed centuries of cultural domination and religious missions to start a reverse flow of the religious tide East to West. These religiously inspired epiphanies are the unforgettable lightning bolts that separate and organize time into history. The prose of routine is given the rhythm and measure of poetry through the universal occurrence of seasonal, religious commemorations, festivals and feasts, and the cyclic re-emergence into time of enduring myths.[3] They give the future a focus, pointed toward days of judgment, rebirths, second comings, apocalypses, and Armageddons. They break up the run-on sentence of time with the punctuation of holiday, ritual, and calendrical rhythm.

Religions provide not only history, but also community—direct, shared participation with other people. Congregation, church, pilgrimage, holy land—bodies surging side by side, animated by the same historical picture. Religions are by no means the only social institutions to provide community, but all religions do so. Elias Canetti, who won the Nobel Prize for literature in 1981, provides both a basic psychology of groups and also vivid examples of the way religions utilize them. He wrote in his major work of social psychology, *Crowds and Power:*

> There is nothing that man fears more than the touch of the unknown ... It is only in a crowd that man can become free of this fear of being touched ... The crowd he needs is the dense crowd ... As soon as a man has surrendered himself to the crowd, he ceases to fear its touch ... The pilgrimage to Mecca is a slow crowd, formed gradually by tributaries from many different countries. The obligation to perform this journey at least once in a lifetime colors a man's whole earthly existence. Anyone who has not been on this pilgrimage has not really lived. The experience of it draws together, so to speak, the whole territory over which the Faith has spread.[4]

Most community experiences offered by religion are less dramatic than the annual, world-wide hajj of Islam. Beyond crusades, or the Mormon trek to Utah, daily religious life may offer kitchens on two sides of town baking for the same table, or multiple hammers pounding two-by-fours on a new steeple. A newspaper columnist from eastern Ohio in 1986 gasped in astonishment when, the day after a fire levelled a farmer's barn, six hundred Amish gathered to floor, frame, and roof well enough to cover hay, what would normally have been a one-hundred-thousand dollar barn, in one day. Religious community may mean someone to come over when your spouse dies; someone to trust when you migrate to a new land; someone who knows the same songs. Religious hermits differ from eccentrics and cranks at least in that their hermitage has a concrete, interpersonal membership despite its solitude. Alexandra David-Neel, the extraordinary French woman who, in the first half of the twentieth century, disguised herself as a man, learned Tibetan, and penetrated the secret and guarded world of Tibetan monasticism in remote trans-Himalayan Asia showed that the extreme isolation endured by Tibetan Buddhist monastic disciples was balanced by their profound devotion to the person of their guru.[5]

In this light I want to stress that by membership, I am not referring to something abstract, like shared myth or literary reference or even to shared life of the spirit, but to something concrete: hands, faces, people. By membership, then, I am referring to the ordering of flux into time and history, concurrent with the actual touch of other people. The people I refer to are those with whom one's relationship is of particular religious significance because of the way it is defined in light of that view of time and history. "These are my fellow Jews; this is my Zen Master; this is my congregation; this is my fellow student on the Path."

This dimension of religious life would seem so unsubtle that it is difficult to write about it without belaboring the obvious. Yet William James, and others who followed in his experiential, individualistic framework, seem to have overlooked it as a core element of religion. They write as if religion were entirely internal, experimental. Aldous Huxley wrote a humorous, heartfelt description of his religious experience on mescalin (in the tradition of James's explorations of nitrous oxide) in *The Doors of Perception*. This whimsical and rhapsodic work set the prototype for psychedelic religious exploration, due not only to Huxley's literary skill, but also to his enthusiasm: "Words like 'grace' and 'transfiguration' came to my mind . . . the Beatific Vision . . . for the first time I understood."[6] But Martin Buber scathingly attacked Huxley's entire direction: "The true name of all the paradises which man creates for himself by chemical or other means is situationlessness . . . because they are in their essence uncommunal, while every situation, even the situation of those who enter into solitude, is enclosed in the community of logos and cosmos."[7]

For Buber, logos and cosmos, the words by which we think and understand, and the complex whole world we relate to are intrinsically products of the human collectivity, of cultures that generate language and shared reality. In his view, every profound experience, every truly religious experience, has roots in cultural antecedents and must be given back to the human community as a tool for others, as part of the web of life. Huxley would no doubt agree—his writing itself was an implicit agreement. But his writing may have lost the emphasis that Buber had, and Buber was echoing Plato. For Plato, the awakened life occurred in dialogue, person to person, not through books or lectures: "It is only after long association in the great business itself, and a shared life, that a light breaks out in the soul, kindled by a leaping flame, and thereafter feeds itself."[8]

Through membership, religions extend individual life so that it becomes part of a longer and broader flesh. As soon as there is a growth in other spheres of religious life, it is reflected in membership. In Chapter 1, the graduate student began to feel witnessed significance, rejoined a church, and experienced a diminution of his narcissistic isolation. In Chapter 2, the Rabbi felt increasing lawful order, and then took his parishioners more seriously. In Chapter 4, the son of the biologist actualized his calling lockstep with the gradual erasure of his paranoia; direct engagement of real people followed: his therapist, fellow students, and teachers. Without opening himself up to a sense of membership, his sense of calling would have remained merely a fragment of self-image, a cognitively held but unfulfilled identity. In Chapter 4, I described how the sense of calling can deteriorate into self-aggrandizement; a possible cause for this is an underdeveloped sense of membership, in which history becomes compressed into immediacy, and community shrivels into self, until time and membership disappear behind a charismatic, melodramatic "me and now."

Religious membership is not the same as social membership. When I talk about religious membership I am not referring to the number of cards in a man's wallet, or the amount and number of dues he has paid; I am not talking about how involved a woman feels, or how many people she knows. I am not talking about joinerism. Religious membership has to do with the emerging out of nothing of the face of the infinite as it shines from real faces. Religious membership has to do with the intuition that the warmth of life itself, like the transmission of life from the world's first father and mother, is alive in any hands you hold.

A tragicomic example of the distance between membership and joinerism was provided to me by a Catholic priest who sought psychotherapy due to pressure from his superiors. This highly placed son of the ivy league arrived in a red convertible with radio blaring. He prided himself on the status of his jobs, the wealth and social register ranking of his friends, the quality of the scotch he tucked under his belt, and his ability to outwit or hoodwink anyone he met. His outlandish bravado had only become a liability in his middle age. Throughout his twenties and thirties, his genuine creativity and wit, the splash of color and joie de vivre that trailed out behind him like a rainbow-colored wind sock, had kept him swirling upward through increasingly desirable parishes. The devil-may-care freshness and cute daring of the affected revolutionary was colorful jewelry on the robes of a young priest. So this scion of the best families and best schools was not only a distinguished member of the world's biggest church organization, not only the household guest of the oldest and wealthiest families, whose weddings and baptisms he performed, but he was a speaker, a trustee, a member of the most desirable political and social organizations. His world began to sour in his forties, when his absenteeism, tardiness, and erraticism began to raise the ire of parishioners, who flagged his superiors. His alcoholism was beginning to become visible. The most amazing feature of his personality to me was his bald cynicism. This self-preoccupied, onanistic trumpet believed in nothing, held to no values, stole from department stores, copped drugs, took advantage of teenage boys, with style. To him, it was the game of life. Like a bathhouse Nietzsche, he felt rules and religion were for the losers and weaklings. The years of his treatment in psychotherapy are another story. Suffice it to say this Fauntleroy around town, who liked to tweak me with his exaggerated disbelief at my boring small-town existence, was as lonely, sad, and fragile as a widow. Like a nineteenth-century romantic heroine, he whirled about the ball but felt totally alone. Getting to know the unconnected dismay that underlay his cynicism only reemphasized to me the distinction between religious membership and sociability.

What I mean by membership is also a far cry from compliant attendance. A depressed, paranoid victim of child abuse attended church regularly and participated in every sacrament, but still felt unable to get along with anyone, and, sometimes, unable to go on living.

Paranoid schizophrenics will invent membership: worlds populated by imagined others. They seal their isolation through fantasy without *participating* among others. Their delusional worlds of helpers and pursuers reflect the creative and destructive aspects of membership.

The need for membership can deteriorate into a destructive force: discretely bounded, paranoid in-groups. In James Jones's Jonestown, the boundaries between membership and outsiders were rigid and absolute; all outsiders were feared and distrusted, and the future of world history was personalized and compressed into myopic, futile destruction.[9] Unfortunately, rather than representing an exotic error in an otherwise clear human record, Jonestown exemplifies a common, almost universal stage of large groups, upon which religions also play.

The British psychoanalyst Wilfred Bion demonstrated that when human clusters congeal into functional groups, capable of accomplishing tasks in a coherent manner, they follow predictable developmental stages, analogous to the development of an infant into adulthood.[10] One of these predictable stages is that of "fight-or-flight." At this stage, whether one is observing a psychotherapy group, or the British Army, or a church, according to Bion, one will observe that the group is galvanized by a common, unifying basic assumption.

> The group has met to preserve itself, and this can be done only by fighting someone or something or by running away . . . action is essential . . . the individual is of secondary importance to the preservation of the group . . . a leader is even more important . . . he should have a bit of a paranoid element in his makeup, for this will assure that if no enemy is obvious, the leader will find one . . . He is expected to feel hate towards the enemy.[11]

According to Bion, an "us-or-them" paranoid attitude towards the outside commands an increase in inner group coherence: "Now that we must fight *them* off, we must all band together and really cooperate."

In religious groups, there is no exemption from this stage. The chosen people, the apostolic privilege, the divine elect, the bearers of the irrefutable Word—this privileged feeling for themselves leads religions over and over to create "pseudo-species"[12] that breed hatred, exclusion, enmity, and ill will. Religions may be no worse than nation-states in their responsibility for shattering humanity into factions that deny each other's humanity, but they have been no better. As Freud and Erikson have pointed out, the sacrifice of autonomy and thoughtfulness to which the individual submits when he becomes part of the divinely sanctioned in-group, is compensated for by the excited inflation of feelings that accompanies the fantasized immortality, conquest of personal death and of human history that the religious herd incites. Freud wrote: ". . . nature rises up before us, sublime, pitiless, inexo-

rable . . . the elements . . . diseases . . . the painful riddle of death
. . . one would expect a permanent condition of anxious sus-
pense and a severe injury to man's innate narcissism . . ." But,
Freud elaborated, cultural ideals, particularly art for the intellectuals, and humanized depictions of nature in the form of
gods for the masses, provide narcissistic satisfaction in the
power of the human collective with which the ephemeral individual can identify. People not only delight in their own ideals
and gods, but they get pleasure and narcissistic relief from the
right to despise people from other groups who have "wrong"
ideals.[13] Erikson expanded Freud's ideas:

> Envisage man, the most naked animal . . . he would bind his group
> together and give to its existence such super-individual significance as
> inspires loyalty . . . in times of threatening change and sudden
> upheaval the idea of being the foremost species must be reinforced by
> a fanatic fear and hate of other pseudo-species.[14]

Freud, Erikson, and Bion are linked in psychoanalytic
theory. They understand group aggression to spring from underlying fears of vulnerability and death, and from a conse-
quent need for group coherence, for which aggression is a key
tool. Canetti, whom I quoted above, sees the individual as
lonely, terrified, and in need of a comforting touch, but he
describes the existence of "warring packs" as derived "from
earliest times"—that is, a given of existence. He understands
this to be a potential form of any sort of human aggregate, and
since religious packs have no exemption, he postulates simply
that there are religions that exist to be warring packs. He uses
Islam as an example.[15]

A religious group frequently revels in the belief that it is
the favorite child of a tyrannical, brutal, all-powerful father-
god. This is the same fantasy that spares and haunts the life of
some incest victims. The victims of father-daughter incest may
have been saved from more destructive situations by striking

a compromise with a sadistic father. By becoming the pet victim of her father, a daughter may be used but not destroyed. Her position is one of degraded, yet specially chosen, and specially powerful, elect offspring. Children of the same sadistic father, who cannot accept this compromise, may be destroyed outright. In one instance I am aware of, a daughter submitted to her father's sexual demands and grew up to be intensely unhappy, guilt-ridden, and self-despising. She hated herself, and wondered in retrospect why she hadn't been stronger, more defiant. In therapy, she recalled how two of her brothers, who had been rebellious (for her father's needs were polymorphous perverse), were spiritually and mentally broken in front of her eyes by her father's relentless, ruthless cunning and mockery. Both boys ended up insane. The daughter, though unhappy, made it out into the world. Her role in the life of her family of origin had been an adaptive, lesser-of-two-evils, choice. But wherever she went, subsequently, she felt herself at odds, alternatively enraged or submissive, unable to simply or safely join.

Freud thought that the universal presence and power of incest taboos proved the need for a restraining force on the yearning for incest. If the yearning were not so great, why would there be such ubiquitous, stern laws against it?[16] Erich Fromm followed Freud in confirming the importance and pervasiveness of incestuous yearnings and taboos, but he differed with Freud's concept of incest. Fromm pointed to a social dimension of Freud's hypothesis: incest at the societal level constitutes not merely overt sexual behavior with relatives, but it is the feeling state of trust, love, and care tightly enclosed within the boundary of endogamous groups.[17] According to Fromm, the belief that a person should marry only within one human group—a very widespread belief indeed—is simply an expanded form of incest. Fromm implies that when a Hindu Brahmin feels he must only marry a Brahmin, or when a Jew or Catholic feels he should only marry a Jew or Catholic, he is using religion to justify acting out the *feeling* of incest. Thus, much religious life deteriorates into the promotion of consanguineous fortresses, in which sexuality and its accompanying nurturance of the young is chained in loyalty and fear to a jealous, vengeful projected fantasy "God." This "God" is used to rationalize incestuous, paternal, sadistic lust—all maintained by the accompanying fantasy of special favor, and special protection, from that omnipotent male/Father/God, because one has submitted to Him and His rules. Submission, endogamy, and protection are prominent themes in many organized religions.

Reflecting over the past few pages, we can see that religions bond people into groups, and that religious groups share some destructive aspects with other human groups and elaborate some destructive forces all their own. They may participate in fight-or-flight paranoia; excited, delusive triumph over the fears of vulnerability and death through the vilification of others; pseudo-speciation and the denial of others' humanity; war packs whose essence is to create and maintain a state of war; and incestuous pseudo-families that proffer magical protection from an imaginary father, at the cost of perverse submission to someone else's will.

But religious membership may go further, down the group path of aggression and incest, to Jonesville. Suicidal martyrdom justified by the cause is a familiar part of religious history from the colosseum of ancient Rome to the suicide car bombings of contemporary Beirut. The great Scriptures, rich in complexity and diversity of message and interpretive potential, are not exempt from their contribution to this destructive aspect of the yearning for membership. Throughout them are the mines of this soothing, divisive sentiment: that one group has a special dispensation, that everyone else is outside the inner sanctum, and that enmity with a suggestion of violence is the expected outcome.

According to the Doctrine and Covenants of the Church of Jesus Christ of the Latter Day Saints:

> And verily I say unto you, that they who go forth, bearing these tidings unto the inhabitants of the earth, to them is power given to seal both on earth and in heaven, the unbelieving and rebellious . . . And also those to whom these commandments were given, to bring it forth out of obscurity and darkness, the only true and living church upon the face of the whole earth . . .[18]

According to the Koran:

> . . . We said, "Go to the people who have cried lies to our signs"; then We destroyed them utterly, and the people of Noah . . . We drowned them, and made them to be a sign to mankind . . . Muhammed is the Messenger of God, and those who are with him are hard against the unbelievers . . .[19]

In the New Testament:

> For nation shall rise against nation, and kingdom against kingdom . . . And ye shall be hated of all men for my name's sake . . . I have chosen you out of the world, therefore the world hateth you . . . he that is not with me is against me . . .[20]

In the Old Testament:

> In Judah is God known; his name is great in Israel . . . Pour out thy wrath upon the heathen that have not known thee, and upon the kingdoms that have not called upon thy name.[21]

Naturally, the scriptures aren't limited to this attitude or even predominantly guided by it. But it is there in them, and a writer is responsible not only for his total effect but also for the way his words permit him to be misunderstood. There is no limit to the evil and destruction that has been rationalized by this aspect of religion, which may spring from group nature antecedent to religion per se, but which religions have so frequently failed to modify and instead have fed upon. John Hay, a Catholic writer, traces Hitler's mass murder back to a pervasive relationship between the core of Christianity and Judaism. Starting with a quotation he agrees with, he continues on his own:

> "More than six million deliberate murders are the consequence of the teachings about Jews for which the Christian Church is ultimately responsible, and of an attitude to Judaism which is not only maintained by all the Christian Churches, but has its ultimate resting place in the teaching of the New Testament." The Christian tradition, which made "the Jews" responsible for the death of Christ, first took shape in the Fourth Gospel . . . John almost invariably employs the phrase, "the Jews" when the context shows, and other evangelists confirm, that he is referring to the action or to the opinions of the High Priests and the Ancients . . . John, by his repeated use of the phrase "the Jews," puts into the mind of his readers the idea that they were all guilty. This condemnation of the people of Israel, in the name of God . . . has strengthened the tradition of hate, a tradition which has disfigured the whole history of Western Europe.[22]

The Holocaust survivor who came to therapy psychotically depressed cannot be understood in a vacuum. History could help us understand and help him; so could a study of the fundamental psychological elements of religion. To deal with the depth of his depression, it was necessary to consider the biology of antidepressant medication and his early family life and relationship to his parents, but most importantly the problem of religious membership. This man was being torn apart on the rack of membership.

I will return to his particular case, but, to understand it fully, we need to turn around and see how the hunger for membership can grow outward, beyond embattled, self-justifying, paranoid, warring, incestuous, suicidal, murderous violence into identification with a large group membership that functions not with an exclusionary boundary but which reaches out to embrace humankind. As membership seasons and ripens, identification is its hallmark. The need deepens beyond comforting submersion in the surrounding touch of the crowd, or group narcissistic inflation, into empathy: the recognition of the identity of the human spirit in self and all others.

At the unconscious level of group function, according to Wilfred Bion's theory, the rageful, fearful, basic organizing assumption of fight-or-flight is supplanted, when an optimistic, hopeful group organization develops that emphasizes not separation and exclusiveness, but pairing. Bion analogizes this stage to the mingling of the sexes to procreate and reproduce the hopeful next generation, the proverbial messiah.

Canetti describes how warring packs, whose entire focus and being revolves around group murder, can be transformed into packs of increase, which thrive on growth and incorporation. What these psychological observers of large group function describe for groups in general may underlie what happens when religious groups cease to define themselves by who they are against, and when they become instead self-extending and welcoming. The same four scriptural texts that contain a frowning, finger-pointing tone of voice in other places exhort their devotees towards open-armed, pan-human membership:

> We claim the privilege of worshipping Almighty God according to the dictates of our own conscience, and allow all men the same privilege, let them worship how, where, or what they may . . . we believe in doing good to all men . . . If there is anything virtuous, lovely, of good report or praiseworthy, we seek after these things. [The Articles of Faith][23]

> . . . aggress not: God loves not the aggressors . . . Surely We sent down the Torah, wherein is guidance and light . . . and We sent Jesus son of Mary, confirming the Torah . . . [Koran][24]

Love your enemies, bless them that curse you . . . thou shalt love thy
neighbor as thyself . . . I was an hungered, and ye gave me meat
. . . I was a stranger and ye took me in . . . I was in prison, and ye
came unto me. [New Testament][25]

And he shall judge among the nations, and he shall rebuke many
people: and they shall beat their swords into plowshares, and their
spears into pruninghooks: nation shall not lift up sword against nation, neither shall they learn war any more. [Isaiah][26]

How could a religion survive the test of time if it didn't
open membership downward to the scorned and broken, and
outward to all other groups? As the need for membership
ripens, it becomes the source of ethics, rather than morality;
that is, it leads to codes of conduct based on the awareness of
the universality of pain and suffering, rather than merely on the
fear of retribution for misdeeds. The need for membership
ripens in those who, like Gandhi, "seek the divine in every
man."[27] It may even expand beyond humanity to a sense of
membership in the community of living things. This expanded,
embracing, empathic ethic is not limited to formally denominational fellows. It represents a culmination of religious psychological development, and because at heart it is at odds with the
chant of the horde, it is more often found in individuated souls
whose membership is open-ended rather than under one theo-
cratic roof.

Freud wanted to alleviate humankind from what he felt to
be the illusion of religion, and he yearned to do so by means
of a futuristic education project that would achieve
". . . the same aims that you expect to be realized by God
. . . the brotherhood of man and the reduction of suffering."[28]
Erich Fromm later pointed out that Freud's aims didn't supplant religion, but were the essence of religion.[29] Anthropolo-
gist and poet Loren Eiseley could stand beside an archeological
dig, and, looking down over scattered artifacts and bones of a

prehistorical burial site, he could feel his brotherhood with those bones through their "essential human gesture."[30]

Empathic identification is not only a developmental attainment; it heals, or helps to heal, isolated individuals to whom it is extended. Surely, this is one of the healing elements of most forms of psychotherapy, and it has been widely identified by religious healers in many cultures as a variable they can manipulate to help sick souls. Johns Hopkins psychiatrist Jerome Frank gave a convincing, cross-cultural depiction of this. In his book *Persuasion and Healing,* Frank argued that religious healing by shamans, or in group ceremonies in primitive societies, contains some of the same active ingredients as are found in contemporary Western psychotherapy. One of these ingredients is a healing restoration of the sense of religious membership, which Frank variably describes as reintegration, or closer relationship, with the group. His illustrations capture the way in which healing ceremonies highlight, or emphasize, the refurbishment of membership in the lives of the sick member. Frank also studied religious healing in the Western world, using the pilgrimage to Lourdes as his example, and again found that this religious form of psychological healing contained efficacious ingredients, among them ". . . a climactic union of the patient, his family, and the larger group . . ."[31] Since the publication of *Persuasion and Healing,* a host of articles in the psychiatric literature have pointed to an apparent curative power for various psychological and psychosomatic forms of distress through the experience of being incorporated and confirmed in membership in a religious group.[32]

This principle has been dramatically harnessed by Alcoholics Anonymous, in which a readily available and endlessly reconfirmable sense of membership, coupled to religious beliefs, has been a key element in successful treatment of alcoholism in probably millions of cases. "A.A." provides, in treating the alcoholic, almost continuous social support, in the form of nightly and daily meetings, and sponsors who function like parents and family, but it provides also a religious rationale, to turn the social support into a form of membership. The principles of "A.A." read: "We made a decision to turn our will and our lives over to the care of God . . . made a list of all persons we had harmed, and became willing to make amends to them all . . . we try to carry this message to all alcoholics."[33]

The sense of membership may expand beyond one's denomination, tribe, sect, or church, to humankind, and it may extend beyond humankind to all lives. St. Francis of Assisi retained his place in the church, but expanded his sense of membership beyond other Catholics:

> St. Francis of Assisi, feeling and knowing—not merely "believing"— that every living creature was veritably and actually a "theophany or appearance of God" . . . acted in accordance with his convictions, preached to his little sisters the birds. "Oh wondrous thing! whereas St. Francis had made the sign of the Cross, right so the terrible wolf shut his jaws and stayed his running: and when he was bid, came gently as a lamb and laid him down at the feet of St. Francis . . . And St. Francis stretching forth his hand to take pledge of his troth, the wolf lifted up his right paw before him and laid it gently on the hand of St. Francis. Then quoth St. Francis: 'Brother Wolf, I bid thee in the name of Jesu Christ come now with me, doubting nothing, and let us go stablish this peace in God's name.' And the wolf obedient set forth with him, in fashion as a gentle lamb."[34]

Regardless of the veracity of this legend, it expresses an ethic treasured at least by those who preserved and promulgated it. We have seen how religious membership can function to divide humankind into socially incestuous, exclusive, group hatred, and how it can also develop into an ethical, pan-human embrace; and now it is easy to see the same issues at work in the relationship between humans and other forms of life. In a landmark article that appeared in *Science* in 1967, Lynn White wrote about the historical roots of the ecological crisis:

> Human ecology is deeply conditioned by beliefs about our nature and destiny—that is, by religion. Christianity inherited from Judaism a story of creation . . . God planned all of this explicitly for man's benefit and rule . . . it is God's will that man exploit nature for his proper ends. St. Francis tried to depose man from his monarchy over creation and set up a democracy of all God's creatures. I propose Francis as a patron saint for ecologists.[35]

This is a long way from the Koranic injunction ". . . slay the idolaters wherever you find them, / and take them, and confine them, and lie in wait / for them at every place of ambush."[36]

The extension of a sense of membership with all life is news in science and a quaint elipsis in Western religious history. It is the basic position of Buddhism and Jainism, two Indian religions founded side by side approximately 600 B.C. Jainism, which seems very little known in the West, is a religion of millions of Indians, and has had an enduring influence on Indian culture over two and a half millennia. Among other fundamental principles, it sees all things as possessed of souls in ceaseless transmigration, based upon the Karmic law of good or evil action (see Chapter 4), which it shares with Buddhism and Hinduism. For the Jains, everything is alive. *Any* act of violence will harm the doer through the law of Karma. To pull up a potato or a carrot out of the ground is considered a violent act against a living, pain-experiencing fellow creature. Accordingly, root crops aren't eaten by Jains. Most of us do not feel brotherhood with potatoes, but Jain radicalism found its way into the mainstream of twentieth-century history through Gandhi, who grew up in an area of India surrounded by Jains, and who specifically referenced his own budding concern with nonviolence to the teaching of his Jain neighbors. These neighbors stressed the ancient virtue of *ahimsa,* non-harmfulness to all. The man who stood closest to being Gandhi's spiritual guru was a Jain.[37]

In Buddhism, a similar pacifist strain is not merely the product of the practice of compassion—a virtue stressed by

Buddha—but represents an aspect of membership. According to one of Buddhism's preeminent interpreters in the West, D.T. Suzuki: "Man is, after all, part of Nature itself . . . Nature is divine . . . I am in Nature and Nature is in me . . . a fundamental identity . . . It is the bosom whence we come and whither we go."[38] Suzuki has pointed out, in an essay aimed at psychoanalysts, that even the kind of affection, admiration, and reverence for nature expressed by a poet like Tennyson differs from Buddhist influenced art, as found in the Japanese Haiku poet Basho, because the former looks at nature sympathetically, while the latter speaks from inside nature with nature's own voice.[39]

While many elements of religious psychology point us towards eternity (see, for example, Chapters 2 and 7), membership is that aspect of religious life that implicitly stretches us out toward infinity. The tension inside narcissistic inflation becoming openheartedness becoming kin to bird and wolf; reflects the possibility that stretches from uniqueness becoming multiplicity becoming infinity.

Mysteriously present in the probability of inertness is the palpitation and flush of life, an ark of forms floating together on the waters of the unknown. The leaves on trees each year outnumber the stars, and every leaf reaches out to the one sun that also fuels my words. The many-in-one is an awareness that can be initiated by surging in a dense mob. It also can be known by working one case at a time toward the alleviation of suffering and the brotherhood of man. Whether lost in perverted forms or ringing pure, an element of religious life is to see ourselves in the heart of all beings, and to see all beings in our heart.[40]

Despite decades of professional success, family life, and apparent security in America, the Holocaust survivor carried inside him the feeling that he was a meaningless chip floating on the random surges of a blind, dead ocean. With a derisive, caustic laugh, and a wave of his hand, he would dismiss anything I implied, or anything in his interactions during the week, that smacked of what might be called good faith, but which to him only was evidence of coddled naivete. I learned to stifle what began to feel boyish and spoiled in me. In his wry, sarcastic way (a form of gallows humor he preserved even in his despair), he referred to himself and anyone else when the fancy took him, as "failed abortions." It seemed to me he dwelled in a world where death seemed natural and life was the exception. But his stories of the past were filled with terror, an infectious terror, and so I imagined that deadness was at least a defense, a hope, against terror. Since he had in fact overcome his past, and built a new life, I focused on the question: why did his daughter's marriage change things? If life were meaningless, what difference would it make if she married a Jew or not? If life were meaningful, how could that rest on the marriage of his daughter?

A good question. (He still liked good questions!) His insight was that he felt a part of his family, but of no one or nothing else. Your family is all you've got. He couldn't trust anyone. Even other Jews couldn't be trusted. In the camps, when people got hungry enough, cannibalism broke out, and he could see in the eyes of people around him—the eyes of Jews—what he meant to them. Why then would it matter if his daughter married a non-Jew? He pondered what it meant to be Jewish, when he neither believed in God, nor could pass his Jewishness on to his grandchildren. It meant something, he couldn't say what. It meant historical bondedness. At least these people had suffered, or might suffer, what he had, known the same reality he knew; they were his brothers, his people; they could never reject him for being a Jew! Yet he was unable to join, be a Jew, himself. Jews were treacherous—everyone was. Worse, joining was a trap. That wooden synagogue.

Instead of membership, which was blocked to him by cynicism and terror, he demanded incestuous substitutes. He wanted his daughter's loyalty. The issue wasn't, who would she be married to, but, was she *loyal* to him? Now, his daughter had blocked that hope. She was disloyal. Abandoned, betrayed are too mild for what he felt; he felt devastated, set afloat from his only bond to the future, his only hope, his only shoreline, his only identification. He swore: "It is simply impossible for her to do this. After what I went through. She knows. She can't possibly know. I've told her. But she can't understand."

He wanted to escape the membership of the wooden synagogue, the membership forced on him as a curse, but he couldn't escape membership. Another survivor he knew told him of a group in another state, led by a rabbi, for families whose children had intermarried. He went to the concrete cinderblock basement with folding chairs underneath a synagogue, where this group met. These people could understand him.

Here was a person who in the name of religion had been denied membership in humanity, and had been branded with burning irons of memory such that wherever he went the smell of horror accompanied him and scared away others. Even well-wishers shirked and rationalized. His past adjustment to his rebuilt life had been heroic and cosmetic. His world hung on one thin thread, a thread he himself had weakened by providing his daughter a safe, healthy, promising American life. She had become loyal to life again, not just to her father. Now he dangled on nothing and fell into despair, and at the bottom of despair he found other pained people climbing up. Oh, human spirit! He started to climb up. "If these other people, real religious Jews who really believe that stuff, can accept their kids' intermarriage, why can't I?" This rabbi, who had written on the holocaust, was a rabbi, to his discredit, but he was no naive fool (a reference to me?).

He drove two hours to attend that rabbi's synagogue—still an atheist—but he had friends there. And why, exactly, had he continued seeing me? He excused himself by needing medica-

tion, but I imagined that dependency is one form of membership. He knew he needed help. He liked good questions.

There is no big success story to his psychotherapy. His
depression moderated. He remained on medication. Unlike the
Christian student in Chapter 1, for whom witnessed significance and membership went together, the survivor continued
to feel stripped of witnessed significance and lawful order. He
had only been able to feel them while psychotic—imagining
himself as self-expressed, as divinely inspired, and as accepted
and sanctioned as the greatest artist. Without his psychosis, he
was bereft of those pieces of himself, and even while psychotic,
his grandiose delusions had been mood incongruent—he had
wept imagining such unreal redemption from his daily lack. He
continued to use me like a cane, a tool, a listening post, an
obedient son, a reliable father. He remained cynical about psychiatry. I continued to tether him in to humanity like a child
with a slightly out-of-control top. I don't imagine interpretations substitute for the therapeutic role of providing sanctuary
for those who can believe nothing. At times we simply reach
out to driftwood for its crooked beauty. Despair is often empirical and can't be treated; it has to be disproven. A psychiatrist
is not a church, not a tradition, and can't provide membership.
But in the magical visions of Sung dynasty landscape art, inspired by Zen Buddhism, it is the slenderest bridge that led to
the forlorn place of ultimate knowledge about what we are.
Psychotropic medication, raised up, raised down, adjusted to
this side effect, to that symptom, is the sacramental sharing
that carries across the thinnest bridge the message of a tenacious, attentive human presence.

III

◊ 6 ◊

Release

. . . I lay down my burden and surrendered myself to the voice of the river, and I became a vessel, and out of me poured the fountain of life . . .

A biochemist sought therapy in a state of extended, low-grade panic. She couldn't concentrate, couldn't make simple decisions. She kept looking over her shoulder for something she felt was overtaking her, yet she could see nothing. She felt she was having a nervous breakdown, going crazy, yet wasn't sure she could participate in therapy, since she couldn't figure out what the problem was, what to talk about. She resented also the dependency she imagined therapy involved. Over months of twice-weekly sessions, a central problem emerged: she felt locked in a struggle to control her life so completely that she felt out of control.

Everywhere she turned—to her husband, inside herself, and to me—she could feel power slipping like sand through her clenched hands. She was incredulous and furious, that she, who had deep faith in God, felt she stood on quicksand, deserted, betrayed. She wanted her way, now; but *which* way was hers? Her husband was a successful executive. His next upward career step was pending, and it would require relocation to another part of the country. She loved her home, her town; she wanted her children to complete high school where they were comfortable and known—and she had sworn ten years ago that she would never move again. So, she found herself in a bitter, covert wrestling match with her husband.

Her husband had built his career while she had been at home with small children. Their frequent family moves had followed the dictates of his career. As a young mother, she had felt powerless, trapped, just a wife. He also had bullied her with rages, and occasionally with his hands. After almost a decade of cowering and resenting, some twelve years ago, she had finally sought therapy for the first time, and it had helped her to break out of her masochistic depression. She took direct control of her life. She stopped her husband's physical violence with a clear ultimatum. She completed her long-hanging Ph.D. dissertation and launched into her own career. Shortly after that, her husband's job required a move; she agreed to it on the grounds that it would be their last. Now, after a decade of stability, her own research was locked into cooperative grants and equipment that would constitute a substantial loss of momentum if she were to move. And now, for the first time in a decade, her husband was considering another move. She felt determined to stand firm—to stay.

But her external war for consistency and control with her husband was complicated by an inner conflict. It was as if she were in both horizontal and vertical battles at once. Since that first therapy twelve years ago, she and her husband had gradually nurtured a tree of affection and camaraderie. His corporate power had put him in a position to administer charitable funds and services, which she admired. They hiked together. He supported her career and respected her intellect. He helped her run the small sheep farm that she kept for relaxation but worried about so often. She felt she wouldn't be able to stand herself, forgive herself, if she stood in his way, merely for her own selfish drives. Yet, she also wasn't going to regress ten years and let him "push her around." She felt she couldn't win, because if she asserted her own career needs she would be hurting the husband she had grown to love and would be hurting their marriage. If she reneged on her own career priorities, however, she would make herself frustrated and resentful again, thereby hurting both herself and her marriage. The low-grade panic that had brought her into therapy was a spiraling paradox of control. She wanted to control herself and her husband at the same time that she felt obliged to control her need for control.

Her religious beliefs only aggravated her situation. She wanted to live a Christian life. A keen student of the Gospels, she felt certain that Christ commanded a simple, devoted, charitable life more consistent with self-sacrifice than with academic, research, career success. She felt urged towards a self-denying Tolystoian saintliness, at the same time that her feminism and her memory of her early married years exhorted her to stand up for herself. Unable to resolve this conflict—in fact, unable to think about it, admit it to herself, without months of therapeutic uncovering—she felt driven, restless, bereft of relaxation or peace, compelled to complete her research, fantasizing and worrying that she would have to just give it all up.

Her head split with severe, recurrent migraines that made her look stiff and pale. They frequently were triggered by our sessions. She was bitter with self-contempt for being unable to hear or find God's voice, which she felt was the true way out of this dilemma. She experienced her very need for more therapy as a measure of her spiritual failure, her distance from God and his commands. In her interactions with me, she was obsequious yet controlling, rushing in to punish or chastise herself in the form of pseudo-insights, disparaging *sotto vocé* asides about what a nut she was. I was almost dizzy from the multiplicity of conflicts she was elaborating: herself versus her husband, her feminism versus her religion, her past views of her husband versus her current views, her religion versus her science, her religion versus therapy, dependency on God's voice versus dependency on me . . .

Patients will talk about their need to relax, to lay their burdens down, to relinquish the effort to control, to be relieved of guilt and anxiety, to be free of tension, and to find inner peace. This is the need for release. It is uniform in process, but it is a composite of contents.

The need for release is related to, overlapping with, and often misunderstood by psychodynamic therapists as *superego-id* conflicts. In the latter, a person is caught in an internal struggle between primitive urges and stern injunctions. The urges, sexual or aggressive feelings and actions, churn and surge inside, ready to break through into destructive behavior. In those instances where the person lacks enough mature, integrating ego-function to contain or rechannel these urges, they are held in check only by the harsh, rigid, punitive superego. The superegoid conflict is personified by the fundamentalist minister struggling with his own hate and lust. The superego is the simple-minded, authoritarian, moralistic injunction that provides the lawful order of orthodoxy (see Chapter 2). The biochemist felt she could slap or strangle her husband, but she reminded herself that Tolstoy and Jesus were pacifists.

A superego-id conflict may trigger a yearning for release, but release exists as a human yearning before and around the edges of this primitive conflict. Release is not limited to the soothing of internal conflict; it includes the ability to accept reality, the inevitable, and the capacity to extend trust toward the world. A prerequisite to attaining release is the faith to let some control slip away, since in any case there are limits to each individual's sphere of control. Release means relief from one's internal conflicts, but it also includes faith in other people and in the future. Since every individual is limited in time and space, each must find some analogue to "Thy will be done." The capacity to speak and feel this universal exhalation of release may in turn have developmental antecedents of relaxing in a mother's arms, or of bowing to a benign father's will. The need for release is not merely related to a superego-id conflict, or is it simply outward turning, or merely trust and faith in other people and in other spheres—it is preeminently tied up with psychosomatic integration, the mixture of the control and dependency we have with our bodies. On the one hand we tell our eyes to open or shut, our arms to swing or be still, our mouths to speak or be quiet. We thus establish control over and express ourselves through our body. On the other hand our body deals out pain, illness, hunger, grey hair, wrinkled skin, and ultimately it will drag us into decay and death. "Thy will be done" also refers to our bodies, and the capacity to assume this attitude is one of the psychosomatic bedrocks of integration with the biological substrate of our lives. Even sleep, coming or eluding us, is a letting go. The biochemist could check her aggressive impulses only through self-conscious commandments; she trusted no one but herself (even psychiatrists were in the business of inducing rather than alleviating dependency), and her rigid body rebelled with migraines.

Affirming acceptance and release are entwined. But the former has more to do with an internal and interpersonal wholeness; while the latter is a synthesis of psychic conflict reduction, interpersonal trust, and psychosomatic integration—all forged into one religious function. Release is one of the jewels of existence, one of the fountains of life, one of the most sought-after treasures of emotional development, athletic health, and spiritual practice. And religions have focused on it, studied it, hoarded it, dispensed it, until the religion and release have become almost inseparable. Erich Fromm expressed it like this:

Self-awareness, reason, and imagination have disrupted the harmony which characterizes animal existence . . . Being aware of himself, man realizes his powerlessness and the limitations of his existence. He visualizes his own end . . . [he] is in a state of constant and unavoidable disequilibrium . . . this results in an imperative drive to restore a unity and equilibrium . . . We must understand every ideal as the expression of the same human need, an answer to man's need for equilibrium and harmony . . . there is no one without this religious need . . .[1]

Listen to the way Williams James tied the two, religion and release, with one knot: "The transition from tenseness, self-responsibility, and worry, to equanimity, receptivity, and peace . . . this abandonment of self-responsibility seems to be the fundamental act in specifically religious, as distinguished from moral, practice."[2]

For James, the abandonment of self-responsibility is the fundamental act of religion. Religions promise respite, sanctuary, security, a covenant with the faithful, which allows for the surrender of strife. Religions all seek to enable their adherents to replace effort and vigilance with a sense of safety, continuity, and confirmation in the presence of the uncontrollable and unknowable processes of self and world. Put your hands in the hand, the Lord is my Shepherd, lay down your sword and shield, be as little children and the lilies of the field, enter the promised land of milk and honey—this is the familiar refrain of hopes and promises of all religions. "In the shadow of thy wings will I make my refuge"—beautiful Psalm 57! For Tolstoy, the essence of Christianity was two words: "resist not."[3] At the center of the Buddhist path we find: "Since there is an Unborn, Unoriginated, Uncreated, Unformed, therefore escape is possible from the world of the born, the originated, the created, the formed."[4] The Koran, which means literally "The Surrender," promises ". . . gardens of Eden underneath which rivers flow."[5] Religions meet the need for release with the poetry of surcease from responsibility and effort.

Here is Jesus: "Take no thought for your life, what ye shall

eat, or what ye shall drink . . . Behold the fowls of the air: for
they sow not, neither do they reap . . . yet your heavenly Father
feedeth them . . . Your heavenly father knoweth that ye have
need of all these things . . . But seek ye first the kingdom of God
. . . and all these things shall be added unto you . . . take
therefore no thought of the morrow . . ."[6] In his challenge and
promise we can hear the speaker's attempt to supplant survival
anxiety, the basic biological drive for certainty of food and
shelter, with higher values, larger goals. But before that can be
done, a release of the grip is necessary.

The mood of yearning for release dominates Black American spirituals, which were composed under conditions of slav-
ery that precluded ease or harmony. Both the heaving, sighing
sorrow and the transporting, repetitive, rhythmic excitements
seem to capture an emotional locus that could be found, independent of brutal realities, in group, religious, musical release.
The words alone without the music, are only outlines, as
demonstrated in such universally known songs as, "I'm gonna
lay down my sword and shield, / Down by the riverside"; or
"Swing low, sweet chariot, coming for to carry me home."
Release is touchingly equated with returning home, or with
being rocked in a nuturant, protective bosom of Abraham.

Because release means the relinquishment of personal control and power, the acceptance of limitations to one's abilities
and even one's life, and acceptance of the body that will decay
and die, it shades into acceptance of meaningful death (Chapter
10). It is said that Nehru, throughout his lengthy premiership
of India, kept on his desk a poem of Robert Frost. While he
struggled with poverty, underdevelopment, the bloody parti-
tion between India and Pakistan, the war over Kashmir, border
wars with China—while his beloved wife was dead, and his
mentor, Gandhi, assassinated—he kept a copy of Frost's
"Stopping by Woods on a Snowy Evening." On the surface,
this poem is about a man and his horse stopping by someone
else's woodlot on the night of the winter solstice, to watch snow

fall for a moment, before proceeding on their way. But many readers have taken it further. The solstice is the "darkest evening of the year"; a man is facing his darkest moment, his greatest trial. The one who owns the woods—and who really owns woods, but the Source of creation?—has a house in the village (a church?) and is not watching the man who, in the trial of his darkest hour, must struggle alone. The man's horse, sweet animal friend, cannot understand the human trial, and shakes his playful harness bells to ask if there is some mistake. A cold, impersonal, yet peaceful universe surrounds them:

> The only other sound's the sweep
> Of easy wind and downy flake

The man, the poet, the statesman who kept the poem on his desk, yearns for . . . is it release . . . is it death?

> The woods are lovely, dark and deep

But finds he is restored enough to drive on:

> But I have promises to keep
> And miles to go before I sleep
> And miles to go before I sleep.[7]

Walt Whitman, who seemed blessed with continuous volcanic surges of release (from what underlying tension?), could chide his fellow humans: "I think I could turn and live with animals, they are so placid and self-contained . . . They do not sweat and whine about their condition, /They do not lie awake in the dark and weep for their sins, /They do not make me sick discussing their duty to God, /Not one is dissatisfied . . . or respectable or unhappy over the whole earth." Whitman felt apart from profane human existence, because of the depth and conviction in his own experience of release. "Swiftly arose and spread around me the peace and knowledge that pass all the argument of the earth."[8]

Underlying the yearning for release is the problem of ambivalence. Release from superego-id conflict, release from a need for controlling an ultimately uncontrollable world, release from enmity with one's own body (the source of pain and death)—all of these revolve around and find their solution in the core of ambivalence, the center of life. Because release is contingent upon the mastery of ambivalence, it is closely related to religious love (Chapter 8) and meaningful death (Chapter 10). The imaginative, anticipatory, and memory-filled capacity of human life, the multiplicity of commitments, hopes, and fears, the complex tapestry of prolonged early learning woven into the living, contemporary, archeological layers of cultural inheritance—these enable each individual to hope all things, imagine all things, yearn for all things, and dread all things. The animal that developed the capacity to foresee carries the burden of the future in his imagination. The animal that stores up past experiences must pluck out unceasingly the worm of guilt. We cannot live riveted to the unhindered immediate, like a fox pursuing a rabbit. Guilt, anxiety, these drifting clouds of higher level tensions, build into the human situation the yearning for permanent psychological shelter. If only we could be free of all second-guessing, all knowledge of death, all yearning for the as-yet-unfulfilled and just unambivalently be!

The yearning for release is the yearning for an unreserved, open, and receptive letting go of mental, physical, and social control into the onflowing process of the world. It is the wish to float and stream. Like two hands on one body that are the same yet opposite, enantomers—release is the enantomer of calling: the same need to relinquish the grip on life and listen to what calls, but the opposite of doing. Release is the freedom to let the world be what it is. Because it requires a no-holds, unambivalent permitting, it requires the faith of love behind it.

That is why it is so exquisitely a religious function, for in a world without a truly lawful order, full release would simply be madness. The trap of life can be sprung into release only where there is the faith in an harmonious exfoliating of the "now." In a state of release, we can see the unguided, upwelling sap of being leaf out into allrightness. A lethal and trustworthy world we can rest on blooms unhindered and unstructured.

> What life can compare with this? Sitting quietly
>   by the window
> I watch the leaves fall and the flowers bloom,
>   as the seasons come and go.[9]

The Japanese Zen poet, Seccho, who wrote those lines in a state of release, was echoing an aspect of Buddhist teaching with which he could be sure his readers would be familiar. According to Mahayana Buddhist legend, after Buddha attained enlightenment, the highest god and creator of the universe, Brahma, appeared before him and pleaded that he teach his discovery to the world. Buddha snapped off a sprig of the Udumbara plant (which has invisible flowers and which the ancients believed to be flowerless) and . . . held up one of its flowers! The whole universe of gods and men assembled in front of him, expecting more—a sermon, a flash of lightning—except for one man, Mahakasayapa, who smiled. "Buddha then said: 'I have the wondrous mind of Nirvana, peaceful rest. This I entrust to you, Mahakasayapa.' "[10] Release is expecting nothing more, seeing the invisible essence, and smiling at the impossible flower of the world.

To attain release we must lay down all our daily modes of coping, protecting, attaining, and striving, and this explains why religion is so often taught through paradox. For example, D.T. Suzuki describes the quest for satori, or enlightenment, in Rinzai Zen Buddhism in Japan: the disciple is pushed with all his ardor and might, endlessly, year after year, to solve an unsolvable puzzle. He must try until trying is exhausted. When the last layers of his will have finally been snapped and he sinks down exhausted, another mode of living emerges, a mode that is the natural upwelling of forces deeper than, and free of the slightest trace of, personal will. Instead of willing his life, the disciple now experiences his life to be the spontaneous and playful unfolding of the life of the world in him. The experience is described as one of transforming release.[11]

This approach to freedom through the implosion, the exhaustion of control, is also described in Martin Buber's *Tales of the Hasidim.* For example, Dov Baer, the Great Maggid, is quoted as saying: "You must be nothing but an ear which hears what the universe of the word is constantly saying within you . . . God loves . . . the man who breaks his heart for God." This strenuous willing to finally break and deplete will, so that the deepest well of life can now bubble up to the surface, is echoed by Rabbi Pinhas: "To pray means to cling to God, and to cling to God means to loose oneself from all substance . . . the prayer a man says, the prayer, in itself, is God."[12]

The technique of paradox developed by Viktor Frankl for use in psychotherapy shows a common stance with the willed unwilling of will, to produce a breakthrough into release, as found in the Rinzai Zen and Hasidic traditions. Frankl calls his technique paradoxical intention. He prescribes and exhorts his fearful patients to do the very thing they fear, to the maximum extreme—an approach reminiscent of implosion behavior therapy. A young physician had a fear of perspiring in public, so "I advised the patient, in the event that sweating should recur, to resolve deliberately to show people how much he could sweat . . . this procedure consists in a reversal of the patient's attitude, inasmuch as his fear is replaced by a paradoxical wish." This technique, Frankl believes, cures through the detachment it creates from self-preoccupied and self-important worry, through the humor implicit in it, and more importantly, through teaching and dramatizing a fundamental existential lesson: we are not free from conditions, but we are free to take a stand toward conditions.[13]

Frankl himself does not comment on the religious traditions that antedated and paralleled his thought. His own psychological philosophy, developed under horrible, insurmountable conditions of Nazi death camps (see Chapter 8), is based on existential philosophy and emphasizes man's will, his capacity to shoulder a burden and accept suffering by finding a meaning in it. But it also contains a paradox: the cure to neurotic suffering is to will the feared, to embrace the inevitable, so that one's personal will pushes in the direction of life, rather than recoiling from it, no matter how horrible life may be. The paradox of willing the inevitable leads to a release from withholding, withdrawing, and neurotic substitutes for committed living. Willing what you don't have to will, and thereby ceasing to have to will, is a tool, like willing what can't be willed, until you can't will. Both dissolve the willed separation of the individual from the stream of life. For Frankl, neurotic fears and compulsions represent false control of life; when they are drained by paradoxical intention, true control, inner freedom, emerges. The inner freedom of an existentialist choosing to embrace fate, rather than to merely submit to it, may not be the same as a Zen Buddhist monk harmoniously flowing from blooming to fading flower. Yet there is a close kinship between the religious spirit that inspired Seccho's paradoxical poem, in which enlightened pleasure in a simple activity, like looking out the window, can be had only when a fear of personal death, the fading of one's own flower, is mastered; and the "existentialist" spirit of Viktor Frankl, who nonetheless falls back on a religious image, leaves us in awe with his undaunted joy and courage:

> Our generation is realistic, for we have come to know man as he really is. After all, man is that being who has invented the gas chambers of Auschwitz; however, he is also that being who has entered those gas chambers upright, with the Lord's Prayer or the *Shema Yisrael* on his lips.[14]

The quintessential expression of release is the Twenty-Third Psalm:[15]

> The Lord is my shepherd; I shall not want.
> He maketh me to lie down in green pastures: he
> leadeth me beside the still waters.
> He restoreth my soul . . .

Along with the image of the lawfully ordering father, this exquisite poem evokes the completely released state of life. All the verbs belong to the Lord; the human author is inactive. He receives and is cradled upon life, trusting; he is an anonymous member of the flock guided by infallible hands.

> Yea, though I walk through the valley of the shadow
> of death . . .

Here he, we are active. God maketh, leadeth, restoreth; David just walks forward.

> . . . I will fear no . . .

The force of his, our human will is a negative, a paradox, as we have seen; he wills only to not fear.

> . . . for thou *art* . . .

Being is in God; David walks forward, doomed, free, released, becoming. Comforted, prepared for, anointed by another,

> . . . my cup runneth over . . .

Completely released, he is timeless, and actively *dwells,* because he is filled with the being of the Other.

Tagore wrote: "Thou has made me endless . . . this frail vessel thou emptiest again and again, and fillest it ever with fresh life."[16]

But the need for release can deteriorate into passivity, acquiescence, resignation, masochism, and depression. The other side of the position: "God willing," may be that Man isn't. When the sense of agency, causality, responsibility is removed by indoctrination, or broken by overwhelming odds, the yearning for release can be used as an opportunity to rationalize psychological paralysis and inertia. In traditional religious cultures, where society functions on the basis of ancient rigid codes, where individual vision and initiative are crushed until they are snuffed out, "Thy will be done" is the phrase that sanctifies hopelessness and defeat. ·Psychiatrist Steven Dubovsky had these impressions of psychiatry in Saudi Arabia:

> Very difficult to manage is an almost universal attitude known as *in' shallah* (as God wills), a pervasive belief that good or bad outcomes, including whether one becomes ill, improves or dies, are entirely in God's hands. As a result, patients may not obtain immunization, follow through with a medical regimen, or remain in the hospital, while they convey a passivity that mimicks helplessness . . . the treatment of depressed patients may be made more difficult by their conviction that they will improve only if God wills it and that they themselves need not—and cannot—do anything active to aid in their treatment *(in'shallah)* . . .[17]

Authoritarian religions slur the boundary between the mature capacity to surrender to existential inevitables, like death, with the political concept of surrendering personal autonomy to human authority. The case examples in Chapters 1 and 3 illustrated this. The graduate student in Chapter 1 felt that the fundamentalist Christian call to surrender himself to God was really a substitute for an attempt to personally subjugate him. The violinist in Chapter 3 experienced the Church's idealization of martyred saints as part of what he felt to be an attempt to break his spirit. Patients who have abandoned punitive religions, which had been previously imposed upon them during childhood, are often plagued by an inability to trust anyone. They confuse compromise with acquiescence, participation with subjugation, because they have for so long felt subjugated by their religion. They also suffer from an inability to integrate their bodies with their sense of self, since bodies, with their sexual drives, cannot be trusted when relaxed and have to be watched vigilantly, lest "the devil" emerge in the form of erotic fantasies and wishes. Ironically, tragically, people who stay within authoritarian religions may have more capacity to trust others and their own physical selves, since their subjugation, mind and body, remains acceptable to them, unconflicted, and, in its own childish way, releasing. They accept imposed, external control, and inside the walls of that life-long schoolyard they can relax. The rebels from Fundamentalism are branded by an unslakable thirst for emotional release.

The yearning for release through dependency is a very common human problem that emerges in psychotherapy. Under the burdens of their lives, people forget that the state of release captured in the Twenty-Third Psalm was not written by a lifelong, passive sheep, but by a warrior.

For example, the son of a minister drove himself relentlessly towards career success, forcing himself to sleep as little as possible. (His older sister who had done the same thing had eventually committed suicide.) He felt he was fulfilling his father's injunction "to be all he could be." He lived in a frenzy and yearned for release. He disliked his father's religion, which he equated with moral injunctions to more hard work. He married a Latin American woman who had left her country of origin, lonely and dissatisfied, and was determined to attain success in America. He saw her as an Amazon, a ball buster, chasing the American dream, and free in her dispensation of venomous rage attacks when thwarted. Tiptoeing around her, terrified and unhappy, he admired her, and in his imagination he magnified her tantrums and ennobled them as demonstrations of her power. The angrier she became, the more frightened of her he became, yet he craved this vicious cycle, too, since it was only *under* her wing that he could stop scrambling, achieving, and striving and could stay at home, read beside her, relax, and get some sort of release. He wanted her to protect him, take care of him, alleviate his responsibilities. He purchased a marginal, compromise release at the cost of his dignity and autonomy.

A similar deteriorated extension of the need for release can emerge in guru worship when it descends into slavish obedience to projected omnipotent images of leaders and heroes. Surrender to a guru, to obtain a sense of release, is probably one of the most widespread religious practices in the world. It occupies a central place in Sufism (a branch of Islam) and in Mahayana Buddhism, the dominant religion of Tibet, Japan, and widespread in Korea, China and the Far East. It is central, as well, in many branches of Hinduism. Devotion to the guru is as effective as it is absolute. In Ranade's account of *Mysticism in India,* there are numerous examples of revered mystical saints who attained their glory through this path of absolute, self-denying devotion. The saints recount how all their desires are fulfilled by their guru, how the greatness of the guru cannot adequately be praised, how religious deliverance is to be found when the guru becomes the sole absorbing topic of the devotee's attention.

> Is it possible to add lustre to the sun? . . . the grace of the guru comes down in floods . . . the Guru, like a true mother, swings the spiritual aspirant to and fro in the cradle of his heart . . . as when the sun shines on the horizon and the moon fades away at dawn, the vision of the guru eclipses the universe . . .[18]

In this way of life, we find the unalloyed, relentless culmination of James's observation about the surrender of self-responsibility. Meher Baba, an Indian spiritual master who died in 1969, and who mingled Hinduism and Sufism with his original, personal vision, wrote:

> In thinking day and night of the Master the disciple *nearly* achieves the ultimate objective which is the aim of the diverse practices . . . By putting the work of the Master above his own personal needs, he *achieves* the aim through complete renunciation . . . In sincere surrender to the Master . . . in obeying the Master at any cost and serving him selflessly, and in loving the Master above everything else, he *becomes* one with the Master as Truth and thus attains Godhood— the goal of all search and endeavor—through his grace.[19]

The late Chogyam Trungpa, a Tibetan-born Mahayana Buddhist teacher who was popular in America, recounts as exemplary a classical Tibetan account of the relationship of disciple to guru in which the disciple ". . . had to give up everything he had, not just his material possessions, but whatever he was holding back in his mind had to go. It was a continual process of opening and surrender."[20] The principle of the practice, so widespread across history and culture, is clear: to find release from anxiety, uncertainty, ambivalence, through total surrender to someone else's guidance. It is a personalized form of the commandment in Deuteronomy: "You shall love the Lord your God with all your heart, and with all your soul, and with all your might,[21]" upon which Paul Tillich based his concept of faith as being a state of "ultimate concern."[22] But God is one thing, man another, so that the dependency intrinsically present in guru worship is vulnerable to the worst possible perversions of dependency.

Psychiatrist Alexander Deutsch studied a cult that began as a "sidewalk ashram" on a park bench in Manhattan in the early 1970s.[23] The cult leader, Baba, "welcomed home" his devotees (an image reminiscent of the spirituals), encouraging them to "let go," that is, "detach from desire, ambition, worry, guilt, and one's sense of individuality to experience peace and unity with God." Deutsch called Baba's role one of "superego replacement." This evolved into making surrender to Baba as the central goal and focus of his devotees' lives. Baba eventually deteriorated into violence, bizarre behavior, and a conversion to fundamentalist Christianity. Those of his followers who stayed until he dissolved his Family showed, according to Deutsch, "child-like dependency . . . a vacuum in guiding values . . . and a need for an omnipotent object . . . submissive and self-deceptive behavior."

In a remarkable example of courageous and curious journalism, Frances FitzGerald documented the history of Swami Rajneesh in America. This eccentric, flamboyant, and highly literate Indian Guru built a creative nation-state of followers in America. Along with sexual licentiousness, generous social concern, literary effusion, and civic originality, the cult focused on blind faith in the guru. The determination to believe someone without reserve gradually shifted into believing anyone and anything. The cult deteriorated from its initial ideals into violence, drug abuse, paranoid fantasies, interstitial armed conflict, until it was dissolved and scattered by the United States government. The chilling quality of FitzGerald's expose comes from the juxtaposition of the devotees' ebullient and infectious will to believe in a joyously released divine state on earth, beside the nefarious manipulation of that desperate innocence. Surprisingly, many of Rajneesh's followers, attracted by his widely referenced books, were psychiatrists, psychologists, and other psychotherapists. Education is no bulwark against profound yearning.[24]

Although the word "Guru" comes from Hindu India, the phenomenon can be found everywhere. James Randi and others who have investigated faith healers in Christian America document the pathetic gyrations of minds driven by a desire to be released from physical suffering and from the ambiguities of reality. Interviews with long-time believers of evangelists revealed them ". . . to ignore paradoxes and to excuse blatant errors of fact presented to them by the preachers . . . they actually take pride in their ability to believe in spite of contrary evidence." Unshakable conviction brings release from the tension of thought.[25]

Of course, deep conviction may be the product also of serious, careful thought. Not every guru is a psychopath, and not every devotee is a fool. Shunryu Suzuki Roshi was a Zen master of impeccable integrity and the internationally respected author of *Zen Mind, Beginner's Mind,* a book considered by many to be a masterpiece at the literary level of the ancient Mahayana Buddhist Sutras.[26] Before Shunryu Suzuki died, he was careful to select his Dharma heir to carry on his work as Zen Master. He chose an American, Richard Baker, to receive the mantle of "Roshi." This elevated Baker Roshi to a position of unquestioned respect that he occupied for more than a decade. As a Zen Master, Baker occupied an august role vis-à-vis his disciples. He manifested absolute reality in human form and was the hand-picked exemplar of a 2500-year-old lineage. When some of his disciples, who were trustees of the San Francisco Zen Center, presented him with evidence of his sexual misconduct and fiscal abuse, he assumed the posture of religious teacher and refused to discuss the matter. But his Zen disciples held firm, and eventually dismissed their Zen Master from his post at the center! When a journalist asked Richard Baker what he thought of his students he said, "I'm proud of them."[27]

An Indian meditation master has clarified that while ever-deepening devotion to the point of absolute devotion is essential on the Path, this is entirely different from blind devotion. The student must understand, intellectually challenge, and experientially test the teaching, so that his devotion deepens because of a culmination of rational thought coupled to confirming personal experience.[28] In such a system, the release from doubt is an accomplished fruition of systematic testing of doubt.

Surrender to a religious leader, with its attendant release from ambivalence and self-worry, brings an enormous surge of hopeful, constructive energy. This has been clear from the Vatican to Rajneeshpuram. It is subject to corruption when the leader claims exemption from the rules he imposes on others, instead of exemplifying those rules; and when the leader has arbitrary power, instead of himself being subject to his own religious antecessors and to a coherent tradition. Unfortunately, blind faith is as releasing as any other, a topic I will return to in the discussion of Sacrifice (Chapter 9). The topic of gurudom also overlaps many other religious elements. Disciples may find and seek, along with release, a sense of witnessed significance from the attention and favors of the guru and a sense of lawful order and affirming acceptance from the beliefs and practices of the cult. A calling is sometimes, though not always, dispensed; membership is a given, as is worldview. Gurus may provide human love in one or bidirectional flow; they often demand sacrifice, and may contribute to a meaningful death. Sweet, simple, unquestioning devotion to a benign guru may also produce a redemptive encounter, leading to a release from anomie and a reenchantment with the world.[29]

Release may also be sought in dionysianism: orgiastic, intoxicated immediacy. Drugs, alcohol, and sex, with their capacity for oblivion, are to release as sugar is to food: they temporarily ease the pains but add no substantial muscle. A lawyer who felt a failure, unable to satisfy the high standards of achievement set by his father, had to "get it on" every evening with his wife. That wore the marriage thin. Therapy that gave him understanding of his damaged self-esteem, and helped him to set and achieve attainable goals, also provoked his return to religious participation. This enabled him to use sex expressively and appropriately, rather than as a form of evening anesthesia. I have treated a number of sexual compulsions that, at root, revealed a perverted quest for religious dimensions of life (see Chapter 3; I will say more about this in Chapter 8).

The shift from anxiety, tenseness, and dread to peace and equanimity through religious release may represent a regression to infantile dependence coupled to denial of harsh realities and an avoidance of responsibility to uphold and maintain the social order. Or, it may represent a synthesis of new sets of possibilities within the personality such that a warrior-king could also feel himself to be a sheep—possibilities that include the capacities for spontaneous, free-flowing engagement with self, others, and life, moment by moment. The need for release can grow into grace: the sense of being filled and surrounded by freedom to pursue one's own path to the Kingdom of Heaven. Not the absence of something to be done, a calling, and not a frenzy of antagonistic obligation, but the direction, the tools, the conviction, the energy, the way. "Knowing nothing need be done is where we begin from."[30]

The ripening of release in grace is described by St. Augustine. After a long struggle to will himself to cease his sinful pagan ways, he was at last converted to Christianity, and he wrote: "Oh Lord, I am Thy servant . . . Thou has broken my bonds . . . By your gift I had come totally not to will what I willed, but to will what You willed."[31] As we saw when discussing D.T. Suzuki's description of Rinzai Zen satori, or Buber's Hasidic Tales, or Frankl's technique of paradoxical intention, release involves a relinquishing of personal will, and a realignment with the will of God, or fate, or Nature. For almost two thousand years, St. Augustine has remained the epitome and spokesman of grace within Christianity. He wrote: "For peace is a good so great, that even in this earthy and mortal life there is no word we hear with such pleasure, nothing we desire with such zest, or find to be more thoroughly gratifying."[32]

William James wrote:

Regeneration by relaxing, by letting go, psychologically indistinguishable from the Lutheran justification by faith, and the Wesleyan acceptance of free grace, is within the reach of persons who have no conviction of sin and care nothing for the Lutheran theology. It is but giving your little private convulsive self a rest, and finding that a greater Self is there. The results, slow or sudden, great or small, of the combined optimism and expectancy, the regenerative phenomena which ensue on the abandonment of effort, remain firm facts of human nature . . .

He added:

. . . you see why self-surrender has been and always must be regarded as the vital turning point of religious life . . . One may say the whole development of Christianity in inwardness has consisted in little more than the greater and greater emphasis attached to this crisis of self-surrender.[33]

As we have seen while looking at Gurus, this religious development is by no means limited to Christianity.

Grace requires prerequisites. A calling must be present to get beyond pointlessness and inertia. To focus on one's calling, one must trust others to carry on with the rest of what needs to be done, and that requires a sense of membership. To be able to relax in one's own body, it is necessary to be able to affirm, accept, and channel one's inner life. A sense of lawful order, like membership, enables concentration that doesn't feel like neglect or exposure. Release, then, matures into the capacity to resolve ambivalence, to relinquish the endless possibilities of other choices and improved safety, to sleep at night because the day is done, to stand by what has been accomplished. To seek the Kingdom of Heaven or higher human goals, one must be able to focus, concentrate, and brush aside the chaff. People who can find no release complain, "Everything is up to me; without me everything would fall apart; I can't leave anything to anyone else, or just let it go." But when release is found, it is linked to a faith in the continuity of life, and in the constructive, reliable presence of other people, places, and times. It ripens into a sense of an adequate, ample portion for one's own existence, coupled to the self-replenishing fountain of creation. Then peace and relaxation rather than spelling neglect and vulnerability are energizing and refreshing. The sense of release bears fruit in rightness. Not that the world is finished, but that it is all right. There follows the capacity to float on tiredness, darkness, and sleep with confidence in both one's own and others' dawn. From here it is one step to pass into death with faith.

> But for the Beauty that seeks its own awareness,
> We ourselves would not exist.[34]

This couplet by the great Indian Moslem poet, Ghalib, evokes the flavor of life in which individuals are seen as expressive culmination of one unfolding unity. It is echoed in Buddhism: "It is to live aiming at the manifestation of life in each and every thing we meet, and to see everything as an extension of our own life."[35] The Mahayana Lankavatara Sutra speaks of "One uninterrupted chain of causation . . . one flame of uniform nature rises up . . ."[36] There are limits to how far we can go on, how much we can do, but our projects, children, and inspirations, the creation creating in and through us, endures, carrying our blessed hopes beyond us. The universe is expanding. We must sleep to dream.

The minister's son drove himself relentlessly because he doubted that anyone could love him for anything other than his accomplishments. Years of testing his therapist's reliable warmth in therapy finally enabled him to relinquish achievement as the core of his identity. He basked in the warmth and affection of the relationship. His panic to produce moderated. He permitted himself freedom and pleasures he had never known before. He fell in love for the first time in midlife, overcame his impotence, and finally dared to adopt religious practices meaningful to him but anathema to his father. He divorced the wife he had married out of dependency and fear. But he continued to trail behind him a herd of half-fed obligations.

The biochemist delved in therapy into the causal history of her relentless, low-grade, power struggles with her husband, herself, and me, that led to her blinding tension headaches. Her father was a workaholic doctor whom she hardly saw. Her mother, in overcompensation, ran a tight, upright home. She turned Catholic religion into stern, black-and-white injunctions that proved a mother is always right. Their life revolved around the Polish Catholic church in the Chicago suburb where they owned a home and several acres of land. The only distance the future biochemist could maintain from her overbearing mother was to join the 4H Club, whose membership was drawn mostly from surrounding farm communities. She loved her one sheep. She picked on and pushed around her sister, whose more conventional feminine ways made her contemptible and enviable. In the absence of a moderating father, and feeling squashed by her mother, she yearned to feel powerful and in control. But she craved a man's attention. Against her conscious intent, she clung to boyfriends. Yet she couldn't acknowledge her need. When she went away to college she felt spied upon and vulnerable to all men. She quickly singled out a boyfriend who was physically strong, angry, rigidly Catholic, and lonely from the early death of his mother from multiple sclerosis. Through his needy loneliness, she controlled him with her relentlessly nurturant attention. By their junior year, when he became captain of the football team, she appeared to be his docile steady girl. Impulsive sexual intercourse meant to both of them that now they *had* to get married.

She split power into extremes of weak and strong, instead of being able to find more fluctuant, complex, middle grounds.

So, on the one hand, she dominated and bullied her insecure husband with her superior wit, education, and intelligence; but, on the other hand, she became a cowering, physically battered wife of an overwrought football-hero executive.

A similar split emerged in her religious life. She was both more religious than the rest of her family, yearning to be a true apostle, yet was also a scientist, an agnostic, a skeptic. In other words, she was covering all the bases, in charge on every front: the most modern, rational scientist; the most devout, literal Christian. The price was crushing inner tension and desperate need to control everyone all the time. During therapy, she had a series of religious experiences.

She presented them to me with awkwardness and hesitancy. Divided in her own religious life, she felt blessed, singled out by God to have these experiences, but also embarrassed, preposterous. Driving home from work one night on the interstate, she felt impelled to take an alternative route. She stressed to me that this was not a whim, not a choice: she felt impelled, an ego-alien feeling she had never experienced before. Continuing down a two-lane state highway towards her home, she came upon a one-car collision. Two teenagers had driven off the road, hitting a concrete post of a cabled retaining fence. The boy, who had been drinking beer, was bleeding from cuts, but the girl, who was not bleeding, was apparently knocked unconscious. The boy, guilty over the beer, was unable to act. The biochemist quickly took charge, dared to knock on the door of a nearby house, and phoned the State Police. After the ambulance and the accident report, she left with thready pulse, weak knees. She delayed in telling me this incident for several months.

On a second occasion she was shopping and felt similarly drawn, absolutely coerced by an inner compulsion, to quickly skip several aisles. When she turned the cart into the third aisle, an elderly woman fainted and fell to the floor. The biochemist rushed over to her, took her pulse, and began mouth-to-mouth resuscitation. A stir surrounded her; in moments the firemen arrived from the firehouse next door and took over. The next day she told me of these two incidents: "That was all. No voice, no lights, nothing special. But that strange compulsion. I could feel my feet being lifted and placed as if controlled from outside me." She told me that, as a young woman, she had a secret yearning to be a Christian missionary doctor, rather than a suburban, academic biochemist. These recent religious experiences signalled to her that God was impelling her to be that doctor. She felt He wanted her to give up her self-protective, material life, " 'But go rather to the lost sheep . . . Heal the sick, cleanse the lepers . . . Provide neither gold nor silver nor scrip for your journey, neither two coats, neither shoes . . . ' " But she also felt she must be crazy! How could a feminist scientist imagine, not merely that God existed, but that She would single out individuals for special favors out of the swarming billions of people in the world. How arrogant! She wanted me to tell her she was crazy. That would be safer than having to uproot her life and transform herself. She had told her priest about these two experiences, and as he counselled her about the ways of God's will, her scientific self took over, watched over her shoulder, and felt that he and she were absurd fools. Now she wanted me to take a side, tell her what these events meant psychodynamically. Didn't they relate to her obsession about control, about who was in control of her life? I replied that, though it made sense to me that she was yearning to be able to give herself up to a man, and that a displacement onto an elusive God might be easier than apparent capitulation to her husband, still, that wouldn't account for the coincidences in her experiences. These were her experiences, not mine. I myself feel uneasy with facile psychological reductionism.

This led into an open discussion of what she felt about me. "You're someone I can trust. There's nothing to be gained or lost here. You won't tell me what to do. I love you, but it's different. It's not a sexual feeling. You seem neuter to me, like

Christ. You look like Him. This is embarrassing. But this is the only safe place I've ever had."

She had felt (we further analyzed) that all women were competitors, like her sister or her domineering mother. Her sister's success as a florist and docile wife and mother aggravated the biochemist's sense of being defeated as a woman. All men were aloof prizes, like her father or husband, who had to be caught, then counter-controlled. By experiencing me as neuter, she could also toss aside her need to control either of us and just relax.

Over a brief series of sessions she decided that, if her husband had to move, she *would* move. It wasn't capitulation. It wasn't selling out feminism. She continued to forward her career energetically. She loved her husband, she was married to him, she would encourage him to stay put, but if he felt he *had* to move, she would respect his need. She interpreted her change as affirming the caring and affiliative capacities she had read about in feminist psychology.

We did not refer to the religious experiences again. She remained very forthright in her expressions of affection for me. But she reminded me of her fears of loss of control through dependency, and, shortly thereafter, her symptoms relieved (no headaches, her subjective anxiety gone), we stopped.

I imagined that her therapy had enabled her to separate sexual love from human love (see Chapter 8). In her unconscious, she felt herself a martyred Christian saint, who never had yielded to sex, and, simultaneously, the boss of her bureaucratic husband. Through the therapy, I imagined she was more able to accept her sexual bond to him, to more fully marry, negotiate, compromise, share with him, because she could trust that impulsive adolescent sex was not her only route to love and marriage. She knew she could feel "neuter" love, because she felt it in therapy. She herself had created a situation in therapy in which she could experience and practice "religious love" for me.

Her knowledge of her capacity to love enabled her to lay down her sword. She could be part of others without conquering them. She had discovered a new way of being part-of. She had stripped herself in front of me, yet had been safe. In a dream towards the end of therapy, a baby she had neglected fell off a cliff, yet was found safe in her real mother's arms.

She had discovered that control was not the only safe bond. She could now also relax herself in the presence of another. She no longer had to fight off her body. Since sex was not the only form of love, she did not have to shut down her bodily feelings every time there was a pleasurable danger of feeling close to someone. Instead she could count on her heart to feel love, and her body to feel sexual, usually at the right time and place. Her headaches left.

She no longer had to fight off her husband; she could participate with him. She no longer felt taken advantage of when she gave up control. Just as love no longer immediately threatened to deteriorate into sex, now sex no longer meant impulsive loss of control. It had a measure of regulation, loss of regulation, and cooperation.

As for those religious experiences: they helped her unmask herself in front of me—the passions of her caring, her hopes for herself and the world. They helped her feel out-of-control, yet safely guided in a lawfully ordered world. She could be led by an Other, benignly. They helped her put herself in a powerless, needy position towards *me*—and she could watch me not take up staff of interpretive authority but let her pick it up on her own. I refused to tell her what she meant, refused to join the battle of science versus religion. She could be free, herself and herselves, not ruthlessly logical and indubitably correct, but complex, variable, diverse. As a child, she built up a battery of controls to get what had never been freely given. Giving and receiving in therapy, she could relinquish her rigidity and permit more of life to unravel. She could live, well . . . better . . . without resolving all the world's problems.

What do I make of the outer-felt impulses, the unusual coincidences in her religious experiences? I think it is a mistake for a psychiatrist to feel either obliged or capable of explaining everything to himself. Even Freud felt a navel of the unknown in every dream.[37] The mere existence of life, consciousness, love on this hurtling stone in a universe of uncountable galaxies, each with hundreds of billions of stars, is the backdrop which we must use as the working foundation of every human encounter. We stand on thin cloth over the void. To purvey and facilitate this attitude is closer to a psychiatrist's work than to judge and slice reality. We must be pillowed in the safety of real relationships in our own personal corner of the universe. Then we can lay our heads down and sleep, suspended as it were in the swinging hammock of the stars. That suits me better; that is the route to release, somewhere between anthropomorphic projection and imagining we possess scientific knowledge on a cosmic scale. Just as I implied with my behavior in her presence, so I believe that I cannot resolve all questions on one or another side of a dichotomy of science and religion.

The great religious traditions can be heard as absurd, pseudo-factual authorities trying to dispel ill-ease of the unknown, but they can also be read as counseling us to release infantile, narcissistic anthropocentrism, while we stride forward to vigorously engage immediacies. The Koran: "He created the heavens and earth . . . he created man out of a sperm drop . . . He cast on the earth firm mountains, lest it shake with you, and by the stars they are guided . . . so haply you will be guided . . ."[38] A capacity for suspending judgment and continuing engagement with people and worlds leads to a freer trajectory than placing oneself in a seat of false control and false knowledge. While we carve our small stone statue to fill one cornice, other hands carve the temple. As amazing as the biochemist's coincidental experiences seem, they are to me no more inexplicable than eyes, and language, and the Australian bower bird.

Once noticed, the yearning for release will quickly be observed as a dominant note in many psychotherapies. The parenting child who attains worldly success but must remain parent to all parents feels trapped under a mountain of obligation. This theme, of the overly responsible child grown up to a life of chronic tension, haunts the lives of many professional psychotherapists. The guarded borderline patient, the superficial narcissist circling through a maze of "spiritual practices" and "new age healing," will frequently be found to suffer from an incapacity to yield any measure of control to anyone or anything.

In Chapter 5, I discussed how Alcoholics Anonymous skillfully utilizes membership in service of healing. "A.A." stands with its other foot planted on release. Its practices are based on the insights of William James in *The Varieties of Religious Experience,* which I have quoted several times in this chapter. "A.A." believes that the alcoholic who wishes to stop drinking becomes trapped in a vicious cycle of will. Like St. Augustine, the prototypic repentant drinker wills to stop sinning, but his inability to do so makes him feel more sinful and more out of control, so he drinks more. "A.A." treats him by demanding acknowledgment of his helplessness; he must turn to an other, outer, higher power; he must be deflated in the depth of himself, and turn himself over to God (as he understands Him). Through prayer and meditation, "A.A." believes the alcoholic can live by God's will, not his own.[39]

Because the yearning for release is such a common issue in psychotherapy, yet is fraught with paradox, and dangers of regression, subjugation, and infantilization, I would like to give one more example.

A teacher became preoccupied with religion. Every day he had apparently revelatory experiences, cosmic coincidences and messages. But these cloud-parting truths lingered only hours or days, then evaporated, to be replaced by more divine signals intended for him. He sought out a series of non-traditional "alternative therapies," and despite flattery and reassurance and encouragement, the divine coincidences persisted and he continued to feel worse. Finally, he sought therapy, reluctantly, guardedly, knowing yet hurt by the fact that he needed help on this side of the clouds.

His search for otherworldly help became understandable to me when I heard about the pain he felt in this world. He was undergoing a second divorce. Years ago he had left his first wife; now he had driven his second wife away with his ceaseless criticism and openly verbalized doubts about their viability as a couple. Highly competent and creative, he worked hard as a science teacher, then came home to work again, building a boat in his garage. He was pressured, productive, anxious, unsatisfiable. Despite substantial worldly accomplishment, he felt irritated, raw, under-the-gun every day, yearning for some magical release from a reality that held no ease for him, no matter what he did. As the therapy started, he made it clear he was planning to keep one foot out the door. He flung a gauntlet at me: how could I help him since I must disbelieve in his experiences because I was in the scientific Western tradition? I eased to the side and refocused on him and his own life.

His father was a prominent scientist with unrelenting standards. His easily overwhelmed, passive mother expected him to take care of her, rather than vice versa. He had to achieve at school, then come home to clean the house; no output was enough or too much. He became anxiously placating to his mother and surly and truculent toward his father. In college, he capitalized on the 60s and became rebellious and anarchistic, mocking and cynical as a student leader. He was a Dadaist disbeliever in everything and a heavy dope smoker, who still managed to attain very good grades. Trying to slough everything serious and potentially burdensome, he clung to the safety of college success while he also sought the comfort of not-caring. His apparent devil-may-care attitude was a control device to dampen his fear of failing; his driven hard work and good grades belied his pose of nonchalance.

The same style of broadly based, divided defense against failure and criticism led him into half-hearted marriage, with half-cared-for children. He sought therapy in the same way, ambivalent, half-in, half-out, so in control that he was out of control.

In some ways, therapy with this intelligent and curious teacher progressed easily. He took the lead, took control, in unraveling the patterns that got set in his past. But he also operated from a supercilious, hyper-independent position in relation to me. He kept me boxed in, telling me what I stood for—Freudian rationalism and scientific reductionism, a predictable, atheistic, machinery world. That's what he knew psychiatrists to be. That's what his father had been. He used his experiences of cosmic coincidences and personal divine indicators to stand above me. I did not feel his experiences presented me with powerful questions, as had the experiences of the biochemist. Instead, they seemed like psychologically needy and driven fantasies of isolated self-importance, against a backdrop of emotional isolation. I knew if I challenged him, he'd leave. If I interpreted his experiences psychologically, I'd confirm his negative transference that I was a scientific spoiler like his father. Instead of trying to reorganize his intellectual understanding of his experiences—as an interpretation does—I tried the opposite. My comments to him were focused on opening more space around his experiences. After all, assuming this or that conjunction of events was a divine message was his own intellectually imposed constrictive interpretation of those events. I sought his trust by encouraging his movement toward the same suspended open-mindedness he expected of me. The therapy and his thought processes shifted from assertion to description, to free association. I was fairly quiet.

After a year and a half of therapy, he described the reversal of his cautious and testy transference as "a breakthrough . . . risking your criticism and contempt by just speaking my mind in here . . . and finding to my surprise a sense of basic goodness. I distrust it. But I feel something like gratitude." He worried that therapy, like religion, might be a soothing "opiate" that would render him apolitical.

After another six months of therapy, during which he was building a new relationship with a woman, he said: "For the first time I can admit to myself that I really need and want someone in my life. In both my marriages I was always looking around, had one foot out the door. It wasn't that I wasn't satisfied; I was just afraid of being left behind. To admit this need puts me in danger. But I think if [my current woman friend] leaves me now, I won't be shattered. I won't like it. But I feel there's an inner coherence in me. It's a kind of faith. It comes from the way I talk in here. I just let go, let the chips fall where they may, and let you make sense of it. I don't have to *do* everything to make it happen. My father will always be my father. My children will always be my children, even if they yell at me. That's the way I feel with [my new woman friend]— I let it out, let it spill out. If it's going to work, good; if not, I might as well find out. That's different from always trying to control and be dictator." This man had experienced the process of free association as a profound release.

This growth was accompanied by a dramatic decrease in religious preoccupation, but one real religious affiliation: instead of waiting for quirks in the unfolding day to reveal hidden teleology to him, he joined a yoga center, and threw himself into active membership. The science teacher found out: "I don't have to be perfect." He lost his yearning for a magically orchestrated universe and let himself be known by one real woman and one real doctor. He practiced releasing his body, in a world in which he was not the only center. His love of nature, which inspired his science teaching, rose to the surface, and he captured my heart with descriptions of rain dripping off trees at the yoga center at dawn.

My work with him reminded me of the way that personalized and desperate religious fantasy can express profound religious yearnings, yet block their fulfillment in greater rivers of truth. Erich Fromm wrote that all neurosis is private religion; that is, all narrow, self-inflected foci of life are substitutes for life's true purposes and goals.[40] In this case, the permission to think and speak fluidly and freely in someone else's presence restored a basic trust in self and other, that led to new confidence and capacities in life. The teacher could relinquish fancifully self-referential religion, when a sense of witnessed significance and human love enabled him to soften his fear of being found inadequate; and he could flow, in word and body, more easily among the tree-lined banks of this real world. "Swiftly arose and spread around me the peace and knowledge that pass all argument of the earth."

◊ *7* ◊

Worldview

. . . when I looked up I saw one hand spinning the divine
wheel of the world . . .

". . . the scene of their lives upon which all men look, is conceived
by them as having some order: chaos is not a possible vision of the
world for anyone."[1]

"No matter where you meet a man on his way, he always holds over
against himself to some degree, in some way, that which he does not
know as well as that which he knows, bound up together in one world
. . . not with the sum of its parts, but as a synthesizing apperception
. . . But this world never arises except out of the totality of the human
race to which it belongs . . . waking men add in common to the world
shape itself . . ."[2]

". . . human beings cannot live in chaos . . . religious man feels the
need always to exist in a total and organized world, in a cosmos
. . . every construction or fabrication has the cosmogony as paradigmatic model. The creation of the world becomes the archetype of
every human gesture . . ."[3]

"Of all phenomena, mind comes first, mind matters most, mind is the
source"[4]

A young lawyer pushed himself to seek therapy for what he had to finally acknowledge to himself was drug addiction. Every day throughout law school, and now on his first job, morning, noon, and evening, he smoked pot. He rolled a joint and had a hit while still in bed; the joint would reemerge in his car, or in bathrooms, throughout the day; and when he got home, he lit up his water pipe.

He described to me the double world in which he grew up. His father was a prominent lawyer and acclaimed civic leader of a small industrial city, who constantly pressured his athletic son towards the highest standards of success. The father was equally skillful in getting his name on boards of directors throughout the city and in hiding from everyone outside his family his alcoholism. The young lawyer had grown up in a home in which his father would be unable to get up, would sleep the night on the living-room floor, or would vanish one weekend night only to reemerge the next at 3:00 A.M., beating on the locked front door with his fists and hollering threats up to his wife. When sober, the father would waft his teenage son through town, grooming him to join the law practice, and letting the town lay eyes on him. Everyone would reassure the boy what an admired, ideal citizen his father was.

During the boy's teenage years, his father's alcoholism worsened: threats became wife beatings. The boy clenched his fists. His mother's mental life deteriorated; she was hospitalized for several depressions, then a mania, and was put on lithium carbonate to treat manic depressive illness. Then the father made a bullying, sexualized advance on his own daughter, and the boy, a lanky, sixteen-year-old co-captain of his high school soccer team, stepped in between. He threatened his father and felt ready to kill him. The clarity of his own murderous feelings was indelible. After acknowledging to me that murderous conflict—a desire to finally lay out that drunken son-of-a-bitch, and the horror that it was really he who was saying and thinking such thoughts, clashing up against a fleeting vision of suicide to control or punish himself, or just to terminate the tension—the young lawyer quit smoking dope. He ran five miles a day for two months. He told his father, who was now sober and for whom he now worked, that he was taking a long vacation, and he told me the same—no discussion. He took off with a friend for a three-week backpacking trip in Montana.

Patients will imply the need for a cosmos, not a chaos, outside and around them—the need for a cognitive-emotional sense of a world that is integrated, whole, meaningful, coherent, beautiful, sacred. This is not merely a need for an overwatching father or a properly functional system, as in the need for lawful order. This is a need to feel interactively functionalized into the tissue of life. People yearn to feel incorporated into the radiant beauty that shines through, and silvers the edges of, every child's spontaneous reaction to sunlight and flowers and animals and heavenly bodies. People intuit that each of us lives inside a greater life. While our internal homeostatic regulators control the level of circulating hormones, thereby modulating the relationships of tissues and organs into one organic, integrated body, externally oriented regulators monitor and guide our integration with the living organ system of the biosphere. Psychological homeostatic regulators—sensual pleasure, intuition, appetite, psychomotor restlessness—move us around the sun-dappled, oxygenated, food-bearing earth. We feel ourselves to be part-of.

One arena of our psychic energy is to monitor and integrate our immersion in the all-around. Our primary delighted apprehension of our surroundings produces an intuition of sustaining partnership with all living things. We recognize our own animation and vitality reflected in the limbs of running creatures and the ceaselessness of leaves and waves. Yet at the same time we face the dawning of the great sorrow, of cruelty, war, destruction through hatred, the dead bird on the grass, the grandparent gone for good, the relentless intrusion of time,

death, loss. This fundamental drinking in by the child of his or
her environment, is the seed-crystal out of which the adult will
feel a need for a worldview. A worldview is a wholistic vision
by which a person integrates what is sensed with what is
known.

A worldview may be variously conscious or unconscious.
For poets, intellectuals, anthropologists, the making-conscious
of their worldview may be a critical, lifelong task. Others may
live with a labyrinth of associations that form an animating, yet
never-fully-visible worldview. Still others, dulled by disappointing fate, may have weak and tentative connections to the
world; or they may paste on decals of ready-made worldviews
borrowed from other social strata or from religious sects. Similarly, worldviews of people may vary in the degree to which
they are personal and idiosyncratic, or patent, generalized, and
adopted. Sometimes we hear a person speak and sense, with a
thrill, that he or she is opening a new vein of ore, has stood on
the peaks of a mountain range we ourselves had never seen
before. Other times we are aware that someone is mouthing a
line, clinging to his or her minister's or mother's picture of
things. Worldviews vary also in their relative simplicity or
complexity, in their relative rigidity and fixedness, or their
flexibility, permeability, and intricacy.

A worldview will explicitly or implicitly provide an orientation around the great religious paradoxes. For example, do
we have free will, or are we fated to our destiny? This is not
just an argument for philosophers, theologians, and psychiatrists. With more or less articulateness and consistency, the
question of free will is written into the lives of old men dying
in cancer wards, in hell-fire-and-brimstone sermons in clap-
board churches, and in political rallies. Or there may be an
absence of the question in the above examples. A person will
stand somewhere or slide back and forth along a continuum,
regarding the idea that we are choiceful, free, responsible,
agents, or that we are buffeted about by cosmic and planetary

forces that determine where and when we are born, whether we will be subjected to famine, lymphoma, or hereditary wealth. This need for synthesizing, embracing gestalts, which exceed information and knowledge, and which resolve life's paradoxes, is the essentially religious need in humans. Unlike the six needs discussed in the previous six chapters, the need for a worldview is the stronghold of the religious *per se*. Worldview is not just a cognitive matrix but an organic intermingling. "The love of life, at any and every level of development, is the religious impulse."[5] The word "religion" is etymologically related to "ligature." The binding, holding force of religion refers to its role within individual personality (see Chapter 3) and between individuals and groups (see Chapter 5). It also refers to the binding of impression, sensation, intuition, fact, and experience into a worldview.

To fulfill this need, organized religions have spoken through, even created, the arts, preeminently scriptural poetry and sacred language, but also drama, music, dance, painting, sculpture, liturgy, and ritual. For flexible modern religions, science and social science have also served the artistic, imaginative, mythopoetic role of contributing to worldview. Worldview is also the realm of myth and symbol.

Valmiki the Poet looked down into the water held cupped in his hand and saw into the past. Before he looked, he thought the world was sweet poison. Men seemed to be living in lies, not knowing where their ways went. The days seemed made of ignorance and doubt, and cast from deception and illusion. But in the water he saw—a dream, a chance, and a great adventure. Valmiki trusted the true and forgot the rest; he found the whole universe like a bright jewel set firm in forgiving and held fast by love.[6]

Valmiki is the legendary author of the *Ramayana,* Hinduism's epic religious legend and mythic cornucopia. The *Ramayana,* like the archetypical stories of the great founders—Moses, Job, or Jesus; or Siddhartha Gautama, who became Buddha; or Mohammed; or Krishna—serves as proto-type, a template of reality from which millions of lives across generations can stamp out an organized worldview in the otherwise undifferentiated ocean of the universe. "The myth reveals something as having been fully manifested, creative, exemplary, since it is the foundation of a structure of reality."[7] Clearly, the "world" as seen in the worldview of myths, is not limited to physical realities, but it speaks to what is possible and desirable in the realm of imagination and spirit. So when Valmiki merely looked into fresh water cupped in his hand—water that is after all the medium of life, a universal solvent in which our bodies and minds are suspended, the Mother Ganges everywhere, the rain, and the bones of plants—when Valmiki looked into the water he saw the world in its entirety mirrored there. What he saw was not just the stuff and things of the ocean of time, but the spiritual, human, divine world of meaning, possibility, and care. And the magic of his Sanskrit slokas, like the Arabic of the Koran, the Hebrew of the Old Testament, the Pali of the Buddhist Suttas, is the doorway into a brave new world.

Dreams are often the route to an expanded worldview. Particularly when not reduced to intellectual concepts, they sweep in fresh winds of scenes, people, and events. They bring together all that has been experienced, as well as landscapes, characters, and moods that are fresh creations, antedating experiences for which their emotional fullness may eventually pave the way. They also bring secrets to the surface, and they put red pencil marks under motives and impulses. Above all, they portray a world with an infinitely receding horizon and an endless cast.

The need for a worldview can deteriorate into urgent believing. The hunger for coherence, coupled to the soothing sense of harmony its presence can produce, may turn a worldview into an idol: a static, frozen imitation of reality that is clung to for comfort and security. Religions rush in to cater to this addiction. Orthodoxy is the sculpture garden of ideological, historically concrete pictograms, desperate ritualizations and repetitions, anthropomorphic iconography, and breathless formulas. Much of religious life has functioned as an assemblage of wishful escapes, pretty pictures to inspire mollifying daydreams. But individuals free of orthodoxies can also produce deteriorated worldviews—solipsistic, idiosyncratic excitations; hallucinating half-pictures; and fragmentary intoxications. This is the realm of the isolated psychotic. Without the option or capacity for religious traditions, people may generate worldviews that reflect their limited information and singular perspective. They do not forgo the need for a worldview, but build one with limited tools and defective material. If they are less than psychotic, their worldview may be deficient in other ways: frantic narcissistic highs, with their self-important, over-inclusive revelations that are meaningless a week later, and which functioned only briefly to stave off their closely coupled despairs. The psychedelic era and its offshoot, the spiritual supermarket, were realms in which worldviews were tried on like new clothes, and discarded.

But this need can grow into sustaining visions, tradition-based or seminal. Here we find the lawful, awed, curious, reverential beacons to individuals or to larger groups. William James referred to religion as the realm of the "more."[8] Kazantzakis wrote: "By believing passionately in something which still does not exist, we create it. The nonexistent is what we have not sufficiently desired . . . Seeing a blossoming tree, a hero, a woman, the morning star, we cry, Oh! . . . this is the only bit of immortality in us . . . we must impart it to the rest of mankind . . ."[9] He concluded "God is being built."[10] Worldviews are born, elaborated, synthesized, clarified, crystallized, modified, through the lives of poets and paradigm-forging scientists, cultural founding fathers, prophets, seers, creative social thinkers, political activists, folksingers, psychologists— wherever people breed numinous, fertile gnosis.

Exemplary is the nature-poetry of the Old Testament, the Koran, and the Vedas. "And the earth was without form, and void; and darkness was upon the face of the deep. And the Spirit of God moved upon the face of the waters. And God said, let there be light . . ."[11] Or the voice of cosmological witness in the Bhagavad Gita:

> Even as the mighty winds in the vastness of ethereal space, all beings have their rest in me . . .

> At the end of the night of time all things return to my nature; and when the new day of time begins I bring them again into light.

> Thus through my nature I bring forth all creation, and this rolls round in the circles of time.[12]

The fruit of the need for a worldview is the realm of ecstasy: standing outside oneself, knowing reality as it is. Ecstasy in its traditional meaning does not refer to transient excitements and euphorias, but to wholistic vision unimpeded by narcissism. It is the capacity to slip out from the realm of one's own skin, one's own hungers, needs, and one's own fate to stand on the neutral ground of impersonal perspective. Tribal religions may seek to induce ecstasy through intoxication, sleep-deprivation, exhaustion, and rhythm. Buddhist and Hindu texts may invoke this state with cosmic, world-shattering imagery, cycles of time, units of measure that last 4,320,000 years only to repeat, again, and again, and again;[13] or they invoke serial universes and limit-destroying concepts. Ecstasy, rather than being a delightful escape valve, is always bound up with death.[14] The capacity to imagine, experience, even participate, in one's own death is a prerequisite to ecstasy, because any enlarged perspective will swallow up the short duration of each small life. The practitioner of Buddhist meditation must, among other things, meditate on his or her own death.[15] Shamans of diverse cultures must have visions of their own dismemberment to rise to their full investiture in their role.[16] Scientists, too, who seek real knowledge, go to medical school and dissect cadavers or peer through telescopes and try to formulate what they see in terms of light-years.

Religion is an equation about "what is the nature of the universe" (see Chapter 1), and worldview is the solution to the equation. Ecstasy is a high order solution that solves many complex equations. This fruition of a religious need is not cognitive, but characterologic. It is the product of an organization of personality, based on an embracing engagement of the outer whole, so that the depth of the finite unit has a direct luminal channel to the infinite. Religious transcendence raises the unit above self-concerns in order to view creation. The most important by-product of a mature worldview is wonder.

Albert Einstein wrote: "The most beautiful thing one can experience is the mysterious. It is the source of all true art and science."[17] Rachel Carson: "A child's world is fresh and new and beautiful, full of wonder and excitement . . . I should ask that [the] gift to each child in the world be a sense of wonder so indestructible that it would last throughout life . . ."[18] Walt Whitman captured this state in a brief poem:

Beginning my studies the first step pleas'd me so much,
The mere fact consciousness, these forms, the power of motion,
The least insect or animal, the senses, eyesight, love,
The first step I say awed me and pleas'd me so much,
I have hardly gone and hardly wish to go any farther,
But stop and loiter all the time to sing it in ecstatic songs.[19]

But wonder is not always so harmonious and benign. In the extraordinary epiphany of the Bhagavad Gita, there is a more powerful and complete vision:

By the hundreds and thousands, behold . . . my manifold celestial forms of innumerable shapes and colors.

See now the whole universe with all things that move and move not, and whatever thy soul may yearn to see. See it all as One in me.

If the light of a thousand suns suddenly arose in the sky, that splendour might be compared to the radiance of the Supreme Spirit.

Trembling with awe and wonder Arjuna [the spiritual seeker] bowed [and spoke], "All around I behold thy Infinity: the power of thy innumerable arms, the visions from thy innumerable eyes . . . Nowhere I see a beginning, a middle or end . . .

I see the splendour of an infinite beauty which illumines the whole universe . . . But the worlds also behold thy fearful mighty form, with many mouths and eyes. I see thy vast form reaching the sky, burning with many colors, with wide open mouths, with vast flaming eyes, my heart shakes in terror like the fire at the end of Time which burns all in the last day . . ."[20]

These world-shaking, world creating lines, which first surfaced in a human mind several thousand years ago, were also present to explain the wonder and dread that dawned with the modern era. J. Robert Oppenheimer, the physicist known as the "father of the bomb" has recorded that, at the moment of the first nuclear explosion over the sands of New Mexico, passages from this chapter of the Bhagavad Gita spontaneously arose in his mind.[21]

The founding moments of religion, the visions of creators and scriptural poets, are always bound up with the flood, the knowledge of "all-powerful Time which destroys all things and slays all men." Those who make their worldview conscious will always be men of sorrows. In Buddhism, the perception of sorrow, the inevitability of loss, the inescapability of impermanence, is the first step on the Path, the first glimpse of truth. This is not the same as the sorrow that accompanies affirming acceptance, which is the recognition that all men are bearers of the capacity for evil. This is the sorrow of mortality, time, loss, and destruction. This sorrow is the doorway into Dhamma, the universal Truth as the Buddha saw it in his meditation, and it is the first step away from unconscious existence into awake human life:

> What now, is the First Noble Truth of Suffering? Birth is suffering; Decay is suffering; Death is suffering; Sorrow, Lamentation, Pain, Grief and Despair are suffering; not to get what one desires is suffering . . .[22]

Buddha was not counseling defeat or pessimism, because the *noble* truth of suffering is the first step on the path to the *eradication* of suffering. But suffering is the essential lens, as the microscope is to the bacteriologist. And suffering is intrinsic. All composite things—all bodies, buildings, civilizations—decay and pass away. Time is relentless, bottomless. The universe is quicksand. By confronting this knowledge, Buddha taught, the seeker can see truth. It is the knowing of Shelley's "Ozymandias"[23]: "Look on my works, ye mighty, and despair. Nothing beside remains"; or of Ecclesiastes (which so closely echoes the first of the two above quotes from the Bhagavad Gita):

> The wind goeth towards the south, and turneth around unto the north; it whirleth about continually, and the wind returneth again according to his circuits . . . behold, all is vanity . . . that which is wanting cannot be numbered . . . I gave my heart to seek and search out by wisdom concerning all things that are done under heaven: this sore travail hath God given to the sons of man . . . for in much wisdom is much grief, and he that increaseth knowledge increaseth sorrow.[24]

These ancient pathways into vision through the wilderness of despair and suffering continue to be trod wherever new visions are sought. For Paul Tillich, religious faith could be found only by diving to the depth of doubt.[25] The deeper the doubt plumbed, the deeper the faith. Such a dive would require courage, ultimate courage, the courage to dive into a nothingness of doubt with no known bottom in order to seek an uncertain source of faith in a doubtful world. Tillich's religion was forged while he was a chaplain on the front, with the German army in the First World War. Unrelieved (all his requests for leave refused), he personally witnessed literally tens of thousands of deaths of young men.[26] His most famous work concludes: "The courage to be is rooted in the God who appears when God has disappeared in the anxiety of doubt."[27] Tillich felt that only when shallow, soothing, false faiths are shattered by the profoundest existential despair that accompanies an unshaded vision of infinite time and personal frailty and helplessness, can the real divinity be glimpsed; and in response to the true faith that arises from this naked seeing, comes the courage to live with what really exists.

Similarly, Erikson concluded in his psychohistorical study of Gandhi, whose millennium-forging faith alternated with paralyzing doubts: ". . . a great man may be only as great as the degree of despair that he can allow himself . . ."[28]

Prophets from the desert, having gone outside to gain perspective and see the whole, return with visions that, if they are to endure, slice through denial, and anneal the two strands of vision—wonder and sorrow. Fresh, full vision enables the transgenerational transmission of ecstasy.

> Think not that I came to send peace on earth: I came not to send peace, but a sword.[29]

The young lawyer had been filled with rage and disgust at what he saw around him. He was literally unable to face the day and unable to fall asleep at night, so he kept himself permanently "stoned." His therapy necessitated multidimensional activity, and by no means focused on religious issues. Unearthing the past was no problem; he had little repression—every day he was porous to his unfortunate past. It was not his memories, but his reactions to those events that were intolerable to him. He also needed to face his pot abuse head-on; he could see it with one eye and rationalize it with the other, so that it took some force to keep its real meaning up in front of him. When he had confessed his murderous feelings to me, and when I had stood by him without judgment but also without backing down on the psychological and biological implications of his drug abuse, he placed me in the position of the good father he had yearned for, and he let a corrective emotional experience of firmness and affection flow through him.

He felt he had a religious problem, too. His Catholic background had struck a note in him about a good mystery in his deep past. But he also felt religion had been a hypocritical shield for his father's alcoholism. Several years before seeking therapy, he had gotten actively involved in Transcendental Meditation. He followed the practice, partly hoping it would break the hold of pot—it did, only briefly—and he made friends on weekened retreats. It provided him an alternative, a challenge, a respite from his parents' world. After a number of years it dawned on him that T.M. was really Hinduism. He read somewhere that Hindus worship Shiva, a god of blood [actually another symbol for the destruction of time, cf. the Bhagavad Gita, above]. Did that inaccurate information offend his esthetic; was he paranoid from smoking marijuana; was he looking for an excuse to quit; were his problems overwhelming his initial hopes for T.M.? He quit T.M. and, in that vacuum, sought therapy.

So, in a sense, he bounced off a religion into therapy. The scintillating illusions of marijuana and of T.M. were foil decorations, with which he tried to turn his ugly reality into a holiday world. As he healed in treatment, his social life moved away from drugs, to sports, and from there to a previously quiescent love of the outdoors. He was spontaneously pulled into the tradition of a vision quest (see Chapter 4), a search for a new self and a new world in the solitude and beauty of the mountains. He needed a new view, a window he could look out of, straight. Joining forces with a more experienced friend, he headed for the Montana Rockies to drink in a vision of wild nature outside and find a manly strength within. He returned, proud of his stamina and endurance (a man even though his father had pushed him around; with self-control even though he had had thoughts of patricide). He gloated about grizzly bears, long mileage, heavy packs, and he glowed as he described watching elk herds graze at high meadows above tree line. He daydreamed about practicing environmental law, yearning for a true calling, but he stayed in his father's firm. He did stop his phone calls home every day. He wanted to be on his own and stopped therapy, saying he'd call again in a year, which he didn't do.

This expansion of his worldview served a partly growthful, and partly defensive purpose. It was spontaneous and classical in style, and it provided more of a world he could live in, and more of a self to live in it. It was religion used as a transitional object.[30]

The lawyer, like every person, lived in a complex, polysemous world, which was a mixture of large-group psychosocial structures like Catholicism and T.M., and of his own perceptions, experiences, and inner mixes. One salient aspect of his worldview was a pervasive sense of duplicity. His father was an acclaimed civic leader, yet a bullying, incestuous drunk. Catholicism was redolent with warm reverence, but it served as a sanctioning screen for his crazy parents. T.M. was just a meditation technique that secretly purveyed Hinduism. He himself was a good student and upcoming lawyer, who was a closet drug addict.

Another beam in the structure of his initial worldview was its claustrophobia: alcohol and drug secrets were kept behind closed doors; his father could barely suppress sexual feelings for his sister; his mother had to be locked away from time to time; he himself yearned to be free of this whole despicable world, yet he was in the gravitational pull of his father, a junior member of his law firm.

Another aspect of his worldview was that he was a defective: son of an alcoholic and a manic depressive, drug addict, weakling who couldn't protect his mother from his father. He couldn't break away from his father's professional umbrella or his parents' mediocre, slummy little city in nowhere, Massachusetts.

The mountains he climbed to rectify his worldview provided focused palliatives. Like a child, like a poet, like a visionary, like so many of us, he headed out for nature, for mountains and wilderness. He went to join the authors of the Scriptures and the Gita and Walt Whitman and Rachel Carson; he wanted to hear the vast winds rush through ethereal space, to stand apart, in ecstasies, high and free from his life. There, the seen was the real, there were no secrets; he would be far from the enmeshed rage and sexuality; and he would test himself, prove himself to be a healthy, primeval, civilized man. The violent, Oedipal winds of death inside him could be harnessed to fill the sails of tough, conquering self-imagery. He would commune with animals, which Eliade reminds us is a culturally pervasive symbol of wisdom and spiritual attainment:

> . . . they know the secrets of Life and Nature, they even know the secrets of longevity and immortality. Let us underline this—that friendship with the animals and knowledge of their language belong to the paradisiac syndrome. The shaman cannot leave his body and set out on his mystical journey until after he has recovered, by intimacy with the animals, a bliss and a spontaneity that would be unattainable in his profane, everyday situation.[31]

When I heard the young lawyer describe each high point of his backpacking trip, I heard him echoing Valmiki: "Before he looked, he thought the world was sweet poison. Men seemed to be living in lies . . . But in the water he saw—a dream, a chance, a great adventure . . ." His calculated toying with danger and death—proximity to grizzlies, exposure to cold, carrying just enough food to run out two days early and have to struggle on, racing time and exhaustion—seemed like a well-planned vision quest, a self-directed practice of shamanistic ecstasy, a journey into the gnosis of pain and death, from which he hoped to return reborn and free. The calculation and self-direction may account for why he was only partially successful. He managed, on his return, to individuate somewhat more, to build elements of an autonomous adult life instead of passively and obediently waiting each evening for his mother's needy and entangling phone call. He said he felt serious about the Jewish woman he was dating—which infuriated his parents—but he stayed in his father's firm. Running and soccer took up the slack; he stayed off pot, felt satisfied with his progress in therapy, and disappeared from my view.

A worldview, by its nature, has areas of clarity and solidity, but it also extends through all the shadows and labyrinths. The very concept is intended to suggest a pervasive suffusion, rather than a geometric delineation. Rather than seeing a worldview take shape, a therapist is likely to see many, only at the foundation. That is because therapy is predominantly intrapsychic, and the building of a worldview must be mixed with the active and external, and requires a full glass of health. Thus, as in the case of the young lawyer, therapy frequently *provokes* the generation or reconstruction of a worldview, but less frequently is necessary, or participant in, the concluding phases of this transformation.

A college student was referred by a student mental health service. She needed more help than they felt they could provide. Just before her return to her junior year, she had found her father in the morning dew behind their luxurious house. His head was a bloody, unrecognizable ooze; a shotgun was next to him. Despite professional attainment, he had been seriously depressed, on and off, for years. Psychiatric hospitalizations had brought brief respites; drug addictions had brought relapses. Her adolescence was a cacophonous memory of parental arguments, hospital visits, tears, and apologies, interspersed with posh suburban living, season's tickets to concerts, and good grades. She had been majoring in economics to follow in her father's footsteps. Naturally his suicide stopped her dead in her tracks.

Her grief took the form of obsessive, frozen ruminations about what to major in (what is meaningful, what world can I dwell in that will protect me from my father's fate, from my own memories). Her accomplishments on the cello, which had previously been an embellishment to her intelligence and a strong second suit in college applications, surfaced, but in a particular way. She became absorbed into baroque music; not just playing it, because she modestly felt it could not ultimately provide her a life. Instead, she plunged into the world of baroque music, its history, and the history of the cultures from which it sprang, and the biographies of its creators. She grasped onto a famous quartet, following them from concert to concert, adeptly wrangling her way into an apprentice/assistant business manager role. When she graduated from college, she planned, temporarily, to continue that work. This was not a calling; she understood it was a temporary, youthful life-style, paying little, and geographically unstable.

Similar to the young lawyer, whose vision quest to Montana did not lead to a calling, this patient was struggling with a matrix, a background issue, that had to be solved first. With both of these young people, sham worlds of bourgeois security had been shattered and their concern became not just to find out who they were, but to find a reliable, true world, out of which, at some future date, possibly a calling could emerge. But now the urge to find a true world was needed merely to affirm life itself. For both of them, the forging of a worldview was urgent, clumsy, dramatic, and of whole cloth—unintegrated with the shattered and rejected worlds, whose pieces they would some day have to integrate with their romantic, enthusiastic, yet fanciful and two-dimensional new worlds.

The college student whose father killed himself can also be understood from the standpoint of "psychic numbing," a concept coined by R.J. Lifton.

Psychic numbing is a form of desensitization; it refers to an incapacity to feel or to confront certain kinds of experience, due to the blocking or absence of inner forms or imagery . . . the cessation of what I call the formative process, the impairment of man's essential mental function of symbol formation.[32]

According to Lifton, death anxiety is the core of human existence, and is countered by a continuous process of symbol formation that connects people to a sense of symbolic immortality transcending death. Because we ". . . both 'know' that we will die and resist and fail to act on that knowledge . . ." we are accordingly driven by ". . . a compelling universal urge to maintain an inner sense of continuous symbolic relationship, over time and space, with the various elements of life."[33] The death imprint on the student was so overwhelming that it numbed her, until she could create new modes of symbolic immortality through the timelessness of baroque music. Lifton's phrasing emphasizes "continuity without sameness" in personality, and shares with worldview a sense of the bridging, self-transforming, world-relational aspect of human life. And it stands firmly on the same ground as worldview when it emphasizes that a fulcrum of knowing is imagery of death and destruction. Lifton's phrasing differs from the concept of worldview by focusing more on process than on content; it seems more general and theoretical and has less of the taint of an individual within his or her content-rich world.

Some of the main melodic lines in the symphony I am

calling "worldview" can be heard by listening to what Erikson calls "fidelity."

> Fidelity is the ability to sustain loyalties freely pledged in spite of inevitable contradictions . . . it is the cornerstone of identity and receives inspiration from confirming ideologies . . . In our day, ideologies take over where religion leaves off . . . historical perspectives on which to fasten individual faith and collective confidence.[34]

Erikson later added:

> In adolescence, the quality of fidelity, the capacity to be loyal to a vision of the future, incorporates such infantile trust . . . can reappear in youth and young adulthood as a vital contribution to a larger vision of love and "beauty"; or it can manifest itself in the collective isolation of a utopian or revivalist community . . .[35]

But fidelity has more to do with conscious development and ego strengths. Fidelity to ideology is often the spoken center of a self-conscious worldview, but by worldview I mean to include attitudes, values, experiences, beliefs, and feelings at every level of conscious and unconscious, a mosaic dome that surrounds us every way we turn, a not wholly-integrated summation of our sense of things, which includes not only what we hold to, but what we are haunted by, not only what we attest, but what we continuously struggle to deny. Concepts like "modes of symbolic immortality" and "fidelity to ideology" refer to consciousness and daylight; worldview refers to a penumbra.

A psychotherapist may feel a worldview surround him or her, or fade away, when an old, well-known patient walks into or out of the room, and the therapist is himself soaked in the names and fates of nephews who defied the rules and what happened to them, or in the overtones and innuendos implicit in anecdotes about a grandmother's house on the seashore. In the two clinical cases I have described, there is a difference between the patients' real, complete, worldviews, which *include* alcoholism, patricide, and decranialized brains, and their attempts to consciously correct and re-create worldviews, which include symbols, fidelities, and poses.

The college student found a mode of symbolic immortality in her identification with great, "timeless" music that has survived centuries (this is what Lifton describes as the third of five possible modes, that of identification with works that are creative and have "an enduring human impact"). She developed a fidelity to a specific group of musicians, and to the musicians' ethos of educating and celebrating, which she described to me with a convert's fervor. At the same time, she was doing much more: pushing aside her parents' quest for material security, which had so obviously backfired; distancing herself from her elite college, to travel with the musicians, and thereby relieving her crushing alienation at being psychically scarred and wizened among a campus full of coddled, hopeful "preppies"; and building a historical, musical stage set, on which she could build up a new world to supplement and transcend her spectral, suburban memories and fears.

The healing potential possible through the modification or transformation of worldview is an ancient observation. St. Augustine found release through grace and faith when he surrendered his own will to the Christian God (see Chapter 6). A critical aspect of this change was his willingness to transform his worldview. He had achieved identity and fame as an eminent proponent of Roman reason. At first he was at odds with

> . . . the Catholic doctrine requiring things to be believed which could not be proved. But, I began to consider the countless things I believed which I had not seen, or which had been done with me not there—so many things in the history of nations, so many facts about places and cities which I had never seen, so many things told me by friends, by doctors, by this man, by that man: and unless we accepted these things, we should do nothing at all in this life . . . it struck me how firmly and unshakeably I believed that I was born of a particular

father and mother, which I could not possibly know unless I believed it upon the word of others . . . Thus since men had not the strength to discover the truth by clear reasons and therefore we needed the authority of Holy Writ.[36]

This gentle and almost humorous description of his famous conversion made St. Augustine the spokesman for faith and reliance upon authority (rather than on evidence and reason) for two millennia of civilization. He describes not only a shift in attitudes, but the attendant implicit consumption of a worldview. He could now dwell inside the world of the Bible, which he could not prove to be true, except for his will to submerge himself therein, and the spiritual relief such a total act brought him.

We can see that along with embracing a new mode of symbolic immortality (Lifton's second mode, the theological idea of life after death), and a new, vehement fidelity, St. Augustine also stepped into a new world of relationships, associations, behavior patterns, symbols, and myths: "I saw that many passages in these books which had at one time struck me as absurdities, must be referred to the profundity of mystery." The deep, personal, intimate dialogue he proceeded to carry on with a god he had previously not believed in, was the most fundamental addition to his worldview. "So I dwelt upon these things and You were near me . . ."

St. Augustine's Confessions secured its powerful historical role through the impassioned lucidity of his theology, and also through the candid, disarming flavor of intimate revelation. Because of the latter, it is easy to glimpse the psychodynamics that underlay St. Augustine's years of turmoil, and the psychological explanation of its resolution.

He portrays the Roman culture he grew up in as one of decadent paternalism. With strong disapproval, he describes the widely accepted practice of wife beating. His own father, whom he viewed with distaste, had a harsh temper. His mother, who was a saintly Christian, avoided any possible behavior that would justify beating. In this decaying civilization, three and a half centuries after Jesus, St. Augustine grew up successful as an intellectual, but unhappy, restless, particularly uneasy regarding sex. Desirous, he also yearned to find peace, accept the Christ, like his mother, and become, as St. Paul advised, a eunuch for Christ. As a counterpull to his sexual feelings, he set up the wish to relinquish desire for all other women and accept his mother's religion, join her, and become the true son she deserved. He yearned to reject the sex and violence that his father epitomized, and, by a final, full identification with his mother's world, to obtain instead an all-good heavenly father, the very one who was his mother's real love (and therefore his real father).

Now we can understand why his conversion hinged on the sentence: "Most strongly of all it struck me how firmly and unshakeably I believed I was born of a particular father and mother, which I could not possibly know unless I believed it upon the word of others." The doubt of, and desire to reject, his own paternity became the strongest force impelling him to abandon Roman (his father's) reason for the Christian (his mother's) faith. He obtained the peace of his conversion by avoiding the Oedipal rivalry implicit in his own maleness, and he resolved to remain his mother's good boy, loyal to her, uncritically absorbing her worldview in a totalistic manner, and secure in his relationship to a really good father, God, who wouldn't be violent or sexual and who wouldn't hurt him as long as he remained a faithful eunuch.

This personal psychological struggle and resolution was the substrate for a change in worldview that carried millions of people along in the shift from the Roman Empire to Christian Europe. Individual changes in worldview, when expressed with the force of genius, may constitute a massive historical force.

Through the outer worlds they select, patients not only

mirror elements of self-feeling, but they marry realities. Not all worldview foundations that are built up during therapy are reconstitutive and defensive. Another side can also be seen. Along with the release and delight of new discovery may come the knowledge of historical panorama, personal death, cosmic time.

A computer scientist sought therapy after her second divorce. She was bright, tall, blonde, strikingly good looking, with easy access to jobs, mobility, and money. She was sexually obsessed. Tall and skinny as a girl, she had felt outcast among her peers. In her parents' home there had been ceaseless bickering. She closed the door and felt good masturbating. In her marriages she was demanding, needy, ready for and causative of the rejections that followed. She talked to me endlessly of her relationships, her worldview constricted to narrow material perspectives: sex, cars, money, apartments, and clothes. After four years of therapy, and a richer relationship with a man, she began to remember her dreams.

To both of our surprise, dream after dream was about her being Jewish and caught in the sweep of world history. Soviet spies deported her to Israel; P.L.O. men fired on her in the streets of New York; she was kidnapped by Libyans, and chased by Nazis. Her obsessively personal and petty universe was invaded by the concerns of the struggle for life, dignity, freedom, and peace. A mind that had been locked in a vagina unconsciously swept the front page and the globe for feeling. The contrast between her intelligence and her narrowness became clear. She was deeply stirred by the earth-shaking, terrifying issues of life's profoundest layer, and she was overwhelmed. Her shallow, self-referential life-style was a way of containing the epic turmoil within her. Therapy did not help her change this. She clamped down on her dreams, married for a third time, worried over every nuance of that relationship, and felt ready to stop self-exploration.

Similarly, many patients report dreams of nuclear explosions or war, and while these dreams have a real cultural basis and may have many other levels of meaning—personal, historical, literal, or symbolic—they also represent a movement away from narcissistic preoccupation to life in a larger, frightening, demanding, world. In our day, Christ's sword, Buddha's First Noble Truth, or Ecclesiastes' search for wisdom concerning all things brings a man or a woman up against the threat of nuclear holocaust, planetary terrorism, resource depletion, overpopulation. These confrontations are coupled to wonder: the sight of Montana elk grazing in high mountain meadows, or the jubilant naivete of baroque music. Because people create the world through their hands, pens, hammers, every new worldview integrated with a calling and membership is also a new world. In this way, one person's psychological growth adds new dimensions to the common human reality.

Because in the morning we must face the world and at night let it go, the two great universal acts of courage are to fully wake up and go to sleep. Few wake and sleep consciously. Instinct, impulse, and need continue to govern much of human life. No one is born consciously; some few die consciously, and these are the ones who have tempered a worldview that can carry them confidently into death. The brave new world isn't discovered, it is built. The world is what we dream when we are wide awake. We must build towers on foundations of gossamer. We pass over to our children, our most intricate, complete, intelligent, sustaining castle-in-the-air, which will definitely be broken, or which they themselves must smash. Yet this volatile trinket is humanness itself. Our minds have visions, our hands write and build. Michelangelo's God-and-Adam on the ceiling of the Sistine Chapel touch hand to hand, the organ of creation. One element in emotional health and illness is the capacity to build a world of wakefulness that will stand suspended and inhabitable above the chaos of darkness. Every dream is a scrap of lumber; every clear sentence is a doorway.

When a patient becomes aware of bad dreams about anarchy, global war, genocide, reports it to the therapist, and then struggles to integrate this dream into a waking reality that he or she can live with, we can reasonably hope for the new being. "Every living thing is a workshop where God . . . transubstantiates clay."[37]

◇ **8** ◇

Human Love

. . . I looked down, and knelt, lending my hand . . .

While pathological narcissism may be the product of specific developmental constellations,[1] or may be a more generalized, cultural phenomenon,[2] both the classical root meaning of the word, and its contemporary clinical application signify failure of the capacity to love. Contemporary psychotherapy can be viewed as primarily the treatment of narcissism, of self-absorption, of failure to love. This is what dominates the psychological landscape, as sexual repression did in Freud's Vienna. Among the hurt and pained in need of help, who may suffer from broken marriages, fluctuating or fallen self-esteem, obsessive constrictions, panicky attachments to parents, bewildering isolation, uncontrolled rages, and haunting depressions, the common denominator is an inability to transcend themselves with care and delight, to reach over and touch another heart. My interest in religious issues in psychotherapy has been spurred on by a series of patients who have told me spontaneously, without prompting but after considered thought, that their impaired search for love was floundering because they were seeking religion through sexual intimacy. The binding together, the touch of person to person, is sought concretely, rather than spiritually, and dyadically rather than communally. The substitution of sexuality for religious life constitutes one of the most prominent and pervasive elements of cultural pathology that a psychotherapist encounters.

This same twisting of needs away from what is essential, to what is convenient and quick, occurs in other patients who did not spontaneously label it that way themselves. The psychoanalyst Otto Kernberg has written that narcissistic patients may attempt to turn their psychoanalysis into a religion;[3] and psychiatrist-gadfly Thomas Szaz has criticized psychiatry for playing a more priestly than medical role.[4] Both intend to call attention to the confused search for religion in the secular practice of psychotherapy. People may seek religion in sexual activity; and, when that fails, they may seek religion in the cure for failed sexuality, psychotherapy: a serialized error.

My impression is that, as the thousand-year old wave of tension between scientific, rational, humanistic thought, and predominantly anthropomorphic, authoritarian, and superstitious religious traditions has crested in our time, the vacuum left by receding religions has led to many substitute religious fragments being elevated onto the dais of the holy. One of those substitute fragments may be nationalism and collective, chauvinistic grandiosity. Tillich has commented that the best laboratory to understand the dynamics of religious faith was German National Socialism.[5] As a courageous anti-Nazi who suffered threats and exile for his stand, Tillich knew Fascism firsthand and felt that it revealed the key to faith in the way that sexual perversion revealed the dynamics of sexuality to Freud. He saw nationalism as a fragmented expression of a fundamentally religious urge.

I think that a different shard of the old bowl of religion

has fallen into the hands of psychiatry. This fragment derives from the romantic individualism that underlies contemporary Western life. Many keen psychosocial observers, such as Jung,[6] Rank,[7] and Becker,[8] have commented on the myth of the hero and the role of Protestant individualism in the formation of the psyche of modern man. Recent sociological thinkers have described America as a culture rooted in individualism—not mere individuality—but an "ism," a pervasive value, a deeply ingrained, national-character-shaping "habit of the heart." Harkening back to de Tocqueville, the great French social philosopher and student of America, contemporary sociologists have pointed to individualism as an isolating, socially fragmenting force, the goal of which is freedom *from* others, rather than freedom *to* be or do.[9] This is the underpinning of the modern novel and movie, but more importantly, of hundreds of millions of people's images of themselves. In this view, each person is a solitary, self-made gunfighter, a warrior carving the shape of his or her life into the surrounding society. The emphasis is on self-determination, choice, and control. The gifts and tools that history and culture contribute to each person's capacities to survive, think, and grasp meaning in life are heavily downplayed. Participation in areas of similarity and commonality that constitute the psychic layer of community is scorned as sentimental.

The view that we are autonomous, self-generated units is so much a part of our contemporary worldview that it is often as invisible to us as our own eyes. Yet this view is by no means intrinsic to human self-perceptions. Consider a viewpoint like the Indian term, Dharma, discussed in Chapter 4, in which "One is not free to choose; one belongs to a species . . . one's concern as a judging and acting entity must be only to meet every life problem in a manner befitting the role one plays."[10] This not only clashes with our daily Western experience of life, but it destroys our culture. Dharma can barely inhabit the same psychological universe as Patrick Henry, George Washington, Daniel Boone, Huckleberry Finn, or Butch Cassidy and the Sundance Kid.

India is not the only culture to emphasize what we have in common rather than how we stand apart. Erikson,[11] Henry,[12] and others have highlighted aspects of American schooling that account for why Native Americans may do poorly in school. They fundamentally misconstrue the essential white American task there, according to their own culturally induced norms and values: they try to blend in, to do no better than anyone else, to fail to know what any of the others also fail to know. Native American children may reject the entire idea of becoming differentiated through excellence. They understand themselves through their tribe and community, not as separate pieces.

In the context of a culture that makes the solitary warrior-hero paradigmatic, love can only mean the meeting of two such isolates in transitional romantic encounter: knight and damsel. Commitment, childrearing, participation in and transmission of culture is trivialized. But, since human salvation is always, intuitively, intrinsically tied to the capacity to love, in this context dyadic sexual liaison becomes the sanctum-sanctorum, the inner temple where the holy mystery is revealed. Consenting, uncomplicated copulation is the closest and longest that two human atoms can touch.

Cultures will guide their hurt members toward those modes of help that are construed as relevant and that are in fact available. A Navajo will seek a medicine-man; a Punjabi Moslem will seek a hakim; an eighteenth-century Hasid may have turned to his rabbi. Many of our contemporaries seek existential salvation in private, romantic fusion, and thousands of misdirected Icaruses come thudding down into psychotherapy. Psychotherapy is the net that catches the fragment, falling from the shattered Western religious traditions, where the need for human love has nowhere to turn, and where sexual adventure is mistaken as a channel for love.

Of course, every person has his or her own story, and many discrete life events may prime the stage for such a flight or such a fall. The sociocultural current of romantic sexual individualism forms only a backdrop for the vicissitudes of individual lives. Just like an underground river, which only occasionally breaks the surface to form the source of a stream, the social currents flow beneath the phenomena that emerge in therapy as the failure of the religious element of human love, but those rivers emerge only when the individual life forms a suitable site. Thus, individual stories and psychodynamics and therapies continue to be loci in which the play of greater social issues are augmented or reduced. The interplay of cultural priming and individual history can be heard in the following story.

A sociologist called for help when his second wife left him, and he found himself the father of four children, the ex-husband of two ex-wives, yet living alone. He was gripped by extreme panic. His sturdy, sharp mind was fluttering; he could think only of one thing: getting back in contact with a woman. In fact, when we first met, he presented his problem by saying that he had just fallen in love, and he had! When his wife callously sprung her secret disaffection from him and walked out without warning one afternoon, he had instantly phoned an old woman friend, set up a liaison . . . and felt himself falling in love—a painful incongruous defense against his outrage and dismay. He rationalized to himself that this new woman represented smoldering love that had gone on platonically for years, and, now that his wife was out of the way, this true love could at last be consummated. He simply could not tolerate the absence of a woman in his life, even for a day. Women almost seemed to be replaceable parts. His rationalization and new relationship quickly decayed. He was in fact alone. In therapy he explored his compulsive need to be in contact with a woman, like a rechargeable battery with a twenty-four clock.

His father had run a gas station near Minneapolis; his parents drank and fought; he and his sister grew up among the impersonal hullabaloo of extended German family gatherings, overflowing with beer and food and angry, ethnic prejudices. From that vantage point, he watched people, and became a keen student. But he felt ostracized from the macho world of football and basketball that formed the only available peer group in his childhood and adolescence. Pampered by his drunken mother who admired and vicariously fed on his brilliance, he was mocked by his bitter father for his soft and clean pen-holding hands.

He never lived alone as a man, never found a place as a man among men, but married a plumber's daughter at nineteen. While she worked, he went through college and graduate school. Children and divorce were followed by a driven, hyperbolic Don Juanism—copulation with hundreds of partners. The pseudo-political excitement of the '60s and drugs lubricated these fleeting accidents of encounter. In the middle of this his father died. He remembered soothing himself, grieving, by having sexual relations with three women on that day. His second marriage produced more children and ended in an abrupt divorce. This seemed particularly bitter to him. Burned by the loneliness and a-domesticity of his childhood, he placed family and marriage first among his values. Undoing the mistakes of his parents, he was sober, soft-spoken, a diligent provider and helper. He had worshipped his wives, done all he could for them, and given them all he could of himself. He couldn't understand, nor was it easy to see, why he was alone.

It took a long psychotherapy to clarify. His generosity and availability were in service of a covert control. He felt the world, the world of his father, of frozen midwestern gas stations, cold-cracked, grease-blackened hands, hunting, sports, crude sexual talk, was an alien planet. He sought refuge in the admiration of his mother and subsequent women. This was his sanctuary, his temple, where, as high priest, he could worship the goddess and receive her blessings and protection. Coy of adult friendship or collegiality, entrenched in an aloof, critical posture to human groups, he returned home for compulsive sexual contact with his wives, on the one hand afraid of displeasing them, failing them, and, on the other hand, recharging himself, plugging himself in. His genuinely sweet affection for them was marred by his need to use them for the totality of his human relatedness. Despite a successful career, his work remained at arm's length for him. The more he poured out his needy love on his wives, the more they felt overwhelmed, resentful. The nicer, and kinder, and more "liberated" he was, the more each of them had sensed the desperation and demand, the smothering clutch that underlay his willingness to do anything for them.

His marriages were like a calling—they gave him a daily focus and self-defining task. They were like a membership, the only church to which he belonged. They were his source of lawful order, for he regulated his sense of the steadiness and reliability of the world by the reconfirmation at dusk that somebody was at home to ease his needs. Orgasm was his only release. His marriages were private religions. Without anchor, belief, or affiliation anywhere outside his home, skillfully and facilely earning his living through impersonal statistical analyses, he had set up his own altar, where he worshipped the goddess. This was more than simple dependency. Elaborate rituals of home building, gardening, furnishing; deeply held dogmas about the sanctity of family; excited sexual worship—all drew into his marriages the religious levels of existence, like an osmotic force.

Once in human history, the worship of the Goddess was probably the dominant form of religion of all the neolithic protocivilizations.[13] The Great Mother's pervasive presence may have receded when the basis of agriculture shifted from hoed garden plots tended by women to plowed fields, where men directed animals and displaced women as the main producers of food. Through historical times to the present, formal, organized worship of a goddess has been limited to India. There we still find the Goddess as the focus of devotion for millions. There are different forms to these Goddess cults, which Hinduism embraces in its tolerance for religious diversity. In general, the various forms of worship of the Goddess are characterized by heightened emotionality, thinly veiled proximity to primitive impulses, and fusion with amorphous, primeval energy. The Goddess is worshipped as the point source of the totality of universal energy; in one myth she spins the threads of creation, gives birth to the gods, who then destroy her and absorb all her energy. The Goddess is often iconographically and mythically portrayed as hideous, for she holds the entire universe in her power and thus represents death and annihilation as well as fertility and creation. She may also be worshipped as half of a male-and-female divinity, as in Tantrism, a practice that spread to Tibetan Buddhism from Hinduism, in which sexuality is the main metaphor for the processes of the world.[14]

The religion of the Goddess showed its outlines in the private religion of the sociologist. He feared nonexistence when he was not assured of direct contact with a woman; his fear was a terrifying premonition that everything would fall apart, shatter, be destroyed. It was as if the visible world were only static empty forms, pieces of things (as the Tantric Hindus believe), but its vitality and energy were provided by an invisible yet palpable "sakti," or energy, the emanations of the essence of the Goddess. The sociologist believed none of this; he had never heard of such things. But his feelings spontaneously reproduced these ancient and ongoing beliefs. Although friendly love and affection were valuable to him, the real point of contact was sexual intercourse, through which the danger of the empty male world crashing down to dust was forestalled for one more day by recharge from the sakti's emanation of creative energy. She, his sexual partner, was therefore the source of his life. Her power was enormous. Just as he loved and worshipped her for the beauty of the world he did in fact so gratefully appreciate (preeminently, his children), he also feared her, as Hindu worshippers of the Goddess stand in awe of Kali, whose name is etymologically connected with darkness, time, and death. Therefore, he was in constant fear of her, needing to placate, mollify, and comply. Naturally, he also carried covert envy and hate into such a subservient dependency.

But this man was by no means wholly primitive, and there was a real quest for love in him too. This was the drive behind his long, sad self-revelations. Painful as therapy was for him, he was determined to find the happy home he had dreamed of as a boy in an unhappy one. It was difficult for him to absorb the impact of the paradox I described to him. As long as he was hyper-focused on building that happy home, it would elude him, for an element of that dream in realization would have to include a change in his religion, his real, lived religion, not his atheist ideation. Our journey together had to take us through a polar detour: why was he so avoidant of men? This question led us across basketball courts, hunting cabins, and tenure committees, in the company of his father, uncles, friends, and rivals.

The forms of the sociologist's private religion arose from a stratum of the psyche where love has not yet been born. Historically, early religion was devoid of this affect and ideation and consisted of magic and rituals of propitiation to maintain cordial relations with supernatural powers. He had followed this way because he himself felt powerless, hollow, unable to hold his own. Yet he had felt potent and unstoppable when his mother was behind him. His father's cold, military style of asserting manhood and dominance had left the boy broken, but his mother's exhortations and encouragement had enabled him to apparently jump over (really to sidestep) his father, and to grow in stature far above and beyond their blue-collar expectations. He felt unable to love because he felt incomplete as a man, completed only by the woman inside him. The Goddess he worshipped was the goddess that he needed, feared, and hated. The long, slow stairway of his therapy required him to live on his own, establish self-sufficiency, make friends, handshake and talk freely with men, and, above all, to meet me, live in a world with me year after year, until his fears were deconditioned, strengths were introjected, and solidity held in my presence.

He remarried. Did we fool each other into imagining that his greater autonomy, capacity for honest argument, and more vital career interests enabled him to love rather than worship? At least partly so? I myself was disappointed that he never engaged any meaningful community and never felt or seemed free of a constricting self-preoccupation. His work now did entail more social concern, more caretaking in the balance pans with career building. His new wife seemed more suited to his intellectual world. He described himself as less of a sycophant with her. They bought a cabin on a lake together—was he creating a new altar, or overcoming a past fear to build a mutual new life? He insisted on compromises rather than always making his own, eager concessions. My unspoken feelings were mixed. The goddess has her subtle, loving, modern forms, and the great doctor-poet, William Carlos Williams, wrote:

Mother of God! Our lady . . .
    We submit ourselves
to Your rule
    as the flowers in May
      submit themselves to
      Your holy rule—against
that impossible springtime
    when men
      shall be the flowers
spread at your feet.

The therapist himself had better let go, and the ethic of patience and work needs to be balanced with one of hope and readiness. In Williams's words:

Mother of God
　　I have seen you stoop
　　　　to a merest flower
and raise it
　　and press it to your cheek.[15]

I think that the sociologist, in years of heartrending work, aided by his fine intellect, had taken half a step out of narcissistic anxiety soothed by primitive goddess worship, to sexual love coupled to whole social membership—but only half a step. Maybe the momentum will carry him. Maybe a lithe and loving goddess—spread out through himself, his new wife, his colleagues, and myself—may have already provided the sunshine he needs to flower.

A psychotherapist today will find failed sexual romanticism being used as a splint over the broken bones of human love. The spontaneous reemergence of Goddess worship may be one aspect of this phenomenon. Here is another:

A linguist sought therapy in the midst of a homosexual panic. She had fallen during a skiing lesson; the tender, manual, emergency ministrations of her instructor over her broken ankle had convinced her that the instructor must be in love with her, too. The linguist had admired the ski instructor from afar for months, but she had imagined that the one-sidedness of this feeling would protect her from her own ego-alien lesbian feelings. The touch of the instructor had overwhelmed her. She professed her love, was rebuffed, and, surging in a chaos of feelings, sought help.

The product of strict Catholic upbringing, she felt ugly, maidenish, medieval. She stayed home, mastering Latin, Greek, Norwegian, Old English, and Anglo Saxon. Medieval

English love poetry was her special province. She married the first man to show an interest in her. He was a wealthy photo-journalist, who, she says, raped her orally on their wedding night. She stayed home, in his home now, mastering foreign languages and translating romantic, heraldic poetry for her Ph.D., while he travelled from psychiatrist to psychiatrist, diagnosed as paranoid schizophrenic, returning eventually to exercise his sexual power over her. Confused, lonely, pathetic, unable to turn to her stern, moralistic parents for help, she attempted to elaborate her plight romantically into the same kind of historical fairy tale that filled the books she studied. The hopelessness of her solitary confinement, coupled to her literary imagination, enabled her to weave an unusual defense. She imagined herself to be both a princess in a castle waiting for a knight (she described herself in those days as having knee-length blonde hair and dressing in beltless flowing gowns) and as a prisoner of a madman.

An affair with a married professor broke the spell of her isolation. Psychotherapy, eight years previously with a woman psychiatrist, had helped her obtain a divorce with a large financial settlement.

She was unique among academics I have met, for showing contempt for teaching. She was now wealthy in her own right and was interested only in scholarship. She no longer looked maidenish, but she felt tormented by her unruly bisexuality. She pursued her ski instructor with poetry, surprise secret meetings, double entendres, innuendos, and gifts from Italy. It was a remarkable fictionalization of courtship and love. The ski instructor married. But the linguist's stock broker, himself a man of means, now fell in love with her, so, accepting and encouraging all the initial signs of his interest, she spent her weekends with a pilot!

Unable to imagine herself as lovable, she sustained the phase of romance. She went about town dressed with two white Alaskan huskies on a leash. Pursuit in any direction was its own end, and an interminable one. Her flamboyant, hysterical high jinks, unavailability, and obsession with courtship and hunt rather than consummation covered her sense of having been despised and rejected by her parents, abused by her husband, and a sexual sinner in the still menacing eyes of the church. It was inconceivable to her that she could care or be cared for. Beneath her costumes and courtships was a wandering Jew, a stranger in the land of Egypt.

As she gradually risked exposing more of her life story to me, I heard about her panicky struggles with asthma as a child, and her mother's cold, punitive attempts to stop the attacks of breathlessness, which felt only like rejection. Her sense of degraded abandonment peaked in adolescence, with severe acne, that, like an imp from a painting by Bosch, jumped on her shoulders and convinced her that she was diseased, that God was punishing her for the sin of pride. For in her inner world, some pride remained, bolstered by the fact that she was undoubtedly the best student in the parochial elementary school.

But her sense of being blamed, attacked, and smothered led to hospitalization in a psychotic state toward the end of high school—a horrible episode she could recall only after we had been talking together for several years. She completed high school from the hospital and escaped her unhappy family life by going to the University. She immediately dropped Catholicism, and began, instead, to elaborate her classical learning into a romantic private religion. A secret, clandestine, forbidden love—such a love as a reject might have with a truly all-loving god who would reach down to his most hurt and humbled true soul in her mud hut—such a love as a fairy princess might have when at last, free of witches and toads, she would be discovered by her prince—these were the controlling images that conveyed her forward, out of psychosis, into quiet, private, academically brilliant college years.

Such a naive, girlish, wishful child's love is not the exclusive possession of the wounded, eccentric isolate. William

James considered such a phenomenon to be a common deterioration of saintliness, and he wrote about

> ... a God indifferent to everything but adulation, and full of partiality for his individual favorites ... Take Saint Theresa for example, one of the ablest women ... a powerful intellect ... but the main idea of her religion seems to have been that of an endless amatory flirtation ...

James dubbed "such sweet excess of devotion" as being a "theopatic condition."[16]

In the linguist, her "theopatic condition" rescued her from the insanity of feeling outcast from humanity, like a child leper, but it misled her into a sick marriage, a confusing affair, and then an existence in which sustained fantasy substituted for life. To pursue or be pursued, without end, ceaselessly riding in the hunt, this Olympian Guineverian multisexual satyrnalia had become her religion. It provided apparent membership and calling (she kept elaborate belle lettre journals that she imagined publishing, analogizing herself to Abelard and Heloise), sewed together her culturally rich but chaotic worldview, and helped her affirm her otherwise frightening sexual self. She left therapy, town, and academia to make an extended visit to the farm of a German horse breeder whom she had met on a research trip to Paris, and who adored her, though she would permit not the slightest hint of sex to transpire between them. She was going there to learn jumping.

Although therapy ended without concrete change in her core problem—indeed, it ended while she seemed to be elaborating and extending her obsession with the chase—some important human work had gone on between us. She had very slowly trusted a man enough to reveal her greatest shames to him (looking away from me most of that time). She had exposed herself and gone away unharmed. She protested in shock or fear if I were friendly or kidded her—"unprofessional!"—

but gradually accepted that I was a human being, not a functional system. Even though I was human, male, and friendly, she didn't have to fear my seducing her or her seducing me—for her world was stiflingly sexual, ricocheting with misguided impulses. To keep me distant, she taunted my youth (I was older than she, but, I suppose, in her eyes, didn't look it), and flaunted her wealth and the haute culture she inhabited with her stockbroker. Over time, she drew me close to the secrets of her heart, which was a good experience for both of us. In our last session she shook my hand warmly and thanked me—I was amazed and pleased that she could let us touch. Could she let more reality touch her?

Close to one decade later we crossed paths at an unexpected moment and place. In an awkward exchange in a corridor of a public building, she told me she was working for Oxfam Africa, and was on her way to the Sudan. "Love ye therefore the stranger: for ye were strangers in the land of Egypt."[17]

Every case of psychotherapy, to a greater or lesser extent, is a problem of the failure to love. Sometimes this problem is in focus; sometimes it is a covert contributor to other problems, but, at core, it is always there. Those who can plant and tend love may have pain in life, but not the kind of pain that draws a person towards psychotherapy. Failure to love does not have one cause. The case illustrations used here do not represent a uniform psychodynamic; they do not come from one diagnostic group of psychopathology; they are not all instances of narcissism, in its limited psychodiagnostic sense. Failure to love is not unique to our age, a cultural flaw pathognomonic of the modern or of the American, though it seems to be an epidemic form taking extra sustenance from current culture. The confusion of sex and intimacy with love may be common here today, but failure to love is always a religious problem. It always has roots in the person's answer to the question: what is the nature of the universe in which I dwell? Whatever cultural contributions are made by individualism, romanticism, or the culture of narcissism, whatever unique psychological constellations are created in a person by insensitive or neglectful parents, pre-oedipal or oedipal entanglements, separation difficulties or peer-group traumas of adolescence, a religious dimension is also always present when a human being has knocked on the great doors of life and has been greeted only by a lover running to embrace or by an absence of such a passion, but not by entry into the great hall itself. A failure to love is not merely a problem of the interpersonal or sexual—ascetic hermits may know how to love—but it is a problem of fundamentals.

Overtly or covertly, directly or only through innuendo that tints their descriptions, patients will speak about the need to nurture, to care for, to hold, to heal, and to help. They speak of the need to move one's sense of self out from the depths of one's heart, above and beyond one's own skin, to embrace the Other. This need to give of oneself in unreserved participation is the need for human love. "Human love" is a term that delineates this sphere from sexual, romantic, arousal.

Human love is the traditional concern of religion. Sexual love, unfortunately, has been, at best, neglected by religion, and often disparaged or villified—a woeful mistake, since, while these two aspects of the continuum of love can be poles apart, they also meet and overlap on common middle ground. Love that accompanies and seals lifelong, pair-bonding (romantic, sexual love rooted) enables cultural reproduction the way that mating enables biological reproduction. Transmission of caring and caretaking occurs when the growing generation is satu-rated in the mist of married love. That human beings could transcend the struggle for survival beginning again with each new life and repeating itself endlessly into the future, that they could start again, each time, on the plateau, within the home of those who came before, that they could receive weapons, and drawings, and dances, and gods, that each generation could be one step freer from the raw knuckles that dug for roots—that these things could happen is all a chorus to the song of sexual love that is also human love.

Yet one does not turn towards the Gospels of the New Testament, or the Psalms, or the Vedas, or the Koran, or the Sutras for the poetry of married love, as one does for the poetry of world vision. Religious scriptures that bend to the matter at all do so simply with condescending moral prescriptions and proscriptions. Living traditions of religious practice begrudgingly tend to be more pragmatic and flexible. Buddhism and Catholicism, among others, revolve heavily around celibate men. This tension, between the marriage of men and women and the marriage of religious witnesses to religion, has formed a zone where human love can fly up free from sexual love, but also where human sexual love is rubbed in the mud by the boots of those who substitute power for care.

Since love is a colloquial word that refers to subjective experience, it is used variously. No usage has final authority. Still, human love can be viewed in a rainbow as occupying a portion of the spectrum that is not the same as sexual love, or the same as attachment-dependency. It is not the same as when a person uses the term to imply need. Nor is it the same as narcissistic mirroring, an aspect of life that sometimes marches along under the heading of love. This mirroring refers to our desire to be seen and acknowledged by someone else as we *wish* we were: flattery, social plastic surgery, inducing a pleasing reflection of ourselves in a distorted mirror of society. Nor is it companionship and teammates, though those fine qualities are welcome cousins. Nor is it mating, even dutiful and committed. Human love is life taking care of life. "The world is my household, all living beings are my children."[18]

Human love is the sphere of life often claimed by religions as their very own. Religions provide examples and opportunities for human love. This is the fourth and final dimension to the root etymology of religion as a ligature: it binds the individual together, and to his or her group, and it binds heart and mind into a vision of a world; finally, it unites the tremble and echo of eternity within the solitary soul, with the roar of the current of life. Religions seek to raise up from the dark well inside the person, pure water of being. Only in this way can the stranded, ephemeral drop flow out onto the ocean of eternity. Human love is a pouring forth. Human love refers to the wide angle that opens out from the point of the individual to incorporate increasing areas of life.[19] It is not a feeling, but a meta-emotion,[20] not a sentiment, but a pervasive attitude.[21] That may be why ancient religions often split human love from familial, possessive love. One opens outward, the other builds walls. Warm feelings that unite a tightly limited, self-protected unity of an isolated functional team seem similar, yet differ entirely, from human love. So, in Buddhism, love is understood as embracing all beings, regardless of their relation to the person; if there is any qualification or differentiation of one being from another, this conditional emotion is not recognized as love.[22] Similarly, Jesus first clarified that by love he did not mean familial, functional affection: "I am come to set a man at variance against his father, and the daughter against her mother . . ."[23] And, similarly to Buddhism, he preached an unqualified human love: "Love your enemies, bless them that curse you . . . if ye salute your brethren only, what do ye more than others?"[24]

There is a psychological way to define human love. The best definitions in science are those that are anchored to clear operations: definitions that can always be agreed upon because they are the product of exact, reproducible methods of being clarified. A psychological, operational, definition for human love is that which enables mastery over castration anxiety.

According to Freud, the root terror of life is castration anxiety.[25] The worst imaginable fate is to suffer pain, mutilation, and loss of fertile potential. According to Freud, the mere whisper of a thought of castration in childhood forms a focal point of fear from which a person is always in flight. Yet this focal, triple horror has actually been imposed on millions of individuals within the span of the twentieth century, as in this description from Cambodia in 1978:

> The wife of a Lon Nol soldier, pregnant with the child of the soldier, confessed who her husband was. To make her crime a public example, a young Khmer Rouge soldier inserted a knife into her vagina and sliced upward to her womb, carving out her fetus. He allowed her to look for a moment at the carnage, and then continued ripping up into her chest until she was dead.[26]

To amplify this point, I will only allude to the death camps of Europe in the Second World War, to dissidents in Argentina or Chile or Uruguay under military rule, to heretics in Iran . . . when not merely death, but a castrating, hideous, exemplary death was the intent. Yet individuals who have survived a brush with such captors have provided a fresh definition of human love that is at once empirical and religious.

Love is what binds a person to life when life is otherwise unendurable; love is what people live for, and why people live when life seems not worth living. Here also we see the fusion, rather than the distinction, of personal man-to-woman love with human love. The psychiatrist, Viktor Frankl, wrote, after years of imprisonment at Auschwitz:

> That brought thoughts of my own wife to mind . . . for the first time in my life I saw the truth—that love is the ultimate and the highest goal to which man can aspire. Then I grasped the meaning of the greatest secret that human poetry and human thought and belief have to impart: *the salvation of man is through love and in love.*[27]

While Jacobo Timerman was being tortured for the crime of being a Jew in Argentina, he described similar visions and conclusions.[28] A similar description is given by a Cambodian doctor, H.S. Ngor, of his experiences during the anarchy and mass slaughter there.[26] Beyond pain, mutilation, and hope for the future, is another dimension to human life, a dimension that provides meaning and momentum when everything else is lost or destroyed. Love is the life in the living that lives beyond mere life.

This realm that transmutes biological, survival values into religious, spiritual participation is the realm of love. Here again we can see why a confusion, a tension occurred, between sexual love and human love. Since a loss of reproductive potential, such as imminent death, or the murder of one's family, often compels a person to live for spiritual purposes, some harsh ancient philosophers had reasoned that the imposition of such a loss in a calculated, tactical, manner could produce a cadre of spiritual eunuchs. A less calculating or cruel mind could see instead that love is always present, like the sun behind clouds, like philosophy in a child. Without *inducing* castration, people can confront and master castration anxiety at the psychological level, internally. This insight was behind the origin of psychoanalysis, and, thousands of years earlier, the spiritual disciplines.[29]

In Chapter 7, I discussed how shamanistic ecstasy is always accompanied not only by imagery of personal death, but by visions of mutilation and dismemberment as well, and how ancient traditions of Buddhist meditation (Hindu and Catholic, too) prescribe meditation on corpses, burning grounds, and other elaborately horrible visions of personal death. Down in the darkest corridors of the psyche, every potential fear is hanging in a closet, and through deep, internal probing, a person may shine a light on, study, and possibly transcend the profoundest anxieties of human life, which may be summarized as "castration anxiety." Many are the souls who fly on love without having first been subjected to history's tyrannies; and many are the otherwise safe and comfortable souls who are totally castrated by their anxiety, which oozes up from inner sources without being catalyzed by actual historical events.

In this looser, more generic sense, castration anxieties can be heard in every patient's story. For example, the sociologist felt his manhood torn from him by his crude, unsympathetic father, and his goddess worship was an attempt to find a redeeming and restorative love to make himself whole again. And the linguist felt physically and emotionally mutilated by the combination of physical illness and maternal rejection; she felt her reproductive future smashed by her husband's perversity, and by her own lesbian feelings; and her romantic fantasies were a caricature of the religious love that might restore meaning to the outcast and broken-hearted.

St. John of the Cross offers an edifying example. This sixteenth-century Spanish Catholic monk is ". . . one of the supreme lyric poets of any age or country."[30] Himself an ascetic whose practices seem today to be masochistic, he found the inspiration for his greatest, most widely quoted mystical poems while he had been locked in a dungeon due to a dispute over clerical political struggles. In his darkest moment, in pain in a cramped, breathless, fetid cell he sprang free of the flesh and its needs, to spiral upwards into pure experience of divine love. Part of the power of his writing is that he incorporated the antecedent torture into the transcendent ecstasy, rather than merely escaping it.

> How well I know the spring that brims and flows,
>> Although by night.
> This eternal spring is hidden deep,
> How well I know the course its waters keep,
>> Although by night.
> Its source I do not know because it has none
> And yet from this, I know, all sources come,
>> Although by night . . .

Or, in another poem:

> Bent on an enterprise of love,
> And not in lack of hope,

193

I flew so high, so high above
I caught my quarry on the
     wing.

In order that I might succeed
On that celestial enterprise,
So high in flight I had to rise
I lost myself from view;
Yet even in this last extreme
My pitch of flight was not enough,
But love moved on so high above
I caught my quarry on the wing.

As I rose to higher reaches
Dazzled, blinded was my vision,
And in an utter darkness won
The hardest of victories;
I took a blind, unknowing plunge
Because the venture was for love,
And went so high, so high above
I caught my quarry on the wing . . .

St. John had managed to utilize his captors' torture of him as a spiritual exercise by which he could remain true to his tryst with divine love despite crushing circumstances. Unlike Viktor Frankl, or Jacobo Timerman, or Dr. Ngor, St. John's experience of love did not move outward from the ground of married love. He was a monk. Interestingly, he continued to use sexual imagery in his poetry. His description of how the dark night of the soul leads to pure love has endured four hundred years as the exemplary literary archetype to manifest this universal religious truth. At the same time, it is tainted by the fact that St. John, unlike twentieth-century spiritual writers, had sought out and self-induced physical mortification on his own, before his stint in a dungeon, as a path to spiritual purification, and he leaves us wondering today about contamination of his experiences by masochism. His poetry, however, is not reducible to his character. Nor were his experiences in the dungeon purely passive, acquiescent embraces of his plight. He used his intellect not only to compose and memorize his poems, but to escape! He shredded his blanket into a rope, unscrewed the bolts to his padlock, and jumped to a narrow ledge beside a sheer precipice . . . and lived to write more poetry:

> On a night of darkness,
> In love's anxiety of longing kindled,
> O blessed chance!
> I left by none beheld,
> My house in sleep and silence stilled.
>
> By the secret ladder and disguised . . .
> By dark of blessed night . . .
> My only light and guide
> The one that in my heart was burning.
>
> This guided, led me on
> More surely than the radiance of noon . . .
> O night, you were the guide!
> O night, more desirable than dawn!
> You joined Beloved with beloved one . . .[31]

His journey through darkness clarified his inner light. He neither succumbed to darkness, nor was repelled by it; he embraced it as an opportunity to plunge to a depth of love that he now knew to be infinite. The excoriation of his physical being, a castrating, humiliating imprisonment, catapulted him into the realm of redeeming spiritual life. His commanding, chilling literary power, emanating from the simplest vocabulary and verse forms, attest to his journey to the height of human love. Even a reader repelled by this ascetic's personal life, as was, for example, William James, can feel the conviction in his paradox: by tunnelling into the darkness, he had soared to the greatest heights, and in an utter darkness won the hardest of victories: he had seen the eternal spring of love. His expression rings as simple, clear, and true as Hillary's factual report that he had stood on top of Everest. Despite the environment of Reformation Catholicism, St. John absolutely refuted dogmatic anthropomorphism:

> I entered in not knowing where
> And there remained uncomprehending,
> All knowledge transcending.

Sufi poetry from medieval Islam,[32] Zen poetry of China and Japan,[33] and Bhakti poetry from India[34] provide a world-wide, cross-cultural historical record of what the explorers of religious love found. Largely, but not exclusively arising from nonsexual lives, these documents continue to emanate the light of a dawn where the heart is turned inside out and beats in an eternally contemporary yet still unborn world. They give words to the feeling that is held in common, to the place where every piece simultaneously clicks into the center of the puzzle. "Love," said Martin Buber, "is a cosmic force."[35]

At the pinnacle of the tradition of poetry of religious love is Rabindranath Tagore, an Indian whose life spanned the latter half of the nineteenth and the first half of the twentieth centuries, and whose poetry gathered up the rich streams of classical Sanskrit learning with folk verse. He knew married love, fathered children, suffered the death of his wife and all but one of his children and lived the ascetic life that was imposed on him in his later years. A torrent of writing, filled with worldly, political, libertarian concerns, gushed from him all his long life, all suffused with a vision of divine, creative love:

> You and I have floated here on the stream that brings
>   from the fount
> At the heart of time love for one another.[36]

But can these religious-literary Himalayas, these masters of poetry and suffering, these heroic survivors I have been quoting teach us anything useful, applicable, relevant to our work as psychotherapists in the foothills? I think the scientific task of comprehending human love can best move forward guided by an analysis of its central function in the human personality. Religious love can be understood in a useful way by observing it dissolve isolation and ambivalence. At the moment we observe love functioning, we can establish meaningful generalizations about a sublime function in its pedestrian ubiquitousness. The following descriptions are meant to suggest principles about psychological tasks accomplished by love.

Love resolves isolation. Love springs up from the hard seed of the human religious problem the way wildflowers materialize on the apparently dead forest floor in reply to the spring sun. Each person experiences him or herself isolated in the shell of mind and body. Love is the activity of transcending the isolation of self. Love functions as the bridge. Erich Fromm described the essence of human love as giving, a correct giving that doesn't create indebtedness, but creates others who feel they now also have enough extra to give.[37] In Buddhism, generosity is the first and most important virtue.[38] The same attitude uncorked exquisite poetry from the prosaic lawgiver, St. Paul:

> Though I speak with the tongues of men and of angels, and have
>   not charity, I am become as sounding brass, or a
>   tinkling cymbal.
> And though I have the gift of prophecy, and understand all
>   mysteries, and all knowledge; and though I have all
>   faith, so that I could remove mountains, and have not
>   charity, I am nothing.
> Charity . . . Beareth all things, believeth all
>   things, hopeth all things, endureth all things.
> For now we see through a glass darkly; but then face to face . . .
> And now abideth faith, hope, and charity, these three; but the
>   greatest of these is charity.[39]

When physical and human giving combine in intimacy, "mutual regulation" of two people results,[40] providing the matrix for childrearing and, from there, the entire fabric of life. In the religious sphere, the growth of love is not merely the flourishing of good works—St. Paul warns against that—but the organization of personality around charitable identity. In this view, human love means a deep resolution of the isolation within oneself. Human love blossoms as the movement of identity across the lines of self. This sounds similar to membership, but it differs entirely. Membership is about equality and participation and love is about identity and creation. Membership is the warmth of the barn, but love is the heat of the sun. Membership is about existence; love is about origins. So love is portrayed as madness, a divine madness, a dissolution of profane bodily identity, and, instead, an extension of determination and imagination in service of the other, the future, the next. Love is truth calling beyond understanding. For this reason, it is always linked to faith, the capacity to move forward beyond certainty and guaranteed success into the compelling, generous unknown. Rumi, the great Sufi poet, wrote: "the fledgling pigeon essayed the air and flew off when he heard a whistle and a call from the unseen."[41]

The function of love, to transcend mind and body isolation, requires faith as its end-organ, as volition requires the hand. I have avoided using the word "faith" among the ten psychological building blocks of religious psychology as seen from the clinical perspective, because it is both so elusive and so variously intended. Few words more quickly invoke private, undefinable, fluctuant, innuendos of meaning, and public proclamations, declarations, and rabid convictions. A remarkable psychological study of faith is already available in Paul Tillich's work.[42] In the context of my ten building blocks, faith can be understood as the capacity to follow the directives of ripening human love. It is the ability to open the lines that delineate the self to the widening world of love and to sustain in abeyance the need for closure, for triumph or success, like a bird forever renewing the experience of its first flight—that is faith. As St.

Paul pointed out, the faith to move mountains, unguided by the charitable heart, is nothing. (Faith also interdigitates with release, and worldview, and will be mentioned again in Chapter 9.)

Where human love is compromised or neurotic, we can still see it operate at least partly to overcome isolation. The sociologist lived without salient human involvement, except for his goddess wives, with whom he yearned to merge. This substitute for charity, like any neurotic compromise, kept him trapped, by having given him enough fulfillment that he had looked no further. Yet at the same time it gave him a shallow, strange love, in which he felt he was constantly giving, while his wives felt he was selfishly smothering. Similarly, the linguist cavorted in harlequin romances, showering gifts on her skiing instructor, yearning to give, but alone. In my last glimpse of her, however, she seemed to have attained true charity.

We have discussed what human love is, how it can be defined by its ability to reveal the realm of life that transcends castration anxiety, how it is expressed in religious poetry, and how it functions to overcome isolation, and in so doing, is linked to faith.

Love is the maturing of the seed of life. The seed sprouts into a relatedness that bears. Love is the unborn calling to the present from within. The fruit of human love is generative, differentiated, overlapping, androgynous, mutual fertilization of bodies and souls. Love is this form of knowledge: that our growth reaches out beyond our bodies, beyond what we can see and touch and know. There is no knowing the finality of our path. We are guided by a compass set by creation, that makes us overleaping, like salmon. As Erich Fromm wrote: "Love is a power which produces love."[43]

In order to clarify the relationship between exalted and exemplary states of religious love and daily life and psychotherapy, we look at the functions of love in personality. Love transcends isolation, and it resolves ambivalence. What about ambivalence?

Human beings are born as aggregates of desires, impulses, reactions, and imposed relationships. There is no intrinsic unity to this system. We have seen how one building block of the psychology of religion is the attempt to create inner harmony and unity out of "patchwork" (see Chapter 3). But fragmentation is a problem due not only to inner complexity, but also to external impositions. How should a person relate to the welter of the world? Religions have provided answers by dispensing a sense of lawful order, a worldview, and a calling within that cosmos. Even that is not enough.

Religious psychologists through the ages have set as their goal a capacity for wholeness. If you read enough religious texts, if you talk to enough religious people, this is the point you will see and hear stressed over and over again. They have addressed the problem of how to live fully, not partially. This means they have struggled to understand and master the secret of ambivalence.

Ambivalence means withholding from life. It is the opposite of the attitudes of generosity and charity that constitute human love. Ambivalence constitutes stinginess of being. It is a universal problem. Everyone recoils, protects, withholds, hoards sometime, to some extent, even when open fingers and a flat palm are called for. Paul Tillich wrote: "Neurosis is a way of avoiding nonbeing by avoiding being." To avoid our fears, we avoid living. "He affirms something which is less than his essential or potential being."[44] Rank wrote of ambivalent life as refusing the loan of living in order to avoid paying the debt: death.[45] So, as Tillich continued to point out, life requires faith (an "in spite of"), and courage. Yet exhortation towards these moral virtues does not really capture the spirit of a whole life, which is not merely flying into the gale with grit, but which sings:

> Now is the time
>   in spite of the wrong note
>   I love you. My heart is
> innocent
>   And this is the first
>   (and last) day of the world.[46]

"In spite of" is overcome by love.

It is possible for people to give out full expressions of themselves, without reserve and in spite of uncertainty, in faithfully following the dictates of the charity of being. It is said that Gandhi could place his whole life behind discrete daily actions; he expressed ". . . total commitment to love and reason in every fleeting moment.[47]" John Lennon could convey that spirit with his singing, and he was once quoted as saying, "When I heard rock 'n' roll I forgot everything else." In a personal letter, Winthrop Sargeant, the late music critic for the *New Yorker* magazine, referred to John Lennon as the "troubador"; his passionate giving-himself-over-into grew into a continually recharged fresh vision of life through love: "Oh my love, for the first time in my life, my eyes are wide open." Eventually, he was able to express immersion into one state of being: "Imageless undying love/that shines around me like a million suns/and calls me on and on across the universe."[48]

Love masters ambivalence. Put even more definitively by Erikson: ". . . ambivalence makes love meaningful—or possible."[49] This capacity to love, a product of psychological development, enables us to grow outward, open up, and give ourselves over wholly. Love of children, spouse, friends, ideas, people, places—the more embracing the capacity, the more it approaches the religious idea of love for all. We love to the extent that we can give over to. The actual psychological capacity is built over the orchestrated substrate of complex, personal development and differs from a rhetorical position, an ideation, or a self-righteous rationalization. Nor is total commitment to concrete goals the sign of mastery over ambivalence. Hatred, fanaticism, revenge, and grandiosity can catalyze intense commitments (see Chapter 4), but these tunnel visions do not produce wholeness; they resolve ambivalence in one sphere by augmenting it in another. (For example, the total commitment to fight to death for one's nation often involves splitting off of one's negative identity and projecting it onto the enemy.)

The wholeness of love, which overcomes ambivalence, is linked to other religious elements. In Chapter 3 we saw the integration of patchwork personality through affirming acceptance; in Chapter 4 we saw how whole living has a point, a calling. In Chapter 6 we saw how paradox, pushing towards exhaustion, can produce release from conflict and unified effort, and in Chapter 7 we saw how a whole world, a psychic cosmos, forms. Love will also reveal itself in sacrifice (Chapter 9) and, as we have just seen, must give answers to the fear of nonbeing, Chapter 10.

But love can deteriorate. A common form of this is pious, sanctimonious, aggression such as using Jesus's words as an excuse to torture Jews in the Inquisition.[50] Domestically, passive-aggression can function this way, as when power and paternalism, or nagging coercion and "maternalism" substitute for care. Several of the angriest people I have met were children of the noblest, most self-sacrificing Quaker mothers. These grown-up children had experienced ceaseless "selfless," "saintly" giving as oppressive, guilt-inducing, life-denying manipulation. One of them would burn his fingers with matches in the college library so he could stay awake longer and study harder. He really had someone to please.

Love can deteriorate into the arrogant self-appropriation of another's soul, as in evangelism. The melodramatization of "love" is just a covert threat. Demanding, impoverished dependencies, and convenient, mutual masturbation may masquerade as love. The jilted spouse will plead love, and behind it there is a threat, "If you don't obey, I'll kill . . . myself." So may timid, cunning enmeshment: couples or families who live inside each other, using fusion to avoid engagement with the outer world, and claiming that their hiding places are the spheres of love. Self-proclaimed adherence to abstract religious love can be used to cover over an inability to experience feelings for specific people. For example, in one instance a rabbi was ceaselessly stirring about in good works attesting to his human love, but this external display was merely the flip side of his total avoidance of his family. In his home, there was a snakepit of failed human relationships that he couldn't face, and which his unavailability through good works only worsened.

To understand a person, we have to ask, of what whole is he or she a part? What is this person embracing and held by? With what is he or she filled? Religions represent the various personal, historical, institutional attempts to enable the development of people who are integrated totalities, everywhere interpenetrating with the world: engaged, fully developed persons. A flower is not committed to the sun, but the whole of its being bursts open towards the sky in a transformed and unpredicted emanation of the possibility of light—perennial, enduring, rejuvenating.

Love is a feature of and an outcome of psychotherapy. Yet its activation is not under the control of therapist or patient.

A political scientist came racing into therapy. He was anxious and distressed; he couldn't locate where to begin. His speech was pressured; he was late for every session; he felt and conveyed turmoil, though externally nothing was wrong. He felt he was a hodgepodge of pretensions, lies, and false identities. He didn't know who he was. Every day was a scramble to keep ahead of the chores he had neglected, the dissembling he had done that might catch up with him, at work and at home. His wife was constantly yelling at him; his colleagues expressed their dissatisfaction. He couldn't sleep. What should he do with his life?

He was the son of orthodox Jews from a small city in Appalachia, where Jews were a tiny minority. His father was a gruff, preoccupied merchant. His mother was removed, depressed. He felt on his own, and he flailed about to join in. Everyone else was gentile. He did what he had to do to mix. His brother and sister were ghosts who went their own way. He became an actor—theatre was his claim to fame in high school, where he was also a second string baseball player, and an undifferentiated good student. He scanned the social horizon for the next role to fill. When confused, he took the advice of his father, who had orthodox opinions on everything. Feeling unconnected to his environment, his family, his peers, he developed a desperate skill of false connectedness through placation of powerful others, groups and individuals. He was a practiced joiner and dissembler.

He married a girl his parents had picked, daughter of merchants from a distant city in the same state. They started having kids right after college—that's what they were supposed to do. He continued through graduate school, finding out what was expected of him and doing only and exactly what needed to be done. Just below the surface, he was devious. His mode of existence was to find the way to get by—he plagiarized prose from unquoted references, turned papers in late, had brief affairs with other graduate students, complied to his angry wife in their cold apartment.

He was astute, and successful. He moved up the career ladder, prematurely bald, shirt sleeves unbuttoned, an indefatigable ally to demanding authorities. He was unreliable unless there was something immediately at stake: never home on time, never where he said he would be, staying up too late, getting up too late, bits of take-home pay missing.

His conversation with me was all over the map, a loud, dismayed complaining, themeless, diffuse, pleading. He called me a horse's ass one session, and I told him to get up and get out if that was what he felt. He took it back. He paid late; I asked him to pay on time. He paid one day late; I said nothing, and the next month he paid two days late. He came late and missed sessions.

Therapy is impossible to capture; any one hour has more words in it than any example that I have quoted in this book. There are confidences to keep and appropriate distortions to make, in order to maintain confidentiality in this retelling. Sessions are rich in interpenetrating veins of themes, many beyond the topic of religious issues in psychotherapy. Many years (hundreds of hours) of therapy unrolled with this man. We found three foci: he didn't know who he was; he was continuously in psychic pain; he loved no one.

From me, he wanted an orthodox authority, like his father; or a department chairman, who could be pleased by specific tasks and would accordingly dispense promotions; or a mother who could reassure him that he was good in spite of all, and that he was lovable, as neither his mother nor his wife had been able to do. He couldn't get what he wanted from me.

Why did I let him ramble so far, stray in his attempts to please and impress and get something from me? I do get paid for time. I wasn't always sure where to go. His lectures were interesting. He had a wide range of references, an agile mind, a keen, wired cat in a town full of big country mutts. He could quote de Tocqueville and clarify the news and relate obscure anecdotes from Lincoln's life. He was an expert on baseball, a historian of the last twenty years' World Series. He loved the hills of Appalachia, the split rail fences, the autumn colors, the crazy and shrewd political beliefs and rationalizations of the hill people. He had a great string of hillbilly jokes.

He loved coming to therapy. He loved impressing me, which he did. He loved making me laugh, which he did. If all this pleasing, placating, and amusing me was only a transference of his old style of finding security by seducing authorities, why didn't I confront it and interpret it, revealing to him its childhood origins and manipulative dimensions? Twice a week, he was reliable and on time, like clockwork. I could count on him in a snowstorm! Something was changing. From my few interpretations, he could psych out my attitudes and values and reconstructed a humorous psychological "constitution," which he said satisfied his need for authority and which he attributed to me. He was a very good pleaser.

He shifted his career. From political theory about industrialization and populism, he turned to the political voices of small cities in Appalachia. He got the grants he needed and was gone every summer, talking to the people, reading the papers, tapping into something he really loved and was stirred by. When he returned to therapy, there was somebody to listen to him. He let his colors spill out like kindergarten finger paints, and in that mess a shape had begun to emerge. To really please me, as he desperately wanted to do, he had to please himself: that was the quiet therapist's gambit. This spy of being, this social secret service, found a calling: he studied the attitudes, effects, and acts of power in the disenfranchised. He published a book of interviews with rural immigrants who had attained elected office in small Appalachian cities. He started a second volume on the voting patterns of Jewish merchants in Appalachia. He could be a Jew and a hillbilly and a good boy and a provocative imp and a political scientist all at once, and that was himself.

His marriage began to warm up. He said what he thought. He learned to listen, by imagining in himself how I listened to him and then listening to his wife in the same way. He was both using his old style of imitation and a new style of focused attention. He stopped lying to colleagues—he had no more need to, because his career was strong. His mood shifted to pleased excitement, as if a holiday were always soon coming. He took his wife with him to the Great Smoky Mountains, and fell in love. The three foci we had found early in the work had all been helped and healed. He knew who he was; he felt well; he loved someone. He might have been ready to stop, but he wasn't. He extended the treatment in a year-long internaliza-tion phase, certain of his greater capacities and happiness, determined to feel secure in his new being before he would stop. His fragmented, ambivalent self was focused. His isolated, sly war with the world had become an empathic social career. He described it: "I know I can talk to her the way I can talk to you. We could never touch before. It's so nice to let myself feel loved. I know this is because I've let myself get close to you. I never loved anyone before. I suppose I love you. I've found who I am. I was always envious of other people's careers or houses or cars. But I have the important things. I'm a voice for those who need it. Hell, I'm a voice for myself."

Between a religious conversion and a lucky therapy, there may be a bond. I imagine I heard in his total response to treatment, the religious theme of "bhakti," a Hindu term meaning loving devotion to the Other in every encounter. Did he only love the therapist, who remained after all muted and silhouetted behind his rigorous working constraints? Did he only love what he had gotten, the attention and delighted receipt of his own psychic cornucopia? Was he only pleasing, flattering, in a wishful folie à deux? There is no exact dividing line between bhakti and any other form of love, including transference love, but when the latter is full, enduring, and leads to long-term and widespread generalization, it fades into human love like summer morning mist in the atmosphere. To see someone, who for so long felt deprived of love, at last spring awake into the delighted expectation and excitement of un-abashed, self-unveiling love was a pleasure to experience. This man changed in his core sense of self from fragmented to focused; he changed in a sustained mood that persisted for years; he changed in his narcissistic isolation and loved many others. After the generalization from me to his wife, his previ-ously palely described children and arm's-length colleagues began to be seen and loved in full color—not to mention his tough work.

Bhakti is not so different from the Christian love we encountered in St. John of the Cross, but it is notable for its earthy embrace of physical love, and its flood tide of literary and artistic expression. Rather than excluding or separating, it sweeps up and metamorphosizes the child's love of parents and the youth's sexual romance into an adamantine jewel that can be seen to sparkle in any love, the essential act itself. Unlike Christ's divine, self-sacrificing forgiveness, Bhakti is human. It is born in the dust. It means that, whatever the object, we can spy in the process the goal itself, love. Bhakti is the *process* of loving. Just as the ancient Hebrews saw the world creator as mercurial, petulant, demanding, and unrestrained but portrayed him as an irate patriarch, Bhakti poets have seen the same traits ruling life and fate, but they have imagined instead a god as a child, Krishna.

> Krishna is singing in the courtyard.
> He dances on his small feet, joyous within.
> Lifting up his arms, he shouts for the black and white cows . . .
> Seeing his reflection, he tries to feed it.
> Hidden, his mother watches the play that makes her so happy . . .
> . . . to see Krishna's play every day is bliss.[51]

Isn't there an echo here of the therapy I just described? The dancing, many-faceted, amoral child grows cohesive through loving synthesis in the mother's eyes.

In Bhakti poems, authors slip in and out of role, even gender. Men write as women; gods become children. The poets aim to shatter incidentals and to illuminate the core process, common in diverse forms. After studying Bhakti, Paul McCartney wrote: "To love her is to meet her everywhere."[52] W.S. Merwin translated the Indian poet Ghalib, "There is only one beloved face/but it is everywhere."[53] And Tagore: "By the force that drives my feelings, roses open"[54] and "He is in the

pupils of my eyes: that is why I see Him everywhere." The
Bhagavad Gita is the Ninth Symphony of Bhakti:

> He who offers to me with devotion only a leaf, or a flower, or a fruit,
> or even a little water, this I accept from that yearning soul, because
> with a pure heart it was offered with love . . .
>
> He sees himself in the heart of all beings and he sees all beings in his
> heart . . .
> He who in this oneness of love, loves me in whatever he sees, wherever
> this man may live, in truth he lives in me.[55]

In therapy, two people reach for human love. In the stories
of the sociologist, the linguist, and the political scientist, we can
hear aspects of this process: individuals reaching upward to
find their source and link to life, confusing one need with
another, substituting perverse sex, fictionalized romance,
or authoritarian security operations for a true connection.
Through the process of therapy they take half-steps, hidden
steps, full steps, in their capacity to end isolation and overcome
ambivalence, before they can lend their hands to the hands
reaching up from the dust. Before they give, they must receive
and learn how it is done: not self-aggrandizing, effusive kiss,
but a quiet flow of unstoppable conviction, the way water
shatters rocks to build the beaches of the world. A therapist
cannot give love, and pop-psychology heros who claim to do
so offend our sense of autonomy and dignity.

As I understand it, human love is not *in* any person,
because by definition it is about that which opens, connects,
and transcends bridges. Love belongs to the *between*. It is not
dramatic, loud, or congratulatory, but is quiet and invisible. It
cannot be given, but it begins to flow. It cannot be kept; to learn
it means to pass it on, to convey it. This glory is ultimately
impersonal, because its essence is the perception and expression
of the creative universal in the banal and the particular. The

liberation of loneliness into love is a psychotherapeutic possibility, but it cannot be shot at like a target, caged with technical operations, lassoed with interpretations. It can be conveyed but not taught. It must be let happen by attention to the pain and fear that blocks it. The therapist does not dispense love, but he holds steady in the possibility of its emergence. The example of love the therapist gives is attentive work. Love is not other than life.

◇ 9 ◇

Sacrifice

*. . . I continued on my way, shouldering my own pain as
I followed the signs . . .*

Writing with a nineteenth-century religious voice at the
dawn of the secular twentieth century, William James put it
emphatically: "In the religious life, surrender and sacrifice are
positively espoused . . . that personal attitude which the individual finds himself impelled to take up towards what he apprehends to be divine . . . will prove to be both a helpless and
sacrificial attitude."[1] The espousal of sacrifice is a classical and
widespread religious virtue rarely acclaimed (though often present) in a nonreligious environment. It is a virtue that floats
precariously in an acquisitive society. Today it is quickly condemned, put away with medieval helplessness and confusion,
or Victorian posturing. Why shouldn't we make the most of
ourselves and our lives? Patients in psychotherapy rarely speak
openly of sacrifice. This may reflect today's normative social
values, or it may reflect the general understanding of psychotherapy as a medium for personal growth and self-enhancement. But psychotherapy patients may be grasping for a

psychological vocabulary, in which this word and its attendant modes of being would have a place.

A department chairman from the University was in a panic. When his new woman friend made it clear she wanted to be his lover, waves of anxiety flooded over him and wouldn't stop, even when he returned alone to his condominium, even when night came, even when morning came, even when a week passed. He had been psychoanalyzed thirty years ago. He never expected to face such nameless, irrational, internal terror again in his life, surely not now at the pinnacle of his career. He thought he understood himself; he could easily recount his story.

His father ran the bank in a small city but ran off with another woman, disappeared. His abandoned mother smothered him with kisses, sat him on her lap and compelled him to hear over and over that he was her favorite, that she counted on him to be her man. He felt repelled, burdened, guilty. He dreamed of airplanes. At the age of seventeen he lied about his age, joined the Air Force, fled, and flew. He drank, fought, imitated manhood, but he avoided the girls.

From college on the G.I. Bill, it was one long, easy, downhill run through assistantships, dissertations, first, second, and third books for this brilliant scholar. Despite a childhood of economic, emotional, and intellectual deprivation, a native, robust intelligence flourished in him. He subspecialized in Jewish history, a long-distance tweak to his mother's rural Methodist bigotry. He was aware, too, that he identified with Jews because he felt himself to be an outcast. As a World War II pilot, he had felt inspired by the thought that America was also fighting for the Jews of Europe. He met a Jewish woman. A colleague bet him he'd never dare to marry her, and on these grounds he proposed. The marriage lasted a childless two years and ended with total incompatibility. After the divorce, he entered psychoanalysis, and by the time that analysis ended, he was married to a woman he felt he loved, the daughter of a

farm-equipment dealer. They had four children. She complained he wasn't home enough. He wrote books and flew his
two-seater all over the country. His wife griped and sniped; he
came home less and slowly grew to resent and hate her. When
an offer came to be Chairman of the Department in another
state, he left his wife and children.

He had published all he cared to or needed to for his
career. He watched T.V., flew his plane alone, and began to
think of suicide. He felt unconnected and isolated. He took
many women for a ride but was terrified by closeness.

He craved my attention and concern, and he appeared to
rebound with the help of therapy. He cut a wonderful figure,
striding into my office in a fedora with a cocked brim, regaling
me with tales of a girlfriend at Cape Hatteras and the beauty
of an aerial view of the islands off the coast of Maine. He traded
and bought planes and equipment. But nothing else happened.
The first blush, the honeymoon phase of therapy, never
matured into anything else. When his wife phoned to tell him
his daughter was pregnant, he stayed uninvolved. When his son
smashed up his motorcycle and was in traction in the hospital,
the Department Chairman merely made some long distance
phone calls.

I made two psychodynamic interpretations of his behavior. I told him his flight from his family to become Chairman,
rather than taking his family with him as would be expected,
and his lifelong pattern of rapid departure from people and
situations, even some elements of his fascination with airplanes,
were attempts to imitate and identify with his father's flight
during his own childhood. He was protecting himself from a
child's impotent rage at his callous father, by telling himself in
effect: "What my father did was a good, fatherly lesson for me.
Rather than feel hurt, I'll accept the lesson and do the same."
I also suggested that the panic his new woman friend had
triggered with her sexual availability was the same panic he felt
when his abandoned mother had so desperately and inappro-

priately taken him on her knee and told him that he was her man—a scenario replete with the possibility of traumatic oedipal consummation. Whenever he got close to a woman, that scenario was rekindled.

He understood these insights well. He agreed with them. He added anecdotes to confirm them. They changed nothing.

He needed to be admired, fathered, watched, and talked to by me, but it didn't fill the well of need in this abandoned-infant grown up. Insights were mere diagnostics, like a surgeon telling someone, "A chainsaw severed your finger." After the explanation, the emptiness remained. He himself could not give to his wives or children or potential lovers, because he felt empty and endangered. The emptiness had nothing to do with an absence of life skills. He was masterful with words—he now had authored a shelf of books—he could organize a budget, orchestrate his colleagues, and wheel and deal with the Board of Regents. He could fly and fix a plane and belt down Scotch with World War II buddies at the end of a long solo, before delivering an arcane paper to a morning session of academics. He had striped pants and sports cars, big savings and big spendings, and a transcontinental set of phone numbers. He spoke up for blacks and Jews from his own uninvolved safety. The sieges of terror inside him—who had not had one parent who could give to him—subsided, but nothing welled up in their place.

College tuition was all he had for his children. He was saving for retirement. Painfully, understandably, he was trapped in a narcissism that made him flee any tie that would limit his freedom to fly, that might require him to sacrifice the least fleck of personal freedom. Thinking about his ability to just walk away from his children and his aloof, material relationship to them, one is struck by an apparent selfishness that speaks to the level of sacrifice that is assumed in ordinary life. This self-made man had received little, and self-protection was his habituated mode of being. His petulant rejections of his own children smacked of Abraham eyeing Isaac. Unable to actualize a modicum of sacrifice, he sacrificed others—an aspect of parenting I will describe more fully below.

Sacrifice is the capacity to make inner rather than outer adjustments to distress. It expresses psychological, rather than behavioral, flexibility. Because everyone will grow old, decay, and die, suffering is existential. (Only the luckiest people face merely existential suffering. Most of us must face many additional assaults and losses: deaths of loved ones, ambitions crushed and dreams dissolved, physical illness and pain, social epidemics with their dislocation, terror, or cruelty.) Suffering is inevitable, and sacrifice is how inevitable suffering can be made meaningful. It is the skill of transforming what must be, into what also is possible. Sacrifice is the manifestation of the human capacity to create values that transcend biological survival. Sacrifice is the right arm of love. Sacrifices that actualize ethical principles elevate human life; sacrificial meaning is often held to at the expense of life itself. Human beings may at times relinquish self-enhancement or life, because of what they believe or refuse to believe. A person may demand of his or her time on earth not merely sustained physical continuity, or fulfillment of animal pleasure, but confirmation of having seen, understood, and acted. The capacity for sacrifice is an extension of devotion and dedication. It is the ability to choose what is less than comfortable in order to fulfill a deeper demand. Nor is the sacrificial mode a rare coin, an elite privilege of heroes and saints. Once a mature and meaningful life course has been set, sacrifice moves subtly in and out of daily life like a quiet, irresistible whisper. It is an inevitable and essential ingredient of commitment and steady participation. The capacity for sacrifice regulates the psychic life like a herald, at the crossroads between choice and desire, love and convenience. It is a cornerstone in the edifices of education, professionalism, marriage, parenting, and culture.

Yet the sacrificial mode can easily appear abhorrent, repellant, or frightening, not only because it may be misunderstood or perversely interpreted, but because its nature is to clash with our normal modes of being: comfort, convenience, health, and safety. Unless a sacrifice arises from our own specific situation, we can quickly see in someone else's sacrificial act a merely dogmatic, zealous rigidity—an unskillful constriction of pleasurable living. No realm of life is more personal and value-laden. Are there any criteria to separate "that attitude which an individual feels impelled to take up towards what he apprehends to be divine," from quirky, neurotic, or psychopathological rationalizations for crippling, life-denying behavior?

Sacrifice, as distinct from self-withering, comes from an overfull cup. Just before the wealthy, noble, secure poet turned his life inside out to struggle for world harmony, Tagore wrote: "What divine drink wouldst thou have, oh God, from the overflowing cup of my life?"[2] In true sacrifice, we feel authentic indebtedness rather than guilt. A treasured gift is passed on, rather than a debt anxiously repaid. Devotion is expressed, not dependency—the sacrificial act comes from an immersion in a transporting value, not from a fear of loss of love or approval if the act remains undone. We feel the radiation of reverence and gratitude, rather than idealization and repayment. The act springs from actualizable love, rather than wishful grand fantasy. We see not an isolated act, or even a sustained series of acts, but we see an integrated necessity, functioning within a called life of love in an awake, ordered world.

An interesting example of the clash between normal, healthful modes of life and sacrificial ones can be found in Erik Erikson's book *Gandhi's Truth.*[3] In this generally admiring psychohistorical study of a great religious figure by a great psychoanalyst, there is one chapter (Part Three, Chapter One) in which the author sharply criticizes his deceased subject. Erikson argues that Gandhi made a fallacious, psychopathologically determined connection between nonviolent action and sexual continence.

For Gandhi, nonviolence was inextricably bound to sexual abstinence. His concern with being a sexually continent, seeker-at-one-with-the-divine, or brahmacharya, was hardly idiosyncratic. The religious importance of the self-sacrifice involved in becoming a brahmacharya is surely one of the most compelling foci of Indian civilization, ancient and modern. It is the *sine qua non* of most (but not all) branches of yoga;[4] it is the focus of countless myths and a well of folklore;[5] it is the cause of medical complaints in modern Indian clinics;[6] and it remains the most widely assessed criterion of an Indian's spiritual power. Gandhi's charisma was at least partly the product of his ability to infuse ancient models and legacies with compelling relevancy and energy.[7] That he was a brahmacharya was absolutely essential to his own self-esteem, and to his self-image as the healer of his people; it was also essential for his followers' image of him. For Gandhi, sexuality had to be sacrificed for pursuit of the spiritual life. (Of course, this attitude is hardly unique to India.) And his vision of nonviolence connected it to spiritual, and not merely political, values.

Erikson tells his readers that a central motive for his own impassioned, energetic, and brilliant study of Gandhi was to facilitate world peace, to make a contribution to the efforts to stop nuclear war, to try to understand, amplify, and extend Gandhi's methods beyond their particular cultural settings and historical moment, and widen their applicability and relevance. ". . . I had just come from the disarmament conference . . . Gandhi seems to have been the only man who has visualized and demonstrated an over-all alternative" (*Gandhi's Truth*, p. 51).

Accordingly, Erikson takes sharp issue with Gandhi's view that sexual abstinence is critical to organized nonviolence for which Gandhi had coined a term: Satyagraha. Erikson writes, as if in a letter to Gandhi, "For the future it is important to affirm unequivocally that what you call Satyagraha must not remain restricted to ascetic men and women who believe they

217

can overcome violence only by sexual disarmament" (*Gandhi's Truth*, p. 234). Erikson then analyzes Gandhi's unconscious ambivalence about sex, and tries to demonstrate that the linkage of Satyagraha with brahmacharya was idiosyncratic to Gandhi, and not a universal truth.

Erikson's analysis reveals two psychologies, two ways of understanding, in conflict. Each way has a strength and a relevance but also a weakness and a flaw.

Erikson's own view stresses interpersonal mutuality and self-acceptance. He points out that sex can be the mutual regulation of intimacy by two equal adults, and that each individual must be able to accept his or her own sexual feelings without denying, repressing, or splitting them off. This viewpoint enables him to envision sex and family coupled to wider commitments of love and work. He also points out that a person who condemns his own sexual instincts will become moralistic and repressive of others'—and he recounts anecdotes that reveal covert sexual sadism in Gandhi. Erikson's position is empathic and ethical rather than sadistic and moralistic. But Erikson also tries to equate Gandhi's healing of India with a psychoanalyst's healing of one patient. He seems oblivious to the enormous distinction between a fee-for-service medical task within the bounds of payment, job security, and normative institutions, and a cultural, political, spiritual radicalism that reaches out to humankind across the boundaries of all conventions and institutions. Erikson's vision does not include risk, failure, mass transformation—being beaten or jailed. It is wise and mature but not religious. His picture of life is organized and sane, but it does not lead outside of the everyday, to confront ultimate fears or ultimate meanings. His viewpoint is a rich prescription for maintaining and even improving society, but not for a movement of liberation. Nor does his view threaten society. His stance is cautious, prudent, healthy, normal, insightful, stabilizing. He speaks from a sense of enjoyment of life, but not of an embrace of pain, rejection, prison, or death.

His attitudes remain within predictable and safe channels, corralled away from the terrors of mass conflict and personal sacrifice.

Gandhi, as described by Erikson, was divided against himself. He had to excise his own sexual life. His vision of himself and of all people was split into twos: saint and sinner, man of love or man of sex. He had to root out, attack, and destroy parts of himself, such as sex. In certain moments, he may well have been rigid, fanatical. But he understood his position not as one of psychopathological neurotic conflict over sex, but as a necessary sacrifice of some parts of himself. He felt that becoming a sexually ascetic, spiritual truth-seeker was an essential sacrifice that enabled him to integrate reform, revolution, and spiritual vision into his own daily life and the lives of millions of his countrymen. He freed himself from normative institutions—like fee-for-service jobs, nuclear family life, and governments—and was fearless, a mass liberator, an ". . . impregnator of the sense of the possible . . ." (as William James called saints). No threat of beating or jail could stop him from speaking out from a platform beyond convention or caution. Though it is possible that he was personally grandiose or power-hungry, he had the ability also to reduce himself to a zero, to a naked, cold, hungry, tired, solitary prisoner, and yet continue to hold to his direction of creating a higher human unity. He was split in Erikson's terms, at odds with his sexual drive but whole in religious terms, integrated with the languishing yearnings of humankind: ideals of peace, love, and truth. He was inspired, possibly dangerous. He had awesome power, which possibly ran out of control. His integration was with the aspirations of the soul, and with mastery over the self-protective fears that block the rest of us from fulfilling those aspirations. He was energized rather than healthy. He was sacrificial. He was remarkably abnormal. He was labile, unpredictable, despairing, yet determined, unstoppable, and full of faith.

Erikson scolds his deceased but exemplary literary subject for not having asked his wife's permission to become a brahmacharya. Would Erikson have taken George Washington to task for not asking his wife's permission to camp out at Valley Forge? Clearly, what Gandhi did in the mode of self-sacrifice, Erikson can only understand from the position of healthymindedness. Erikson wishes to clarify the difference between an expanded arena of self-accepting ego-control and self-critical superego-control. Gandhi, following the ancient, venerable image of "tapas," spiritual self-immolation, was seeking a power-producing self-sacrifice; he was not trying to enhance his mental health, but to give away his life in service of a cause: religious reform, political freedom (possibly more personal power).

This dialogue between a psychoanalytic author and his religious subject highlights the difference between technique and reason, and between vision and faith. Gandhi intended to create in himself and his followers, not mature, reasoned, tactical choice, but a state of no-other-choice, like a soldier on a battlefield (for he felt that the essence of nonviolence was to *be* a soldier, but not strike). He tried to produce a state of mind in which the fear of death could be transformed, away from self-protective narcissism, into an embracing identity with the Other. He wanted to turn personal generativity into transpersonal membership, and, to do so, he felt that the personal family must be surrendered or sacrificed. Satyagraha is not the same as being good and nice; it was intended by its founder to be a force: a mixture of potent, manly, aggressive force, with nurturant, passive, female annealing. Gandhi envisioned Satyagraha to be the sexual life force turned away from sex and family, to bear a new family of humankind.

Whether Gandhi was a true visionary for all time, or merely a historically limited leader of a particular movement, is difficult to see; but it is easy to see how idiosyncratic and personal acts of sacrifice can be, and how thin is the margin of even the greatest of them from rationalized perversion. Later on in this chapter, I will point to some individual instances in which Gandhi's understanding of sacrifice continues to resonate far beyond him.

The psychotherapist, like Erikson in his role as psychohistorian, is eminently justified in systematic suspicion of all acts flying under the banner of sacrifice. This virtue must be differentiated from self-deceit and the trappings of unlived life. Where one observer may see a courageous, principled action taken at great personal cost, a critic may observe it as attention-seeking, foolhardy notoriety. Public demonstration and exhibitionism are two sides of a coin. Where the student of sacrificial life sees noble idealism in relinquishment of privilege, the motive-detective may skeptically espy self-denigration, shame, and low self-esteem. Where the priest may observe endurance and forgiveness, exemplary sacrificial virtues, bonding together a long-term marriage, the personal-growth oriented psychic healer may notice only two passive, dependent spouses unable to risk change, growth, or autonomy. For the balanced psychotherapist, it is important to remember that reservation in applause is a far cry from cynicism.

Sacrifice is not only the attitude an individual will take towards his or her divinity, it is also systematically promulgated by all organized religions. Paradigmatic are the Jews, whose scriptures contain the book of Job, and whose enduring history is a serial documentation of the extremity of sacrifice. Clearly, biological life is less powerful than loyalty, belief, and sacrifice. For Jews, sacrifice is ritually proximated via Yom Kippur. For Christians, God's own son was sacrificed on the Cross, and the early founders and followers emulated that sanctified mode while facing lions and persecution. For Christians, sacrifice is ritually proximated via Lent. As we have seen discussing Gandhi, the idea of "tapas" is core to the Hindu way of life. For followers of Islam, sacrifice is unending, and the faithful reveal it through arduous haj (pilgrimage to Mecca), jihad (holy war), and annually at Ramadan, a month-long partial fast. Apocryphal, heuristic legends of the Buddha contained in the Jatakamala[8] describe him as offering himself up as a meal for a hungry tiger, out of compassion for her starving cubs. Religions not only tout this virtue as historically transforming, but they provide occasion and rationales for it, through service, membership, example, and disciplines.

In general, a historical developmental trend can be glimpsed in the religious sacrificial attitude. Its earliest form derives from rituals of hierarchical propitiation, as when a dog displays its jugular vein to a dominant victor. When we read in the Old Testament of offerings of incense or burnt ram, or when we read in the Vedas of oblations of butter poured into the fire or of horse sacrifices, it is clear that we are hearing about people who fear a powerful superior and who have to placate Him or Her with a choice bribe. Rather than live in a capricious chaos, these early peoples imagined a powerful deity, who was absolutely in charge, and then fantasized ways of guaranteeing their own good standing with Him or Her, by sacrificing the prime cut of meat. This understanding of sacrifice remains common; in Chapter 8 I described its operation in relation to the Goddess as revealed in the life of a contemporary psychotherapy patient. Many of the sacramental acts and moral behaviors of members of organized religions today continue to operate at this level of cowering, placation, and protection.

The next stage in understanding sacrifice is protoscientific. The world is understood as lawful; there are gods, whose wills and motives do not run the world but are merely mediators or executives for immutable processes. Sacrifice then is understood as power. We can say that, in this stage, people sacrifice to gods as a magical coercion: if the ritual is correctly performed, it will *compel* the gods to comply. This attitude is more noticeably institutionalized in Oriental religions, such as Shintoism and aspects of Hinduism, than in the religions of the Near East, where faith and relationship to gods undercut the importance of coercive rituals. Nevertheless, just as millions of contemporary Hindus believe that mantras can be used as charms, or that rituals for the dead will influence their fate, Jews and Christians will repeat in psychotherapy their outrage or disbelief when they behaved "good" and yet suffered. Clearly they saw their goodness as an inevitable guarantee of protection. This is sacrifice understood as a legally bonded insurance policy.

A modification of the magical view of sacrifice is found in the Hindu concept of Tapas. Here, one sacrifices oneself. But the goal remains coercion and power.

> What is glorified . . . is the omnipotence of ascetic will power. Through the endurance of self-inflicted suffering the yogi accumulates an immense treasure of energy. In him the universal life force becomes concentrated to such a focus of blazing incandescence that it melts the resistance of the cosmic divine powers . . .[9]

Because Tapas is understood both as self-sacrifice and as universal law, it participates in the next level of development in the understanding of sacrifice: "In the myths of the Vedas, such energy [Tapas] is employed by the gods themselves to many ends . . . especially for the creation." At this level, sacrifice is understood as a universal principle. Not just people relating to gods, but gods themselves must sacrifice and must sacrifice themselves. In Chapter 4 we saw how caste is justified in Hinduism as a product of a creation that emerged from a divine sacrifice.

> The universe is derived from the sacrifice of the cosmic Person, the Purusa; the figure is of the dismemberment of a sacrificial animal; from each of the members of the cosmic Purusa evolved a part of the existing world.[10]

This understanding parallels the widespread archaic religions in which kings, or virgins, were sacrificed, not to please or soothe potentially angry deities, but to actually re-create, and refertilize the world.[11] There may be some parallels to the belief in the sacrifice by God of his only son, the Christ. Sacrifice can be understood to exemplify the pain inside creativity and the nobleness inside compassion.

In the story of Abraham and Isaac,[12] the perception of sacrifice is suffused with the issue of faith. A complex set of meanings around sacrifice emerge. Abraham may be seen to be offering his son Isaac to God like a burnt-ram protection-money; or he may be thought of as sacrificing a piece of himself, his most treasured love, to God. He may be seen as having such faith in God that he can go forward as far as brandishing the knife, all the while faithfully knowing his God will send a reprieve. He may be understood also, as Kierkegaard understood him in *Fear and Trembling*,[13] as so filled with faith that he could take the absurd leap of "infinite resignation," in which he was so certain of the goodness and meaning of God's voice and God's word that he could cast aside all skepticism, all doubt, even all understanding, and move forward unquestioningly and unambivalently under God's command. In this story the act of sacrifice has mythic ambiguity. Between the act and its meaning is the link of faith, a zone of choice, ethics, and relationship. This is a synaptic understanding. We can't be sure whether we have read of cruelty, cowardice, obedience, cunning, paradox, trust, or love. The rich compression of ambiguous possibility in the story of Abraham and Isaac, however, is not purely a developmental advance in understanding sacrifice. The primitive possibility of cowardly compliance is not entirely eliminated. And the story retains the memory—and I'm afraid it must be said, it extolls the memory—of human sacrificial victims. Abraham was nonplussed by God's command because he lived in a world in which sacrifices frequently meant the slaughter of someone else to obtain personal favor with a demonaic god. "It is appalling what a systematic wallowing in human—not to mention animal—blood has marked the history of religions in every quarter of the globe, in high as well as low culture contexts."[14]

In an era when children can be coddled with such unctuous preciousness, the psychotherapist continues to hear frequently the opposite: patients who utilize the secure confidentiality of therapy to express a desire to kill their children, or to abandon them, or to have them disappear. Among other perversions of the human potential, the religious sacrifice has been used to shield and rationalize a common murderous impulse towards interpersonal objects of frustration: kings, virgins, sons, and daughters. Sacrifice provides a channel to rationalize rage, cruelty, retaliation, and displacement of aggression.

Unfortunately, the history of religion is replete with other deteriorated forms of sacrifice. Naturally, if you want to domineer over a mob, how useful it is to inculcate the idea that self-sacrifice is a virtue. Large-group, orgiastic, homicide-suicide, crusades, holy wars, jihads are groomed and bred in this kennel. Sacrifice can be bent away from voluntary self-restraint in the service of higher goals, into painful and embittering self-mutilation that incites murderous, scapegoating rage. Heinrich Himmler exhorted his S.S. men to continue their slaughter of innocents, and he explained to them that their disgust or dismay had to be overcome as a form of sacrifice![15]

The religious sacrifice can dovetail with a perverse understanding of lawful order, affirming acceptance, calling, and membership to produce an agile zombie of destruction. The Assassins are a fascinating and very relevant example.[16] This eleventh- and twelfth-century Shiite Moslem sect (from whom the English word "assassin" is derived), specialized in religiously justified and inspired murder. Their uniqueness lay in the arduous spiritual devotion with which they were trained for an entire lifetime in a religious zeal that would culminate in one act of murder suicide. Though they were a tiny splinter subsect, their power spread over much of the civilized world. An endlessly patient, suicidally ruthless hunter is almost unstoppable, particularly when he construes his act as "hallowed justice." ". . . by one single warrior on foot, a king may be stricken with terror, though he own more than 100,000 horsemen." It is awesome to read of the restrained endurance, the lifetime of cunning sacrifice, with which disciples of this sect lived, in order to penetrate a select, trustworthy entourage and finally pull back the curtain and kill. Knowledge of this revered legacy helps us understand the apparently crazed terrorizing by Shiite men in Iran and Lebanon in the 1980s (see Chapter 4). Their acts of sacrifice are suspended in a net of feeling called, having conviction of a divine order, having surrendered to another's will, having split off their own sense of guilt, and feeling part of an illustrious membership.

Religious sacrifice can also deteriorate into solitary, psychotic strangulations of the life force retrospectively acclaimed as saintliness or martyrdom. Self-restraint becomes an end in itself, rather than a means to a wider spiritual life. Hollow, unsustainable self-aggrandizements and transitory idealisms also get rationalized as heroic sacrifices.

Medieval martyrdoms still percolate down to us and influence the aspirations and behavior of patients in psychotherapy. In Chapter 3, I described how the life of a patient I treated was profoundly influenced by the story of a monk fried alive centuries ago, and by other tales of Catholic martyrdom. In Chapter 8, I referred to "self-sacrificing" mothers who used Quakerism or Judaism to rationalize indirect manipulations of their families. Similarly, health care providers—nurses, social workers, psychiatrists, and others—may often reveal in treatment how they have sought to slake their own unmet dependency needs by giving to others and thereby tying those they serve into a guilty indebtedness.

For example, a social worker whose parents poured all

their concern into her brother, who had muscular dystrophy, became a "candy-striper" in a hospital as soon as she was old enough. Wherever she went, she had her eye out for the wounded. She became a social worker specializing in work with the crippled. Her tireless devotion and overtime hours led to career success, coupled to desperate unhappiness and several job changes. When she bore her own children, she found herself irrationally enraged at them. She had fleeting images of murdering them. "I'm sucked dry. I have nothing left to give. I'm burnt out." Her self-sacrificing years of overtime work were an attempt to meet her own needs, be the good, healthy, ignorable daughter her parents required because they, too, were drained by their son. Here, as so often, self-sacrifice was a mask for deprivation-provoked rage. This is part of the unconscious undercurrent in the story of Abraham and Isaac.

In another instance, a minister's son grew up with a father who was always out of the house, at work seven days a week. The boy's job was to comfort and care for his hurt, depressed mother. He grew up catering to women. He pursued his career, cooked, shopped, and cleaned, while his wife worked neither inside nor outside the home but gave him orders. He was frantic and fragmented when he came to therapy but very proud of his self-sacrificial, liberated, non-sexist marriage.

But sacrifices can grow into the selflessness of "the saving fragment"—those who can give away of themselves from the overflowing cup of their lives. Love is always linked to the capacity for sacrifice, but they must emerge in that order, and the latter is the corollary and measure of the former. Such saving organizations as Amnesty International, Greenpeace, Friends of the Earth, Oxfam, World Wildlife Fund, Physicians for Social Responsibility, American Friends Service Committee—all float on the small gifts of hundreds of thousands of donors and testify to the commonplace, widespread power and efficacy of minute, anonymous acts of financial sacrifice. Hard work and midnight parenting are the proximal forms of sacrifice, easy to hear, important to earmark in the stories of many patients. Others may reveal some mastery of this mode of life through their own character discipline and committed decades. Self-control, patience, and determination should be noted as important folk versions of this classical aspect of life. Psychiatrist Arthur Deikman has posited that the common ground between the healing available through psychotherapy, and through mystical discipline, rests on the capacity to develop an "observing self."[17] Such a personality structure can only develop through thousands of minute acts of sacrifice of impulse, desire, and willfulness.

When sacrifice is linked to a calling, it can be free of caprice. A lifelong purpose and direction then guides both what must be done and what must be left undone. The capacity to sacrifice is also linked to the capacity to find release, because one element of laying the burden down is the ability to relinquish, shuck, sacrifice fulfillment of many wishes, drives, or urges. I have treated many young Americans who imagine themselves to be suffering from deprivation. They complain initially about how poor they were, or how distracted or unsympathetic their parents were. In some instances, however, our psychotherapeutic exploration together has revealed backgrounds of easy cash, high expectations, far-flung vacations; the resulting psychic pain can be understood better as being the result of sanctioned, institutionalized avariciousness. This produces the distress of an individual with a scattered, hungry identity, unable to affirm a self because of an inability to sacrifice multiple, entitled expectations of consumption.

Just as sacrifice is linked to calling and release, it is connected to worldview: a worldview that is coherent and articulated provides integrated meaning for otherwise isolated acts—larger goals and higher claims may catch the person's attention, and lesser trees can be cleared out of the forest. The inner plasticity to hold to a painful affirmation, rather than bowing to convenience or cynicism, is also linked to faith (see Chapter 8). The sacrifice of faith provides tenacity beyond reason to loving acts of uncertain outcome.

Occasionally sacrifice can send its dark red flower above the common colors of the good providers and caretakers, to blossom emblematically. Gandhi's political son, Nehru, recounts how during his own nine years of intermittent imprisonment for his struggle to free India from Britain, news arrived that his wife, Kamala, was dying. The British agreed to release him if he would agree to cease political activity. After inner torment, he concurred. However, word of mouth travelled faster than Indian transportation, and when Jawaharlal arrived home, the bed-ridden Kamala ordered him back to prison rather than let her death be the occasion for his reneging. In fact, he served his term, and she survived.[18]

This Gandhian tradition of sacrifice has bloomed also in America. Charlie Liteky was a Catholic chaplain in the United States Army in Vietnam. When his company was pinned down by enemy fire, he risked his life over and over to drag wounded men to safety.

> In a magnificent display of courage and leadership, Captain Liteky began moving upright through enemy fire, administering last rites to the dying and evacuating the wounded . . . he stood up and personally directed the medivac helicopter into and out of the area.

These quotations are from the citation accompanying his subsequent award of the Congressional Medal of Honor for heroism. How did he escape being shot himself? He didn't. The citation continues:

> . . . it was discovered that despite painful wounds in the neck and foot, Captain Liteky had personally carried over twenty men to the landing zone for evacuation . . .

A description of Charlie Liteky's subsequent life continues:

> At the awards ceremony the following year, in the East Room of the
> White House, President Lyndon Johnson, leaning over to drape the
> Medal of Honor around Liteky's neck, whispered in his ear, "Son, I'd
> rather have one of these babies than be President."[19]

But nineteen years later, Mr. Liteky, at a public news conference, laid his Congressional Medal of Honor next to the wall
of the Vietnam Veterans Memorial in Washington and re-
nounced it, in protest of American policy supporting Contra
armies in Nicaragua. One month after that, on September 1,
1986, he began a fast for life, along with three other American
military heroes, on the steps of the United States Capitol, to
bring public attention to the American role in the Nicaraguan
war. He quoted Gandhi to explain himself to reporters: "This
is a kind of prayer . . . As Gandhi said, those who claim that
the spiritual and political can't mix don't know either." One is
reminded of the words of William James:

> This practical proof that worldly wisdom may be safely transcended
> is the saint's magic gift to mankind . . . the world is essentially a
> theatre for heroism. In heroism, we feel, life's supreme mystery is
> hidden . . . he who feeds on death that feeds on men possesses life
> supereminently and excellently, and meets best the secret demands of
> the universe . . . What we now need to discover in the social realm
> is the moral equivalent of war: something heroic that will speak to
> men as universally as does war, and yet will be as compatible with
> their spiritual selves as war has proven itself to be incompatible.[20]

Charlie Liteky and his three companions fasted from September 1 to October 17, 1986, forty-seven days, ceasing only after
thousands of letters and phone calls, and multiple sympathetic
fasts and demonstrations had convinced them that public
awareness had grown regarding the life and death struggle in
Nicaragua.[21]

As a theme in therapy, sacrifice is in the atmosphere yet most often only as a subtle imprint, just a track in the sand beside a stream. It is present often as a negative rather than as a photograph. Or it can be heard in mixed approximations, or as a recurrent, muted whisper, struggling for expression.

An engineer lost contact with his two little daughters after his divorce. He sent his ex-wife money and felt excised, rejected, inadequate, enough of a failure to be only a failure. About ten years after the divorce, and while he was in therapy for a depression following a second divorce, his first ex-wife came down with stage four Hodgkin's disease. Severely ill from chemotherapy and radiation and cancer, she requested that he take his daughters, and he concurred. One was now a sullen adolescent and a poor student, but the younger was a heavy drug user, promiscuous, and explosive.

The engineer's own adult life reflected his long personal struggle to reparent himself. He was the sixth child and third son of French Canadian mill workers who had had too many children, not enough money, and too much alcohol. After the threat of physical violence between himself and his father, he had left home and worked his way through engineering school. His guiding compulsion was to orchestrate his own physical comfort, take care of his house and home-made furniture. He had been a have-not, and he wanted to compensate. He left his first wife for greener pastures. His second wife left him. She felt starved out by his fussy compulsions, his tool-throwing tantrums, his frequently verbalized doubts that he loved her or anyone.

Now he was faced with an obstreperous, defiant, belligerent teenager, and he was a single parent. But he had already taken therapeutic strides in understanding how his self-reflexive attempt to purchase a new childhood for himself had isolated him in adulthood. At the same time that he was struggling to overcome his own entitled rages, to acknowledge the severe pains of his bleak childhood, and to build a relation-

ship with a new woman friend, he took on the care of his
stranger daughters. He wanted to make up for his negligence.
He wanted to break the chain of misery in which he felt caught
and in which he had ensnared his daughters. But he also
wanted to smoke dope, change girlfriends, and travel. He was
used to being single and not responsible. He was used to being
his own boss.

He tried to incorporate his daughters into his ongoing life.
They were invited, like adults, to parties he held. He found, to
his chagrin, that rather than admiring his self-styled, counter-
cultural and youthful ways, they scorned him as an old hippie.
The younger girl cursed him foully in front of his friends to
humiliate and dare him. He felt mortified. He decided to be
firm and lay down the law. He was the parent, and he would
show it. He gave her a curfew; she opened her bedroom window, climbed down the drainpipe, and disappeared. He took
away her allowance. She retorted that he was only driving her
into dealing, not just using, drugs. He said he would limit
her stupefying T.V. watching; she turned on the T.V. in front
of him and said, "Are you going to physically stop me, you
asshole?"

In therapy he spilled out his struggle, like a man being
drawn and quartered. He didn't even know this girl. She was
a real bitch, and he hated her. He wished she would disappear.
He felt an impulse to thrash or strangle her. But he also felt
guilty. He knew her feelings; they mirrored his own reaction
to his father. Her bravado must cover fear, as his had thirty
years ago. An idealist at work, where he specialized in revers-
ing and controlling environmental pollution, he wanted to care,
to clean up, to heal. Could he? This ambivalent struggle con-
sumed months of therapy. Many divorced parents find a way
to extrude, palm off their children, particularly unruly teenagers—they can be gotten to leave. But the engineer had already
done that to two little girls.

In therapy, he was blown back and forth between two

feelings. No one had helped him; no one could help anyone; what could he do; it was her problem not his—he heard the voice of a comforting, excuse-bearing depression. Hopelessness is a balm for guilt and expectations. But he also wanted to fight: fight his daughter with the same spirit he fought his father, but also fight *for* his daughter against the hopelessness he knew was driving her sneering demeanor. I admired his capacity to at least sometimes empathize with the person humiliating him, but I felt nonetheless that his deadlock was due to a defensive self-righteousness based on his history with his father. In his view, he owed his father nothing. I challenged that as an unrealistic exaggeration. He worked with me too cooperatively, too fluidly, for me to believe that his primary relationship with a man had been so absolutely negative.

He found at last a virtue in his mill-working father that he could identify with and emulate: grit. "If I do one thing, it will be to be the father of this girl" (the younger one was taking all the attention). He continued to explore his past from this new angle: not what he hadn't gotten, but what he had, to strengthen his sense of hope. We all tend to see the future as an extension of how we remember, interpret, and reconstruct the past. The Catholic Church, which he had abandoned with mill work, provided memories of hope. He went back to the Bible. He found his feeling mirrored in the unscientific apostle he thought he had rejected, St. Paul: "If any man among you seemeth to be wise in this world, let him become a fool, that he may be wise."[22] To try to help, or even live with, this girl was foolish, and he decided to be a fool.

The spirit that gripped him was a desire to make good as a person, as he had once propelled himself against the odds through engineering school in the desire to find material success. The money he craved and acquired now became a mere tool to be sacrificed to a different goal. He wanted to break the cycle of abandonment and hostility that he had felt caught in, that therapy raised into his awareness, and that he now saw he had perpetrated on his daughters. He added family therapy to his costs. He came home early seven nights a week. He stopped counting up how much money or time he was spending on the girls. He didn't surrender to his own fury. He absorbed the youngest's hatred and kept trying to figure out and solve each interaction.

Initially he sought rules. "Should I be firm? You're the psychiatrist." Or, "I've got to give her a break; it's not her fault." Neither firmness nor leniency was an adequate rule for the complexity of his relationship with his daughter, because he had to do more than regulate her behavior. He had to live with his own feelings. The rules he sought were an avoidance of what he felt. Describing in therapy his interactions with the outrageous girl, he relived his own interior life: frustration, fury, accomplishment, love, and yearning to be loved. His capricious libertine's life disappeared. He was a hardworking, overworked, single parent—a task to which he abandoned himself with almost tearful fury and joy, because he knew he was winning the battle, not with his daughter, but with his own narcissistic, compensatory, material obsessions. I felt I was observing a small field of personal heroism, where an ex-Catholic scientist was following Japanese Zen Master Dogen's advice, to climb to the top of a fifty-foot flagpole, and when you get to the top, keep on going.[23] To bend and labor in the sacrificial field of parenthood exceeded any flush of life that this previously cynical and guarded quantifier had ever imagined for himself. Sacrifice is the realm where you stop counting.

The two fathers described in this chapter show similarities and differences. Both experienced deprivation in childhood that left them unfamiliar with ordinary parental sacrifice. The Department Chairman was abandoned and remained abandoning. The engineer felt abandoned, but deprived though his background was, he could locate strengths and gifts within it that enabled him to identify with the capacity for sacrifice. He remembered his mother doing her best to buy him respectable clothes for high school. He remembered a Jesuit who was an inspired English teacher. He had internalized in engineering school an image of the solitary scientific quest, the sacrifice of knowledge. Before this therapy ended, he went on a camping trip to Maine with his two daughters, an ordeal, an adventure, a touch of ordinary life. As his house began to resemble a home, and he began to resemble a parent, he ceased therapy, though dramatic clashes with his daughter continued to occur.

A psychotherapist must be alert to pry under the word sacrifice to find rot. But there is another side: where there is no capacity for sacrifice, there is no health. No other issue so clarifies the need for a therapist to revitalize continually his or her capacity for suspended judgment. Fitting the modern temper, many psychotherapists seem quick to point a finger at rationalization and inhibition, while devotion and sacrifice fly quietly past.

In those psychological circles where scientific causality is applied reductionistically to human behavior, then sacrifice is discounted not as a costume for self-deception but as merely determined behavior. What appears sacrificial is interpreted as the product of a field of causal forces. If there is no free will, can sacrifice have any meaning? What is done had to have been done; there was no choice. Even then, I would say, sacrifice means embracing the inevitable. The most rigorous scientific model of our life does not exclude the possibility and necessity of sacrifice, but the word can no longer be understood as saying no, giving up, as in giving up chocolate for Lent. Sacrifice can also mean accepting the picture of necessity without coloring in desires and illusions. The ultimate sacrifice may be simply to live in unshaded reality.

Sacrifice, an extension of love, means participation. It extends the reach of affirming acceptance of self; it lightens the journey of calling and membership. The deepest psychological understanding of sacrifice (rather than a mere behavioral understanding) is to say yes. He who meets the world as it is sacrifices his desires and wishes and holds the collective world-view out into the daylight. In this sense, we can say yes to the way wounded unknown souls say yes through eccentric and idiosyncratic offerings, when illusion is sacrificed (not human lives, not meat) to the actualization of possibility. Not what you refrain from, but what you throw off to proceed is your sacrifice. Life is rushing on; you must give, give up, surrender, sacrifice something cherished you carry, and move on. Authentic sacrifice yields up fond dreams to the actual. To simply assume parenthood was sacrifice for the engineer.

I would not conclude quickly that every self-limiting act is necessarily neurotic—some corrals enclose a ready stallion.

◊ **10** ◊

Meaningful Death

... and now that I feel the chill of death upon me, I can sing of how I was sent forth, and who calls me home.

A retired professor sought help for depression. The slow increments of organically based, intellectual deterioration were destroying him. He had grown up in a small town in Tennessee, where, between his mother's and his father's relatives, almost the whole town was in his family: tobacco farmers and doctors, bankers and alcoholic carpenters. At the age of eight he contracted polio. He spent a month on a respirator, eventually recovering full function, except for a dramatic limp. Throughout his ordeal, his parents were devoted but reserved. The family style and his cultural background exhorted hard work and stoicism. His father taught high school science, and, when the boy turned thirteen, he died of a heart attack. The funeral was restrained; the boy never cried. He understood that, since he couldn't play football, and since he had to uphold his father's standing, his job was to study hard. He did that for the next fifty years.

His career was distinguished. Though modest and self-effacing, he told me that his many books were all impeccable scholarship. His wife was a minister's daughter, who understood her life as one of service to others. She cleared the path ahead of him, so that he could get back to his office or the library untroubled. She raised their children. When they became teenagers, the children complained that they found their father distant, unemotional, preoccupied, depressed. Yet their home was far from gloomy—there was music, an active church life, and three bright kids. There were also sabbaticals in England, Switzerland, and Vancouver.

The professor avoided situations that would point out his crippled leg. Raising babies had been his wife's job, but it was also her job to take teenagers skiing and attend their school events. His job was to study. Colleagues whose professional knowledge was threatening to him were also kept at a distance. The totality of his self-esteem resided in his keenness of mind, the superiority of his intellect. Without this he felt naked in a competitive world. His intellect shone in the sun until retirement.

When his adult children returned at holidays, they were strangers who had a past only with his wife. Though he had planned to go on studying and writing after retirement, he became aware of his memory loss, and his diminished command of words and facts. He couldn't tolerate turning out second-rate writing. His wife's dutifulness had shifted, as her traditional church had also shifted in its attitude towards women. Now, free of her austere and awesome father, and free of her children, and free of obligatory role constraints, she let out her resentment. Her years of service had also produced a rich network of relatives and friends with whom she had deep engagements on her own, independent of her husband. The trips, retreats, conferences were now hers to go to. The retired professor felt abandoned, useless, and a failure. He wanted to die and wasn't willing to wait. His despair had so much fact and conviction behind it, that by the time his wife was able to convince him to see a psychiatrist, I couldn't reach him. He had to be hospitalized to prevent him from killing himself.

Patients will imply the need to face their own death, yet feel confirmed, not shattered. Every person is a piece, a fragment, that will die, pass on, disappear, lose everything and everyone. Yet people can touch, know, express, live out from the source of life itself, which is in us:

> Yea, though I walk through the valley of the shadow of death,
> I will fear no evil: for thou art with me . . .[1]

For each "I" that "thou" may differ.[2] The possibility of a life that feels complete rather than broken off in the face of death is a lifelong project and need.

Plato said that ". . . philosophers are always occupied in the practice of dying . . ."[3] A long historical tradition, winding through Cicero and Seneca, links the philosopher's life to a ceaseless awareness of and preparation for death.[4] Martin Heidegger confirmed that stance for twentieth-century philosophy; he felt that the core of human life was a potential to be authentic, caring, and whole, but this all rested on "being towards death."[5] Nonetheless, religion is that realm of life that can be counted on to both refocus attention on the imminence of death, and to provide "modes of symbolic immortality."[6]

To walk into a religious institution, to open a scriptural text, is to be gripped and shaken into an abrupt reminder of the proximal possibility of your own death. The churchbell, the Psalm, the meditation hall—all toll attention towards death's portentous enigma. The ancient Buddhist text, the Dhammapada, emphasizes over and over: ". . . this body is frail like a jar . . . this body is the foam of a wave, the shadow of a mirage . . . consider this body! A painted puppet . . . decaying, a nest of diseases, bound to destruction and dissolution. All life ends in death.'"[7] This state of mind is echoed in the most famous stanza of the later, more influential Buddhist text, the Diamond Sutra:

All composite things are like
a dream, a fantasy, a bubble
and a shadow;
Like a dewdrop and a flash of
lightning—
They are thus to be regarded[8]

In Chapter 7, the Bhagavad Gita was discussed, with its climactic vision of all-devouring time and mass death. The New Testament conveys the power of imminence with the tone of threat and promise: "Repent: for the kingdom of heaven is at hand . . ."[9] Similarly, the Koran produces the feeling of an immediacy to the ultimate confrontation: "Wherever you may be, death will overtake you . . ."[10] And the Old Testament has its relentless, somber, fierce realism: "All go unto one place; all are of dust, and all turn to dust again."[11]

Religions not only strike the gong of reminder over and over; they also offer a method by which death can be confronted, held, understood, and incorporated into daily life. Erik Erikson has written beautifully about this double role of religion:

Religious ritual . . . offers at regular intervals ceremonial confrontations with ultimate concerns which both reveal and hide the fact of death . . . living bridges to a sense of consolidation which makes it possible to produce, create, and serve without debilitating despair.[12]

According to Erikson, this carefully measured-out exposure and closure facilitates the maturation of individuals, who then can live aware of, but not be paralyzed by, death; so that, when they at last arrive at the Presence, they will have lived well enough to die well enough.

Only in him who in some way has taken care of things and people and has adapted himself to the triumphs and disappointments adherent to being, the originator of others or the generator of products and ideas . . . he knows an individual life is the accidental co-incidence of but one life cycle . . . In such final consolidation, death loses its sting . . . the lack or loss of this accrued ego integration is signified by fear of death . . .[13]

Erikson's haunting prose captures the same wisdom as the twenty-five hundred year old poetry of the Dhammapada: "Those who in their youth did not live in self-harmony, and who did not gain the true treasures of life, are later like long-legged old herons standing sad by a lake without fish."[14] Heinrich Zimmer showed how religious myths attempt to steer their listeners between two perils which awareness of death can provoke: ". . . the peril of indifference or callousness . . . or the opposite spiritual disaster—impotent despair, absolute disillusionment in man's capacity to realize the everlasting, great ideals."[15] In Chapter 5, I discussed how shamans and healers of diverse cultures must pass through symbolic death, dismemberment, and spiritual rebirth to be confirmed in their calling. It is through their encounter with death that they have the opportunity to embody life.

Thus, religions share in common their desire to hold up death as a guide for life, to remind us to live as if the end were near, so that we will live for what will ultimately make us feel confirmed in our ways. Religious practices exhort us to dwell in the future perfect subjunctive: to live so that when we die we shall have lived as if death were our daily guide. We are taught to make death an inlay in the buckle of life, to incorporate *all* of our life in each day of our life, so that we live fully and well. When a contemporary Zen monk was asked why the great Japanese Zen master Dogen wrote so stridently and repetitively about the nearness of death, the monk replied, "Dogen wants us to enjoy life." Not everyone can be paradoxically spurred forward. Unfortunately, scriptures and rituals of religions may

terrify, overwhelm, and debilitate their listeners and may turn
them off, rather than open them up.

In the Old Testament, references to death are usually
invoked in the mood of a feared punishment, a personal retaliation. In the New Testament, death is fundamentally denied: "O
death, where is thy sting? O grave, where is thy victory?"[16]
Spiritual and physical death, resurrection, and immortality are
blurred to appeal to many levels of readers, many different
hopes and fantasies. The historian William McNeil refers to
this phenomenon as the "invention of the religions of salvation," including Hinduism, Christianity, and Mahayana Buddhism, in which human beings for the first time systematically
elaborated the idea of a personal immortality available to the
masses. Before the dawn of the Christian era, religions promised only success in this life, or spiritual immortality, or personal immortality for the elite, like the Pharaohs.[17] But the
world religions of the Christian era specifically elaborated
heaven and afterlives and resurrections to mollify human fears.
In the Koran, death is described as the loss of life's most salient
trait: the capacity to choose between good and evil. Death is
a hideous threat to the living, since it may signal the commencement of unending vicious torture under the guidance of
an inexhaustibly revengeful and sadistic God: ". . . there shall
be a hospitality of boiling water and the roasting . . ."[18]

Some modern writers have expressed their belief that contemporary people have a unique problem, in that we must live
in awareness not only of our own death, but also of mass death,
due to modern history and to nuclear weapons. Psychiatrist
Robert J. Lifton wrote: "For Protean (contemporary) man is
pursued by terror and evil. He has no choice but to live in the
memory and expectation of holocaust."[19] Jonathan Schell's influential book *The Fate of the Earth* had an epoch-making
influence on human civilization with its clear, convincing incorporation of the image of the possibility of the extinction of
life on planet earth due to nuclear holocaust.[20] The lucidity,

precision, and daring of his own thoughts enabled the rest of us to think beyond the horizon of what had been previously thinkable about death. It is not clear to me whether today our fears of sweeping death, based on accurate historical reconstruction of Nazi mass murder in Europe during World War II, and on scientifically informed and eloquently reasoned research into the implications of nuclear weapons—it is not clear whether these are categorically different from fears of the Black Death in Medieval Europe, or fears of the end of the world as contained in Revelations or the Koran, as they were experienced by people of the past. Religions have proclaimed not only individual demise, but violent extinction, just as the ancients themselves witnessed and feared it. Genocide is not new.[21]

> Then the Lord rained upon Sodom and upon Gomorrah brimstone and fire from the Lord out of heaven. And he overthrew those cities, and all the plain, and all the inhabitants of the cities, and that which grew upon the ground.
> . . . and Lo, the smoke of the country went up as the smoke of a furnace.[22]

The need to deal with death, now, so that we are prepared for this unexpected inevitability, can deteriorate into the fanciful, pathetic, paraphernalia of religious superstition, and into the infantile, cringing delusion that led Freud to see in religion a wish to "remain a child forever."[23] In Chapter 2 we discussed how Freud saw religion as a defense against the fear of death.

> . . . there is the painful riddle of death . . . nature rises up before us, sublime, pitiless, inexorable . . . men's helplessness remains, and with it their father-longing and the gods . . . the gods must exorcise the terrors of nature and reconcile man to the cruelty of fate, particularly as shown in death . . .[23]

Too harsh and indigestible reality leads to denial and illusion building. Much of humankind much of the time lives through denial of death.[24] The denial leads to absurd group fantasy-inventions of inexhaustible and indomitable good human parents who live in the sky, presiding over a flawlessly, narcissistically gratifying reproduction of life on earth's ideal daydreams.

Historian McNeil wrote:

> The religious travail of the submerged peoples and the rootless populations of the cities of western Asia in the first centuries of the Christian era marks a profound change in human history . . . Christianity, Mahayana Buddhism, and Hinduism agreed in defining the goal of human life as salvation. All three promised their adherents eternal life in a blissful afterworld . . . and allowed men to face almost any sort of disaster with a modicum of cheerfulness, since, according to each of these faiths, this world was but a prelude to another. Societies in earlier times had never known anything quite like these religions of salvation.[25]

Death can also be avoided, in thought, through compartmentalization; then the need to confront it deteriorates into a technocratic mastery that is temporally myopic. Scientific mastery over one dilemma can be used to deny the power of death anywhere else. Thus, a heart transplant victim, like an Aztec sacrifice, is created as an emblem of the scientific mastery over death, and this one, withered, prolongation, of one half-life, is given center stage, while at the same time entire regions of continents are devastated by famine, and hundreds of thousands of preventable deaths are ignored. The solitary heart transplant creates a compartmentalized illusion of triumph, but the political, economic, and social chaos of famine is overwhelming and easier to ignore. Similarly, as Lewis Thomas wryly wrote (using numbers now fifteen years out of date):

> There are 3 billion of us on the earth and all 3 billion must be dead, on schedule, within this lifetime. The vast mortality, involving something over 50 million of us each year, takes place in relative secrecy

... It is hard to see how we can continue to keep the secret with such multitudes doing the dying.[26]

Similarly, as discussed in Chapters 2, 6, and 7, the struggle to find order, peace, and meaning can deteriorate into an attempt to gain the upper hand over death by inflicting it upon others, making it, apparently, a tool of one's own will.

Psychiatrist Irvin Yalom has pointed out that the fantasy of being "special," which has been interpreted by other psychiatrists as a narcissistic reaction to not having felt special enough to one's parents in childhood, is more likely prospective than retrospective. Feeling "special" is a defense against feeling merely a part of "the multitudes doing the dying."[27] The idea of salvation is an urban idea, an idea divorced from observation of nature, and the delusion of specialness is also a motivated, selective blindness to nature. As Lewis Thomas added: "We will have to give up the notion that death is catastrophe, or detestable, or avoidable, or even strange. We will need to learn more about the cycling of life . . . Everything that comes alive seems to be in trade for something that dies, cell for cell."[28]

Human beings confront death psychologically, creatively, imaginatively, not as a toasted, dry fact. The psychological, emotional, and intellectual armamentarium available for molding death into augmented life will determine whether death is dealt with through fairy tale, manipulation, sadistic emulation, or through growthful, life-enhancing methods.

Just as life must be continuously viewed through the lens of death's eye, death in turn will be seen in the light of the life that is being lived. The writer Stephen Levine, who is also a student of Elisabeth Kübler-Ross, has captured this point in a series of aphorisms: "The ways of a lifetime are focused in our death . . . our fear of death is directly equatable to our fear of life . . . whatever prepares you for death enhances life . . . focusing on death is a way of becoming fully alive."[29]

When patients discuss, or more often, suggest, the prob-

lem of meaningful death, it never rises up as a freestand-
ing, independent variable; it is always suspended on multiple
threads that lead in to it from the living issues surrounding it.
The problem of a meaningful death is a summative, integrative
problem. Psychotherapy patients confront it dissolved in the
solution of many other life dilemmas.

When the need for control and order in life has hypertro-
phied, then the dis-control that death suggests can stimulate
panic as time runs out. When control has been channeled
into career—one of our contemporary substitute religions—as
it was for the retired professor, death proximity stimulates
awareness of love ungiven. The professor told me: "When my
uncle, who was an old-fashioned Tennessee farmer, was going
through his last illness, he was surrounded by and interested
in the lives of dozens of grandchildren. What am I going to do?
Hand out reprints?"

Just as sexuality can be used as a channel to attempt to
solve other religious problems (as was shown in Chapters 2 and
7), it can be used to drown out the growing voice of death
anxiety. This desperate solution seems more common in men.
Those who feel they haven't yet lived emulate youth's most
flamboyant trait: robust sexuality. While younger people will
discuss and show great concern with the quality of their sexual
relations, older men frequently keep public count in front of
their psychiatrist. They want a witness to acknowledge their
banner of immortality, like the man who, when I suggested he
seemed in a panic about aging, laughed derisively at me, told
me I was reading too much Lifton, and reassured me that, like
Picasso, he would be virile at ninety.

In psychotherapy, death is usually a woven-in theme,
rather than a stark one. It is also important to remember that
death itself can be a defense, a symbol for loss, depression, rage,
and other issues. Themes of death in therapy, therefore, can
represent a fresh approach to reality, or a defensive flight from
other problems.

For example, a child of holocaust survivors described himself as obsessed by death. Every relative, location, or cultural reference point his parent mentioned to him as he grew up had been smashed or killed. "Everything around me was dead, dead." He spent his twenties looking for "incredible highs," relationships or actions that were explosive in life force, drugs, extramarital sex, in an attempt to feel more alive. He wanted "the ultimate connection." He yearned to overcome the feeling of ostracism and abandonment in his grim heritage. Death was too real, too imminent, and unnatural, unfair, imposed and tyrannical to him. His obsession with death was partly a hypersensitization, an overexposure, a hauntingly raw awareness, but it was also partly a displacement from his shattered sense of membership. As his interpersonal world deepened over years of psychotherapy, his obsession with death diminished, not because death itself was any less powerful or real, but because his capacity to join and love were no longer dead. The two issues, membership and meaningful death, ceased to overlap, and each occupied its own sphere.

Themes of death can also operate defensively in other spheres. People who are overwhelmed with anxieties about comfort or security may become obsessed with death as a form of implosive comfort. Nothing else seems to matter; other worries can be kept in perspective. Survivors of near-death experiences may need to relive them repetitively in order to attempt to master them. Occasionally, after experiences such as war or accident have been apparently mastered and have lain quiescent for decades, they may be rearoused by an apparently tangentially related event. Fears of death then provide a superstitious warning. The World War II survivor contemplating divorce in 1987 may become preoccupied anew with the European front; the connection is the thought: "How can you ask for more out of life now when you're lucky just to be alive?"

The therapist is equally mortal. Meaningful death is a problem present in every hour of the therapist's work. We can see this clearly by looking at a great psychiatric text. Elisabeth Kübler-Ross's masterpiece, *On Death and Dying,* [30] was a historical watershed in psychiatry, for its empirical, factual discoveries, coupled to a richly empathic and roundly human approach to the actual clinical encounter with dying cancer patients. This book changed work with dying patients forever. It does not bear directly on the main theme of this chapter— how whole lives are lived in response to the awareness of death—for it focuses on the response patterns that emerge in the specifically sick and dying cancer patient. But in reading her text, I imagine I hear the voice of a great explorer opening up new lands, an original investigator like Darwin on the *Beagle,* yet also a Magellan of compassion, strength, and availability steering the great vessel of hope under full sail into dark waters to see what can be known and accomplished there. And it is very striking to me that Dr. Kübler-Ross begins every single chapter and concludes her book with quotes from Rabindranath Tagore. The explorer needs an astrolabe, a sexton; new lands of the heart also need their pole star. The scientist-humanist oriented herself around the visions of the great religious poet. How can we emerge if we are only lost?

The "meaningful" in the term "meaningful death" is not a cognition. When she wrote *On Death and Dying,* Dr. Kübler-Ross was impressed with neither intellect nor organized religion as aids in facing death, for she wrote: "Simple people . . . seem in general to have somewhat less difficulty in facing this final crisis . . . Religious patients seem to differ little from those without a religion . . . we found very few truly religious people with an intrinsic faith." [31] She quotes from Rabindranath: "I stand under the golden canopy of thine evening sky . . . I have come to the brink of eternity from which nothing can vanish . . . Oh, dip my emptied life into the ocean, plunge it in to the deepest fullness . . ." [32]

Not a cognitive ideation, not a social affiliation, but a plunge into life enabled Kübler-Ross to sail along death's horizon. The need for a confirmed life in the face of death grows into wholehearted living, unreserved participation in what Martin Buber called ". . . each mortal hour's fullness of claim and responsibility . . ."[33] This death-confronting, life-affirming spirit that we can hear in Kübler-Ross, Tagore, and Buber, was immortalized in prose by the young man Thoreau:

> I went to the woods because I wished to live deliberately, to front only the essential facts of life, and see if I could not learn what it had to teach, and not, when I came to die, discover that I had not lived . . . I wanted to live deep and suck out all the marrow of life . . . and, if it proved to be mean, why then to get the whole and genuine meanness of it, and publish its meanness to the world; or if it were sublime, to know it by experience, and be able to give a true account of it in my next excursion.[34]

This sort of spirit implies a mastery over the caution in life that is the cover for death anxiety. Without a realization of finitude, there is on one side an opportunity for unending hesitation, prevarication, reservation; and, on the other side, a fear of death may be translated into a fear of all risks and, therefore, a fear of living. We saw in Chapter 8 how the neurotic cannot affirm himself, drive forward to create, actualize, and express the fullness of his life, because full living would require full awareness of death as well. The neurotic chooses to avoid death by avoiding living.[35] In Chapter 6, I discussed similar views in Viktor Frankl's writing and clinical techniques. Withholding of self from life, keeping one's core in reserve for a preserved, unopened future, makes for a half-lived, half-committed life that is apparently endless, all potential, no actualization.

Release and love, such life-affirming forces, always awaken proximity to death. Death drives men and women to love; romance becomes love when awareness of death filters into it. We can love when we can die, and love enables us to walk forward consciously or firmly into life and death. A timid, controlling scientist described to me how he could never turn

up a radio dial to full power, because he always wanted a littl
extra potential to spare in ready reserve for a never-fulfille
future. This constricted behavior pattern dissolved when he fe
in love. Robert J. Lifton has captured this phenomenon per
fectly: "Every significant step in human existence involve
some inner sense of death."[36]

But the mature need for meaningful death does not merel
open up life's tangible ripe commitments. Thoughts of deat
interdigitate with vital immediate issues, they substitute fo
such issues, but they also occupy a unique proper sphere
Death awareness also leads beyond concrete concerns to
lifelong, steady search for the eternal, the undying. What doe
in fact transcend death? This question, at some level, occupie
everyone, and the need for meaningful death, when harnessed
will have us awake early, scanning the treetops and clouds fo
the wings of the transcendent in the autumn skies.

This search for the transcendent can impel people to th
borderline of life and death. An unforgettable account of thi
is provided by the Australian woman Cherie Bremer-Kamp
Her father was an airline pilot; she grew up with the spirit o
adventure, and became a mountain climber. She met her sec
ond husband, Chris Chandler, M.D., when they were both par
of a large expedition to K2, the world's second highest moun
tain. Dr. Chandler had already climbed Everest as part of th
1976 American Bicentennial Expedition. The two fell in lov
and formed a marriage of adventure. They eschewed larg
expeditions, sailed and climbed, and set as their goal to climb
the world's third highest peak, Kanchenjunga, in minimalis
style, without oxygen. In the summer of 1981 they made it t
26,000 feet, in winter, among 200 mile-per-hour winds, an
camped only 2000 feet below the summit, with a view of th
entire Tibetan Plateau spread out before them. Dr. Chandle
died of cerebral edema, and in her futile attempt to resuscitat
him, Bremer-Kamp, a critical-care nurse by profession, tore of

her gloves: "My fingers had become white, like marble. I knocked them together and it sounded as if I were banging two pieces of wood against one another . . . I thought I would have to sacrifice my hands . . ." Eventually, she left her husband's body propped up in a seated posture, gazing out over the vast plateau of Tibet. She thought of dying, then she thought of her two children and began the four-day trek down the mountain in company of their one sherpa guide. She was flown to Katmandu, Nepal, then to Bangkok, then to Anchorage, and then to Seattle; she was hospitalized five months, and had ten operations to remove fingers and toes, and have stumps grafted back on to her knuckles. Her goal is to try to climb Kanchenjunga, again, herself. Why?

When Chris and I were on the mountain together, we felt that this was what we were meant to be . . . The beauty of course is stunning . . . but it's more than that. Chris and I were not conventionally religious people, but being on the mountain is as close to a religious experience as I've ever had. You lose yourself in the environment, and when you see a rock you realize that it's not only a rock but that it's part of a grand design . . . to Chris and me the mastering of danger offers insight into life. The word for "thrill" comes from the Greek words "to penetrate," and for us climbing mountains was a way to cut through the farce of everyday living.

She quoted an American Indian poem:

Do not stand at my grave and weep.
I am not there. I do not sleep.
I am a thousand winds that blow.
I am the diamond glint on snow.[37]

Were these depressed people, compelled to seek thrills to feel alive? Were they impulsive, judgment-impaired fools? In hearing this story, I was reminded once again of the phrases of

William James that also sprang to mind about Charlie Liteky (Chapter 8): that the world is essentially a theatre for heroism, and that he or she who feeds on death that feeds on men possesses life supereminently and excellently, and meets best the secret demands of the universe. Whatever personal or pathological strands may also be present in her story, Cherie Bremer-Kamp manifests the courage to unleash the unreserved spirit of life, over and above death, because her religious inspiration had carried her into a liberating gnosis.

Albert Einstein was quoted as saying:

> A human being is part of a whole, called by us "universe," a part limited in time and space. He experiences himself, his thoughts and feelings, as something separate from the rest—a kind of optical delusion of consciousness. This delusion is a prison for us, restricting us to our personal desires and to affection for a few persons around us. Our task must be to free ourselves from this prison by widening our circle of compassion to embrace all living creatures and the whole of nature in its beauty.[38]

The need for meaningful death can bear fruit as an organic, deeply-felt sense of fulfillment, completion, continuity, which enables one life to pass on courage, hope, and vision in the very act of expiration. A life lived and concluded in this faithful way has as its core a continuous living out from another source, a root. The capacity to build a meaningful death over the span of life requires a sense of witnessed significance, lawful order, affirming acceptance, calling, membership, release, worldview, love, and sacrifice. It is not merely a dependent variable; it has a realm of its own. There must be a sense of an enduring, eternal, outer, other, inner somewhere. In the words of the Nobel Prize winning poet, Czeslaw Milosz:

> Do not die out, fire. Enter my dreams, love.
> Be young forever, seasons of the earth.[39]

Even Dylan Thomas's famous poem captures the spirit:

> Do not go gentle into that good night,
> Old age should burn and rave at close of day;
> Rage, rage, against the dying of the light.

I understand these lines, which Thomas called his "forked lightning," not as embittered, cynical atheism, but as the pure passion of an unbeatable force that he sensed in himself and in all mortal beings. He shocks us in the last stanza:

> And you, my father, there on the sad height,
> Curse, bless, me now with your fierce tears, I pray.
> Do not go gentle into that good night.
> Rage, rage, against the dying of the light.[40]

God's height is sad, because it lacks the fomenting vitality of human lives, like Thomas's own. The poet asks for God's curse as well as his blessing; he doesn't want safety, he wants energy, tumult, creation. This poem is a paean of the undefeatable spirit of life in its tragic and fiery mortal garb. It exemplifies meaningful death, not as sweet, exhausted resignation, but as unrelenting nature. It might as well have been written by a jaguar or a thunderstorm as by a man.

There is a widespread belief, found in Islam, Catholicism, Theravada Buddhism, Tibetan Mahayana Buddhism, that a person's last thought determines what will happen to him at the moment after death. Sometimes this is thought of in a magical way, as when the American Catholic high school students asked their Jesuit teacher whether, if they live as chaste Catholic boys, but happen to have one "dirty" thought at the moment they are killed in a car crash, will they then be condemned to burn in hell, based on the coincidental superimposition of that one thought on their death-moment. As I understand the meaning of this folk belief, however, it is a neophytic form of causal thinking. The point is not that a coincidence of thought and event will provoke a loutish God to leap upon some innocent good boy and skewer him. The point is that there is no coincidence. In a causal universe, the last thought is a product of a life of thoughts. Our deepest habits emerge from a life of habit-building. Our reaction to death itself begins when we are children.[41] In the intensive care unit, doctors can watch the rabbi mutter Hebrew prayers, and the mother ask about her child's welfare—someone else complains about the nurses. Each of these innocent gestures are repetitions of lifetime habits. Taken less literally, this folk belief reminds us that each moment is a launching pad, that we are always living towards dying. Stephen Levine puts it beautifully:

> It doesn't seem to matter whether one has lived twenty years or seventy years, at its end that life seems to have been exhausted in a single moment. The past is irretrievably gone but the sense of being is ever present. Indeed, if one asks someone right at the edge of death if they feel any less alive at that moment than they have at any other time in their life, they will say no. Those who follow life to where it resides in the heart live life fully.

He quotes the Indian poet, Kabir: "What is found now is found then."[42] Lifton's phrase is "continuing open search."[43]

In her book *This Timeless Moment*, Laura Huxley describes how her husband, Aldous Huxley, died, living to the end with his mixture of scientific curiosity and open-mindedness, literary commitment, and worldwide friendship. But the heart of Huxley's last quest was a question and a method that the author of the *Perennial Philosophy* felt would lead him to the deepest truth: "How can I love you more?"[44]

In sad contradistinction, the retired professor, with whose story I started this chapter, was unable to reopen to life, unable to rage like Dylan Thomas or love like Aldous Huxley. From the hospital, he sought exit into a nursing home, using his crippled leg as an excuse. There, his wife informed me, he dried up into a living husk. I believe that this last habit had actually started when he got polio sixty-plus years ago, and when his father's death had left him bereaved; it was also rooted in an arid cultural style.

Meaningful death need not imply heightened drama. It may just as well incorporate measured removal, dignified diminution.

In May 1986, the *American Journal of Psychiatry* published an article by two doctors, one alive, one dead.[45] The deceased author had kept his notes on the cases that he treated as he was dying of lymphoma. He studied his patients' reactions to his illness, and his reactions to their reactions. He sought consultation and at death left his notes to a colleague, who initiated follow-up on the patients in question. Although the deceased author nobly strove to remain engaged and helpful right unto his last, his own case notes and his colleague's follow-up revealed that effort to have been unwise. By and large, concluded the colleague, the patients had been more hindered than helped by this brave effort, and he suggested that psychotherapists must incorporate a sense of timely withdrawal into their work, to balance their sense of ongoing commitments. There is a time to stop.

Rude or sophisticated, people live, work, suffer, and grow in reference to their sense of future that lies beyond the closed door. A meaningful life leads to meaningful death, which on the one hand, is the last moment in a series, an extension, culmination, and conclusion of a chain of routine, life-oriented actions and mind-moments. On the other hand, it is a unique sphere unto itself, in which beliefs, habits, values, strengths, fears, courage, and individuation specifically organized around death prepare each person for their encounter with the loss of themselves and an immersion into the unfathomed. Long before this plunge, we are preparing for the event. The light of life circles a cone of darkness reaching back into us from the future.

When a whole life has been called up from inside a being, and part for part has gone out to meet the world, until every inner secret has become a force to shift reality towards that which joins together, then the fear of the loss of individual existence will have been transcended. This outward-turning, other-serving way perceives a halo of an exalting mystery diffusing out from the edges of the everyday, towards the infinite unknown. Religious ritual, liturgy, symbol—private and idiosyncratic, or public and sacramentalized—is also the realm of the more, the sublime, through which a person can live in reference to what happens when the hour glass breaks, and the sand pours out.

> I saw, in the twilight of flagging consciousness,
> My body floating down an ink-black stream . . .
>   . . . as it drifted on and on
> Its outlines dimmed . . .
> Dark formlessness settled over all diversity . . .
>   As shadow, as particles, my body
> Fused with endless night. I came to rest
> At the altar of the stars. Alone, amazed, I stared
> Upwards with hands clasped and said: "Sun, you have removed
> Your rays: show now your loveliest, kindliest form
> That I may see the Person who dwells in me as in you"[46]

The psychotherapist has only rare opportunities to see a meaningful death evoked through his or her work. More often, we are witnesses to the opposite, like the retired professor who felt suicidal despair at the end of his compulsive, compensatory, lonely life.

A poignant opportunity to facilitate a meaningful death was described to me by my colleague, Dr. Stephen Dashef:

MEANINGFUL DEATH

In her move towards death, this stage and movie actress unexpectedly re-experienced her childhood pain and terror, that once had rendered her unable to use words, and that now, as an adult of forty-eight years, returned with a horror that left her unable even to dream at night. She thought of how to enlist the help of others in killing herself. Here she was, dying in a health care center near the Southern Academy for the Performing Arts which she had come to love, feeling enraged and disdainful of her medical caretakers, and full of self-pity and remorse. Her shoulders and hips ached severely, her muscles were weakening, her legs did not move, and hands barely functioned. Her once powerful voice was growing more halting and softer. She feared the ultimate strangulation of drowning in her own secretions.

A religious counselor had not helped, for her childhood rejection by her own mother had led her away from traditional belief in anything. Feeling again like the three year old foundling child she had once been—now being injected with needles, and unprotected and paralyzed—she desperately asked to talk with a psychiatrist, who was called and came to see her. We met, and agreed to continue twice a week, for what turned out to be twenty sessions before her death.

As a five-year old, she had been rescued from the orphanage by married friends of her biological parents, and had been raised to the best of their abilities. Her adoptive mother had been a concerned, morally rigid woman. Her adoptive father was a withdrawn man given to angry outbursts and physical punishment when distressed, especially about issues of sexuality. At twelve years, her sexual fate was prematurely foreclosed when teachers and her father had humiliated and hit her for sexual exploration with a young male friend. Despite some fantasizing about dating with me, she consolidated her sexual and loving feelings more predominantly in relationships with women.

She read voraciously, loved the adventure of high speed motorcycle and car driving, and exposed herself to peoples of diverse cultures while traveling the world professionally. She had been vigorous, charming and impressive. Only when illness forced her to give up acting had her mood darkened, her pessimism reemerged, and anger and fearfulness returned to dominate her life, especially in the darkness of the night.

Special duty nurses had been coming and going from her bedside, but when a nurse whom she particularly liked left, her childhood abandonment pain repossessed her. For this depression she wanted no medication, which doctors had previously offered, but rather the chance to talk about it, which friends were fearful of doing for fear of worsening her intensely painful state. "I fear losing my breathing . . . I have no protection and no recourse . . . I sleep fitfully . . . I am at the mercy of this disease twenty-four hours a day," she related.

In the next two and a half months she worked on the arduous task of giving up and grieving her supportive, loving connections with others and with bodily life itself. I encouraged her to exercise active choices within limits, and to overcome her earlier, regressive tendency to self-directed rage. As in all therapy, we paid attention to both present stress and past contributions to her dilemma, thus allowing a future-orientation to live on until her death.

In dealing with her present, the illness itself, her self-esteem was enhanced when she actively responded to change. She needed help to let the staff know when she was angry, and to actively solicit the nursing care she desired. This expressed and facilitated her need for witnessed significance. Because she had begun to experience dying as an activity, not a prison, she accepted medication for her physical pain, without guilt, decided to allow a gastrostomy to be performed to slow down her loss of weight, and helped develop and use charts for spelling out words when her speech failed. Her need for lawful order was restored through a responsive relationship with a newly hired physician.

In her final days, after a lengthy discussion in which her wish for life but fear of prolonging her own pain became clear, she decided, with her physician's concurrence, not to be put on a respirator and to let nature take its ultimate course. Her need for release surfaced in massive grieving over the advent of her death, and with rage at her restriction—not being able to shop for friends at holiday time, as they could for her. Towards the end, she said she felt like a rocket ready to take off, ready for the ultimate release from her watch over her body's decline.

Past issues were reworked, too, as they resurfaced. Initially, her need for lawful order had been threatened by her abandonment depression, and her tendency to withdraw in the face of anxiety, physical pain and her loss of precious speech. In expressing and restituting the need for lawful order by requesting and sustaining psychotherapy, she not only talked more actively but again began remembering and reporting dreams. In one dream she saw herself as a hurt animal, which she had the instinct to shoot. Later she dreamed of human connection: her friends and I were present, and she saw herself anchored by guidewires. Following a difficult visit with her father, in which rage and disappointment returned, her awareness of sacrifice and her need for affirming acceptance enabled her to express her sorrow that she had not sustained intimate sexual relationships with men and had not borne children. With this subsequent self-acceptance, her emotional storm subsided.

To the end, her need for calling and membership persisted. She planned a performance, to be done by others, of her favorite scenes from theatre and from film: a prearranged event to be given posthumously at the arts academy. Her worldview—her belief in personal courage and interpersonal love—was transmitted to friends by arranging for their continued visits throughout her final illness, and in personal communications, such as the spontaneous handing of a rose to her therapist after a difficult session. Her need for nurturing love and her transmission of love outlived her distress. After lapsing into a coma for twenty minutes during her final session, she awoke with a beatific smile etched on her face, asked that the therapist hold up her chart, and with much effort, pointed to the word "love." She died her meaningful death the next morning, having shared her life and love with her friends and having received theirs, leaving behind her theatrical performance for their enjoyment and inspiration.

Such a meaningful death is a transition for all who participate. Both the dying and their witnesses feel the need that Elisabeth Kübler-Ross expressed as: "The sense that their communications might be important, might be meaningful to others . . . a sense of service."[48] Solitude, selfhood, resonate with a deepening intimacy forged by the commonality of our shared loneliness. There is a sense of proportion, about what one *had* to do, and what *couldn't* be accomplished. The least religious or superstitious persons will still feel themselves to be in the presence of an unknown. A door opens. Both the dying and those with them who do not close off in fear, feel deepening love, and life itself never feels more ephemeral and indomitable. Those who remain know that something has vanished, but their own lives are supercharged. All of life feels exposed and mysterious. Any psychotherapy that travels into the heart of a person's life will knock upon that door—no matter how many years to go until it will have to open. Serious, life-transforming conversation contains within it space for the expansion into our presence, from out of the invisible, of an unnamable presence that sweeps away everything before it and leaves us trembling and blessed.

Elisabeth Kübler-Ross concluded: "Watching a peaceful death of a human being reminds us of a falling star."[49] She was undoubtedly influenced by the lines that the aging, bedridden Tagore had written:

> That a great hymn
> To light should swell from the inmost cavern of my being
> And reach to the realm of light at the edge of creation—
> That was why you sent for me.[50]

Zimmer, the mythologist, was also speaking for science when he wrote: "Nothing dies, nothing perishes, nothing suffers annihilation utterly. No virtue, no energy is lost. Destruction—death—is but an outer mask of transformation . . ."[51] When our wave of energy rises up, and, in human form, we reach to pick the fruit of life, we are creating and destroying the visible world. Each action, each motion of the hand, and every whispered word is the world flow in transformation. The death we conceive of is our conception and not death the inconceivable.

Conclusion

Psychotherapists continuously listen to the hesitant phrasing, and often to the whole and complete if intermittent clauses, of the universal struggle to speak this one compound sentence:

At the conclusion of life, I would hope to say: I was seen and known, heart and soul, and in the same way knew those who circled me; I bowed to the one who opens in dawn, and I lived in harmony with the order, the principles, the laws of the day; I knew myself, saw myself, and held in one embrace human faults, limits and successes; I did my job, working in the common cause; and I stirred up dust with my feet, tramping along in the undivided march of human history; I laid down my burden and surrendered myself to the voice of the river, and I became a vessel, and out of me poured the fountain of life; and when I looked up I saw one hand spinning the divine wheel of the world; and I looked down, and knelt, lending my hand; and I continued on my way, shouldering my own pain as I followed the signs; and now that I feel the chill of death upon me, I can sing of how I was sent forth, and who calls me home.

Kabir wrote:

If your soul is no stranger to you, the whole world is your home.[1]

Psychotherapy can be practiced as a midwife to this sentence, feeling it quicken in every hour of healing words.

Notes

PREFACE

1. Fleischman, P. *The Therapeutic Action of Vipassana Meditation;* and *Why I Sit.* Buddhist Publication Society, wheel no. 329/330; Kandy, Sri Lanka, 1986.

INTRODUCTION

1. Eliade, M. *Myths, Dreams, and Mysteries.* Harper & Row, Torchbooks, New York, 1960, 17–18.
2. James, W. *The Varieties of Religious Experience.* Doubleday, New York, 1902, 40–41.
3. Jung, C.G. *Psychology and Religion.* Yale University Press, New Haven, Ct., and London, 1938, 59.

1: WITNESSED SIGNIFICANCE

1. See for example: Kohut, H. *The Analysis of the Self.* International University Press, Madison, Ct., 1971. Kernberg, O. *Borderline Condi-*

tions and Pathological Narcissism. Jason Aronson, New York, 1975.

2. Ps. 101, The Holy Bible (Hebrew).
3. Ps. 141.
4. *The Bhagavad Gita,* J. Mascaró, trans. Penguin, New York, 1962, Ch. 9, Verses XVII–XVIII.
5. *Koran Interpreted,* Arberry, A.J., trans. Macmillan, New York, 1955, 109, 113, 142.
6. Matt. 7.7; 5.18; 10.26; 12.36, The Holy Bible.
7. Frank., J. *Persuasion and Healing.* Schocken Books, New York, 1974. See Ch. VII.
8. Bowers, M.J. "Pathogenesis of Acute Schizophrenic Psychosis." *Archives General Psychiatry,* vol. 19 (September 1968), 350–351.
9. Zimmer, H. "Some Biographical Remarks," Appendix to *Artistic Form and Yoga in the Sacred Images of India.* Princeton University Press, Princeton, N.J., 1984, 260.
10. See for example: Zimmer, H. *The Art of Indian Asia,* J. Campbell, ed., 2 vols. Princeton University Press, Princeton, N.J., 1955. See also, n. 9, above; Ch. II, n. 3; and Ch. VII, n. 13.
11. Jung, C.G. *Mandala Symbolism,* Princeton University Press, Princeton, N.J., 1959. See also "The Self" in vol. 9, part II, of the *Complete Works,* Princeton University Press, Princeton, N.J., 1972.
12. *The Confessions of St. Augustine,* F.J. Sheed, trans. Sheed and Ward, New York, 1942.
13. Gandhi, M.K. *The Story of My Experiments with Truth, An Autobiography,* M. Desai, trans. Navajivan Publishing House, Ahmedabad, India, 1927.
14. Fischer, L. *Gandhi.* New American Library, Mentor, New York, 1954.
15. See notes 13 and 14 above; also *Gandhi's Truth,* Erik H. Erikson, W.W. Norton, New York, 1969, 166.
16. See Erikson. Ibid., 448.
17. Buber, M. "What Is Common to All," in *The Knowledge of Man,* M. Friedman, ed. Harper & Row, Torchbooks, New York, 1965.
18. John 1.1, The Holy Bible.
19. Buber, M. "The Word That Is Spoken," in *Knowledge of Man.* See n. 17, above, 113.
20. Ps. 102.

NOTES

2: LAWFUL ORDER

1. Freud, S. *The Future of an Illusion.* Doubleday, Anchor, Garden City, N.Y., 31–36.
2. See for example: Rahula, W. *What the Buddha Taught.* Grove Press, New York, 1974. Nyanatiloka. *The Word of the Buddha.* Buddhist Pub. Soc., Kandy, Sri Lanka, 1967. For original texts in translation see for example: *Buddhist Scriptures,* Conze, E., ed. Penguin, New York, 1959. *Dhammapada,* Mascaró, J., trans. Penguin, New York, 1963.
3. See for example: Zimmer, H. *Philosophies of India,* Campbell, J., ed. Bollingen/Princeton, Princeton, N.J., 1969. *Hindu Myths,* O'Flaherty, W., trans. Penguin, New York, 1975. *The Loves of Krishna,* Archer, W.G. Grove Press, New York.
4. Eliade, M., *The Sacred and the Profane,* W. R. Trask, trans. Harcourt, Brace & World, Harvest, New York, 1957.
5. *Dhammapada.* See n. 2, above, 35.
6. Tagore, R. *The Religion of Man.* Beacon, Boston, 1961.
7. Buber, M. *I and Thou,* W. Kaufmann, ed. Scribners, New York, 1970, 151 and 181.
8. Koran. See Ch. I, n. 5, 105. Also I Timothy, 2:11–12.
9. Edgerton, F. "The Origins of Hindu Speculation," in *The Bhagavad Gita.* Harvard University Press, Cambridge, Mass., 1972.
10. *The Bhagavad Gita,* See Ch. I, n. 4, 71.
11. Tolstoy, L. *The Kingdom of God Is Within You.* University Nebraska Press, Lincoln, Neb., 1984, 368.
12. Eccles. ii.13, The Holy Bible.
13. The Upanishads, J. Mascaró, trans. Penguin, London, 1965, 118.

3: AFFIRMING ACCEPTANCE

1. Job: 40.4, 40.6–7, 42.6–12, The Holy Bible.
2. Koran. See Ch. I, n. 5, 175.
3. Matt. 4.17, 5.29; John 5.24.
4. Buber, M. "The Way of Man According to the Teachings of Hasidism," in *Religion from Tolstoy to Camus,* W. Kaufmann, ed. Harper & Row, Torchbooks, New York, 1961.
5. Rahula, W. *What the Buddha Taught,* rev. ed. Grove Press, New York, 1974, 3.

6. Eliade, M. *Yoga, Immortality and Freedom,* W.R. Trask, trans. Princeton University Press, Princeton, N.J., 1970. 29f.
7. Zimmer, H. *Philosophies of India.* See Ch. II, n. 3, 175.
8. Naipaul, V.S. *Among the Believers.* Knopf, New York, 1981.
9. James, W. *Varieties of Religious Experience.* See Introduction, n. 2, 281–284.
10. O'Flaherty, W.D. *Women, Androgynes, and Other Mythical Beasts.* University of Chicago, Chicago, 1980.
11. John 8.7.
12. "Phaedrus," from *The Works of Plato,* J. Edman, ed. Random House, Modern Library, New York, 329.
13. Buber, M. "Distance and Relation," in *The Knowledge of Man.* See Ch. I, n. 17, 71.

4: CALLING

1. Jung, C.G. *Memories, Dreams, Reflections,* A. Jaffe, ed. Random House, New York, 1961, 170. Following quotes are from pp. 192 and 199.
2. Jung, C.G. "The Development of Personality," in *The Collected Works of C.J. Jung,* R.F.C. Hull, trans. Princeton University Press, Princeton, N.J., vol. 17.
3. Matthiessen, P. *The Snow Leopard.* Viking Press, New York, 1978.
4. Erikson, E. *Identity, Youth, and Crisis.* W.W. Norton, New York, 1968.
5. Erikson, E. " 'Identity Crisis' in Autobiographic Perspective," in *Life History and the Historical Moment.* W.W. Norton, New York, 1975, 18–20.
6. Erikson, E. *Young Man Luther.* W.W. Norton, New York, 1958.
7. Erikson, E. *Gandhi's Truth.* See Ch. I, n. 15.
8. Gandhi, M.K. See Ch. I, n. 13, 198.
9. *The Bhagavad Gita.* See Ch. I, n. 4, 59.
10. Zimmer, H. See Ch. II, n. 3, 152–153.
11. deBary, W.T., ed., *Sources of Indian Tradition.* Columbia University Press, New York, 1958, 13.
12. See for example: Eliade, M. *Gods, Goddesses, and Myths of Creation,* vol. I of *From Primitives to Zen, A Source Book of the History of Religions.* Harper & Row, New York, 1967.

13. Palmer, R.R. *A History of the Modern World.* Knopf, New York, 1964, 144, 158–159, 284–285.
14. Buck, W. *Ramayana.* University of California Press, Berkeley, Calif., 1976. Buck, W. *Mahabharata.* University of California Press, Berkeley, Calif., 1973.
15. Gandhi. See. n. 13, Ch. 1, p. 343.
16. Gandhi. 102.
17. "Apology." In *The Works of Plato.* See Ch. III, n. 12.
18. Thoreau, H.D. "Civil Disobedience," in *The Portable Thoreau,* C. Bode, ed. Viking Press, New York, 1947.
19. von Franz, M-L. *C.G. Jung, His Myth in Our Time,* W. Kennedy, trans. Little Brown, Boston, 1975, 99–100.
20. Eliade, M. See Introduction, n. 1, 75–81.
21. Eliade, M. *From Medicine Men to Muhammed,* Part 4 of *From Primitives to Zen, A Source Book of the History of Religions.* Harper & Row, New York, 1967, 3–25.
22. See for example: Storm, H. *Seven Arrows.* Ballantine, New York, 1972.
23. Erikson, E. "Hunters Across the Prairie," in *Childhood and Society,* rev. ed. W.W. Norton, New York, 1963, 150–157.
24. Smith, J. *The Book of Mormon* and *Doctrine and Covenants of the Church of Jesus Christ of the Latter Day Saints.* Salt Lake City, 1981, History 1:30–33.
25. Buber, M. *I and Thou.* See Ch. 2, n. 7, 92, 102, 103, 108, 109.
26. Isa. 60.19.
27. Mascaró, J. "Introduction," *The Upanishads.* See Ch. II, n. 13.
28. Buber, M. "The Way of Man According to the Teachings of Hasidism," in Kaufmann, W., ed., *Religion from Tolstoy to Camus.* Harper, New York, 1964, 429.
29. Dostoevsky, F. *Crime and Punishment,* M. Scammell, trans. Washington Square Press, New York, 1966.
30. Coyne, M. "Iran Under the Ayatollah." *National Geographic,* vol. 168, no. 1, July 1985.
31. Mehta, V. "Mahatma Gandhi and His Apostles," *New Yorker,* May 10, 17, 24, 1976. See Part II, "In the Steps of the Autobiographer," 122–123.
32. Kazantzakis, N. *Report to Greco,* P.A. Bien, trans. Simon & Schuster, New York, 1965, 16, 207, 416, 422, 480.
33. Erikson, E., "Human Strength and the Cycle of Generations," in *Insight and Responsibility.* W.W. Norton, New York, 1964.

34. Lifton, R.J., *The Life of the Self.* Simon & Schuster, New York, 1976, 148.
35. Tagore, R. *Gitanjali.* Macmillan, New York, 1913, no. 16.

5: MEMBERSHIP

1. Williams, W.C., "The Yachts," in *Selected Poems.* New Directions, N.Y., 1949. 77.
2. Jung, C.G. See Introduction, n. 3, p
3. Eliade, M. *The Myth of the Eternal Return.* Princeton University Press, Princeton, N.J., 1954.
4. Canetti, E. *Crowds and Power.* Continuum, New York, 1962, 15, 142.
5. David-Neel, A. *Magic and Mystery in Tibet.* Dover, New York, 1971.
6. Huxley, A. *The Doors of Perception.* Harper & Row, New York, 1954, 18.
7. Buber, M. "What is Common to All." See Ch. 1, n. 17, 100.
8. *The Philosophy of Plato.* See Ch. III, n. 12, xii.
9. Reston, J. *Our Father Who Art in Hell: The Life and Death of Jim Jones.* New York Times Books, New York, 1981.
10. Bion, W.R. *Experiences in Groups.* Basic Books, 1959.
11. Rioch, M.J. "The Work of Wilfred Bion on Groups," in *Psychiatry,* vol. 33, no. 1, February 1970, 60.
12. Erikson, E. *Gandhi's Truth.* See Ch. I, n. 15, 431–433, 434.
13. Freud, S. *Future of an Illusion.* See Ch. II, n. 1. 18, 23, 24.
14. Erikson, E. See n. 12, above, 431–432.
15. Canetti, E. See n. 4, above, 94–95, 128, 141–143.
16. Freud, S. *Totem and Taboo,* The Standard Edition of the Complete Psychological Works, ed. and trans. Hogarth, London, 1953–74.
17. Fromm, E. *Psychoanalysis and Religion.* Yale University Press, New Haven, Ct., and London, Ch. 4.
18. "Doctrine and Covenants," 1:8, 1:30, *The Book of Mormon and Doctrine and Covenants of the Church of Jesus Christ of Latter-Day Saints.* Salt Lake City, 1981. See also n. 24, Ch. 4.
19. Koran. See Ch. I, no. 5, vol. 2: 59, 229.
20. Mark 13.8, 13.13; John, 15.19.; Matthew 10.22, 12.30.
21. Ps. 76, 79.

NOTES

22. Hay, M.V. "Europe and the Jews," in *Religion from Tolstoy to Camus*, Kaufmann, W., ed. See Ch. III, n. 4, pp. 341, 343, 355.
23. "Articles of Faith of the Church of Jesus Christ of Latter-Day Saints," 61. *The Book of Mormon* and *Doctrine*. See n. 18, above.
24. Koran. See Ch. I, n. 5, vol. 1: 53, 134–135.
25. Matt. 22.39; 25.35–37.
26. Isa. 2.4
27. Fisher, L. *Gandhi*. See Ch. IV, n. 14, p. 154.
28. Freud, S. See n. 13, above, 97.
29. Fromm, E. See n. 17, above, 18–19.
30. Eiseley, L. "How Man Became Natural," in *The Firmament of Time*. Atheneum, New York, 1967, 113.
31. Frank, J. *Persuasion and Healing*. Johns Hopkins University Press, Baltimore, 1961, 59.
32. See, for example: Galanter, M., "Charismatic Religious Sects and Psychiatry: An Overview," *American Journal of Psychiatry*, 139:12, December, 1982, 1539–1548. Caplan, G., "Mastery of Stress: Psychosocial Aspects," *American Journal of Psychiatry*, 138:4, April, 1981, 413–420. Pattison, E.M., and Pattison, M.L., "Ex-Gays: Religiously Mediated Changes in Homosexuals," *American Journal of Psychiatry*, 137:12, December, 1980, 1553–1562. Griffith, E.E.H., and Mahy, G.E., "Psychological Benefits of Spiritual Baptist Mourning," *American Journal of Psychiatry*, 141:6, June, 1984, 769–773. Kakar, S., *Shamans, Mystics, and Doctors*, Beacon Press, Boston, 1982.
33. *Bill on Alcoholism*, Alcoholics Anonymous World Service, New York.
34. Underhill, E. *Mysticism*. E.P. Dutton, New York, 1961, 260–261.
35. White, L. "The Historical Roots of Our Ecologic Crisis," *Science*, vol. 155: 1203–1207.
36. *Koran*. See Ch. I, n. 5, p. 207.
37. For references to *ahimsa* in Gandhi's life and to his relationship to the Jain mystic Raychandbhai, see *Gandhi's Truth*, Ch. I, n. 15; and *The Story of My Experiments with Truth, An Autobiography*, Ch. I, n. 13. For introductions to Jain doctrines, see *Philosophies of India*, Ch. III, n. 3; and Basham, A.L., *The Wonder That Was India*. Grove Press, New York, 1954.
38. Suzuki, D.T., "The Role of Nature in Zen Buddhism," in *Zen Buddhism, Selected Writings of D.T. Suzuki*, W. Barrett, ed. Doubleday, Anchor, 1956.

39. Fromm, E., Suzuki, D.T., and DeMartino, R. *Zen Buddhism and Psychoanalysis.* Harper & Row Colophon, New York, 1970, 1–15.
40. See *Bhagavad Gita,* J. Mascaró, trans. Ch. 1, n. 4, p. 71.

6: *RELEASE*

1. Fromm, E. *Psychoanalysis and Religion.* See Ch. V, n. 17, pp. 4–25.
2. James, W. *The Varieties of Religious Experience.* See Introduction, n. 2, p. 265.
3. Tolstoy, L. "My Religion," in *Religion from Tolstoy to Camus.* See n. 4, Ch. 3, p. 50.
4. Nyanatiloka, *The Word of the Buddha.* See Ch. II, n. 2, p. 25.
5. *Koran.* See n. 5, Ch. 1. This line is repeated as a refrain, 215.
6. Matt. 6.26–34.
7. Frost, R. "Stopping by Woods on a Snowy Evening," in *Selected Poems of Robert Frost.* Holt, Rinehart, Winston, New York, 1963, 140.
8. Whitman, W. "Song of Myself, 5 and 32," in *Leaves of Grass.* New American Library, New York, 1960.
9. Quoted in Huxley, A. *The Perennial Philosophy.* Harper & Row, Colophon, 1970, 63.
10. Quoted in Katayiri Roshi. *Udumbara.* Publication of the the Minneapolis Zen Center, Minneapolis, 6.
11. Suzuki, D.T. *Zen Buddhism.* See Ch. V, n. 38.
12. Buber, M. *Tales of the Hasidim,* 2 vols. Schocken Books, New York, 1947. See Vol. I: 104, 107, 125.
13. Frankl, V. "Basic Concepts of Logotherapy," in *Man's Search for Meaning.* Washington Square Press, New York. 1963. See also Frankl, V.. *The Doctor and the Soul,* R. and C. Winston, trans. Vintage, New York, 1955.
14. Frankl, V. See n. 13, above, 214.
15. Ps. 23.
16. Tagore, R. *Gitanjali.* See Ch. IV, n. 35, no. 1.
17. Dubovsky, S.L. "Psychiatry in Saudi Arabia." *American Journal of Psychiatry,* 140:11, November 1983, pp. 1455–1459.
18. Ranade, R.D. *Mysticism in India.* State University of New York Press, Albany, N.Y., 1983, 49, 50.

19. Baba, M. *Life at Its Best.* Meher Era Publications, Poona, India, 21.
20. Trungpa, C. *Cutting Through Spiritual Materialism.* Shambala, Berkeley, Calif., 1973, 37.
21. Deut. 6:5.
22. Tillich, P. *Dynamics of Faith.* Harper & Row, Torchbooks, New York, 1958, 2, 3.
23. Deutsch, A. "Tenacity of Attachment to a Cult Leader: Psychiatric Perspective," *American Journal of Psychiatry,* 137:12, December 1980, pp. 1569–1573. Deutsch, A. "Observations on a Sidewalk Ashram," *Archives General Psychiatry,* 1975, no. 32, pp. 166–175.
24. FitzGerald, F. "Rajneeshpuram." *New Yorker,* September 22 and September 29, 1986.
25. Randi, J. "Be Healed in the Name of God," in *Faith Healer, Miracle or Fraud. Free Inquiry,* vol. 6, no. 2, Spring 1986, 17.
26. Suzuki, S. *Zen Mind, Beginner's Mind.* Weatherhill, New York and Tokyo, 1970.
27. Butler, K. "Events Are the Teacher." In *Co-Evolution Quarterly,* no. 40, winter, 1983, pp. 112–123. The quote is from *Editorial Comments* by Stewart Brand, 112.
28. Minkin, S. "Exploring the Path to Enlightenment: Goenka on Vipassana Yoga," in *East West Journal,* December, 1982.
29. Babb, L.A. *Redemptive Encounters.* University of California Press, Berkeley and Los Angeles, 1986.
30. Snyder, G. "Four Changes," in *Turtle Island.* New Directions, New York, 1975.
31. St. Augustine. *Confessions of St. Augustine,* F.J. Sheed, trans. Sheed & Ward, New York, 1942.
32. St. Augustine. *The Basic Writings of St. Augustine,* W. Oates, ed., Random House, New York, 1948.
33. James. W. See n. 2, above, 107, 195.
34. *Ghazals of Ghalib,* A. Ahmad, ed. Columbia University Press, New York, 1971.
35. Uchiyama, K., *Approach to Zen.* Japan Pub., Tokyo, 1973, 79.
36. *The Lankavatara Sutra,* D.T. Suzuki, trans. Prajna Press, Boulder, Colo., 1978, 17, 56.
37. Freud, S. *The Standard Edition of the Complete Psychological Works,* J. Strachey, ed. and trans. Hogarth, London, 1953–74, vol. 5: 525.
38. *Koran.* See Ch. I, n. 5, vol. 1: 287–288.

39. *Bill on Alcoholism.* See Ch. V, n. 33.
40. Fromm, E. See n. 1, above, 27.

7: *WORLDVIEW*

1. Redfield, R. *The Little Community and Peasant Society and Culture.* University of Chicago, Chicago, 1960, 95.
2. Buber, M. "Distance and Relation" and "What Is Common to All," in *The Knowledge of Man.* See Chap. I, n. 17, pp. 62, 90.
3. Eliade, M. *Sacred and Profane.* See Ch. II, n. 4, pp. 34, 44, 45.
4. Dhammapada, S.N. Goenka, trans., in "Words of Dhamma" Igatpuri, India.
5. James, W. *Varieties of Religious Experience.* See Introduction, n. 2, 454.
6. *Ramayana,* William Buck, trans. Mentor, New York, 1978, xxxi.
7. Eliade, M. *Myths, Dreams and Mysteries.* See Introduction, n. 1, 14.
8. James, W. Ibid. 458.
9. Kazantzakis, N. *Report to Greco.* See Ch. IV, n. 32, pp. 434, 481, 482.
10. Ibid., 18.
11. Gen. 1.1–3.
12. *Bhagavad Gita,* J. Mascaró, trans. See Ch. I, n. 4, p. 80.
13. Zimmer, H. *Myths and Symbols in Indian Art and Civilization,* J. Campbell, ed. Harper & Row, New York, 1946, 16.
14. Eliade, M. *From Medicine Men to Muhammed,* Part 4 of *From Primitives to Zen, A Source Book of the History of Religions.* See Ch. IV, n. 21.
15. Conze, E. *Buddhist Meditation.* Harper & Row, New York, 1956.
16. Eliade, M. *Shamanism: Archaic Techniques of Ecstasy.* Bollingen, New York, 1964.
17. Einstein, A. Quoted in: *Spring on an Arctic Island,* K. Scherman, Little Brown, Boston, 1956.
18. Carson, R. *The Sense of Wonder.* Harper & Row, New York, 1956, 42–43.
19. Whitman, W. "Beginning My Studies," in *Leaves of Grass.* New American Library, New York, 1960.
20. *Bhagavad Gita.* Ibid., 89–92.
21. Goodchild, P. *J. Robert Oppenheimer: Shatterer of Worlds.* Fromm International Press, New York, 1985, 162.
22. Nyanatiloka. *The Word of the Buddha.* See Ch. II, n. 2.

23. Shelley, P.B. "Ozymandias," in *Poems,* C.F. Main, P.J. Seng. Wadsworth, Belmont, Calif., 1961.
24. Eccles., 1.6; 1.13–18.
25. Tillich, P. *The Dynamics of Faith.* Harper & Row, New York, 1957.
26. Pauck, W., and Pauck, M. *Paul Tillich, His Life and Thought,* 2 vols. Harper & Row, New York, 1976.
27. Tillich, P. *The Courage to Be,* Yale University Press, New Haven, Ct., 1952.
28. Erikson, E. *Gandhi's Truth.* See Ch. I, n. 15, p. 381.
29. Matt., 10.34.
30. Meissner, W.W. *Psychoanalysis and Religious Experience.* Yale University Press, New Haven, Ct., 1984.
31. Eliade, M. *Myths, Dreams and Mysteries.* See Introduction, n. 1, 63.
32. Lifton, R.J. *The Life of the Self.* See Ch. IV, n. 34, p. 27.
33. Ibid., 31.
34. Erikson, E. "Human Strength and the Cycle of Generations." See Chap. IV, n. 33, 125–127.
35. Erikson, E. "On the Revolt of Humanist Youth," in *Life History and the Historical Moment.* W.W. Norton, New York, 1975, 209.
36. St. Augustine. *Confessions.* See Ch. IV, n. 31, pp. 47–48.
37. Kazantzakis, N. *Report to Greco.* 24.

8: HUMAN LOVE

1. See Ch. I, n. 1.
2. Lasch, C. *The Culture of Narcissism.* W.W. Norton, New York, 1978.
3. Kernberg, O. see Ch. I, n. 1.
4. Szasz, T. *The Myth of Mental Illness.* Hoeber-Harper, New York, 1961.
5. Tillich, P. See Ch. VII, n. 25.
6. Jung, C.G., et al. *Man and His Symbols.* Dell, New York, 1968.
7. Rank, O. *The Myth of the Birth of the Hero,* F. Robins, S.E. Jelliffe, R. Buenner, trans. New York, 1952.
8. Becker, E. *The Denial of Death.* Free Press, New York, 1973.
9. Bellah, R.N., et al. *Habits of the Heart.* Harper & Row, New York, 1985.
10. Zimmer, H. See Ch. II, n. 3.

11. Erikson, E. See Ch. IV, n. 23.

12. Henry, J. *Culture Against Man.* Knopf, New York, 1963, 286–287.

13. McNeill, W. *The Rise of the West.* University of Chicago, Chicago, 1963, 19.

14. Zimmer, H. "The Goddess," in *Myths and Symbols in Indian Art and Civilization,* J. Campbell, ed. Harper & Row, New York, 1946. For a discussion of the Great Mother: Neumann, E. *The Great Mother, An Analysis of the Archetype.* Princeton University Press Princeton, N.J., 1963. For a discussion of the underlying family constellation that might relate to goddess worship, see Kakar, S. *The Inner World: A Psychoanalytic Study of Childhood and Society in India.* Oxford University, 2nd ed., 1981, Chap. 3. Also, pp. 160–181 contain an excellent psychohistorical case study of worship of the Great Mother. See also, Bharati, A.. *The Tantric Tradition.* Doubleday, Anchor, Garden City, New York, 1970. O'Flaherity, W.D. *Hindu Myths.* Penguin, New York 1975; 64–69. O'Flaherity, W.D. *Women, Androgynes, and Other Mythical Beasts.* University of Chicago, Chicago, 1980, 65–143. Mookerjee, A. *Tantra Art.* Ravi Kumar. New Delhi, 1971.

15. Williams, W.C. *Pictures from Brueghel.* New Directions, New York, 1962, 83–86.

16. James, W. See Introduction, n. 2, 312–317.

17. Deut. 10.19.

18. This is a paraphrase of the Lotus Sutra, as quoted in Uchiyama, K. *Approach to Zen.* Japan Pub., Tokyo, 1973, 117.

19. Suzuki, S. *Zen Mind, Beginner's Mind.* Weatherhill, New York and Tokyo, 1970.

20. Fleischman, P. See Preface, n. 1.

21. Fromm, E. *The Art of Loving.* Harper & Row, New York, 1956, 38.

22. Nanamoli Thera. *The Practice of Loving-Kindness.* Wheel no. 7, Buddhist Publication Society, Kandy Sri Lanka, 1981. See also: Nyanaponika Maha Thera. *The Four Sublime States.* Wheel no. 6, Buddhist Publication Society, Kandy, Sri Lanka, 1980.

23. Matt, 10.35.

24. Matt, 5.44–46.

25. Freud, S. *A General Introduction to Psychoanalysis* Washington Square Press, New York, 1960, 326–27, 377–78.

26. Rust, M. "Flight from Terror Paved Way to Stardom," in *American Medical News,* April 19, 1985.

27. Frankl, V. See Ch. VI, n. 13, 59.
28. Timerman, J. *Prisoner Without a Name, Cell Without a Number*, T. Talbot, trans. Knopf, New York, 1981.
29. Fleischman, P.
30. Brenan, G. *St. John of the Cross.* Cambridge University Press, 1973, 3.
31. Ibid., 145, 165, 175, 179.
32. See for example: Rumi, J.A. *Mystical Poems of Rumi*, A.J. Arberry, trans. University of Chicago, Chicago, 1968. Or, Wightman, G.B.H., and al-Udhari, A.Y. *Birds Through a Ceiling of Alabaster.* Penguin, New York, 1975.
33. See for example: Basho. *The Narrow Road to the Deep North . . .*, N. Yuasa, trans. Penguin, New York 1966. Or, Ryokan. *One Robe, One Bowl.* J. Stevens, trans. Weatherhill, New York and Tokyo, 1977. Or Stryk, L., and Ikemoto, T. *Zen Poems of China and Japan,* Grove Press, New York, 1973.
34. See for example: Archer, W.G. *The Loves of Krishna.* Grove Press, New York. Or Dimock, E.C., and Levertov, D. *In Praise of Krishna,* Doubleday, Anchor, 1967.
35. Buber, M. See Ch. II, n. 7, p. 66.
36. Tagore, R. *Selected Poems,* W. Radice, trans. Penguin, New York, 1985, 49.
37. Fromm, E. 21.
38. Goldstein, J. *The Experience of Insight.* Unity, Santa Cruz, Calif., 1976, 76.
39. I Cor. 13.1–13.
40. Erikson, E. See Ch. IV, n. 23, p. 265.
41. Rumi, J. 85.
42. Tillich, P. *Dynamics of Faith.* See Ch. VII, n. 25.
43. Fromm, E. 21.
44. Tillich, P. See Ch. IV, n. 27, 66.
45. Quoted in Lifton, R.J. See Ch. IV, n. 34, 42.
46. Williams, W.C. 82.
47. Erikson, E. See Ch. I, n. 15.
48. "Across the Universe," on *Let It Be.* The Beatles, Apple Records, New York.
49. Erikson, E. See Ibid, 155.
50. Hay, M.V. "Europe and the Jews," in Kauffman, W., *Religion from Tolstoy to Camus.* See Ch. III, n. 4.

51. Kakar, S. *The Inner World: A Psychoanalytic Study of Childhood and Society in India,* second ed. Oxford University Press, New York, 1981, 202.
52. "Here, There, Everywhere," on *Revolver,* Lennon and McCartney. Capital Records, New York.
53. *Ghazals of Ghalib.* See Ch. VI, n. 34, 7.
54. Tagore, R. 89.
55. *Bhagavad Gita,* 9.26; and 6.29–31. See Ch. 1. n.4

9: SACRIFICE

1. James, W. *Varieties of Religious Experience.* See Introduction, n. 2, 54.
2. Tagore, R. *Gitanjali,* no. 65. See Ch. IV, n. 35.
3. Erikson, E. *Gandhi's Truth.* See Ch. I, n. 15.
4. Eliade, M. *Yoga: Immortality and Freedom.* See Ch. III, n. 6, p. 50.
5. See for example: Bharati, A. *The Ochre Robe.* Doubleday, Garden City, New York, 1970. No discussion or book on Indian culture lacks for references to brahmacharya: see also, for example, the references in Ch. II, n. 3 and Ch. III, n. 10.
6. Fleischman, P. "Ayurveda," *International Journal Social Psychiatry,* vol. 22:4.
7. Rudolph, S. "Self-Control and Political Potency: Gandhi's Asceticism," *The American Scholar,* vol. 35, Winter, 1956, 79–97.
8. Conze, E. *Buddhist Scriptures.* See Ch. II, n. 2, pp. 24–26.
9. Zimmer, H. *Myths and Symbols in Indian Art and Civilization.* See Ch. VII, n. 13, pp. 115–116.
10. Edgerton, F. "The Origins of Hindu Speculation," in *The Bhagavad Gita Translated and Interpreted.* See Ch. II, n. 9, p. 117.
11. Frazer, J.G. *The Golden Bough.* Macmillan, New York, 1963, 308–330.
12. Gen. 22.
13. Kierkegaard, S. *Fear and Trembling,* W. Lourie, trans. Doubleday, Garden City, N.Y., 1954
14. Campbell, J. *The Mythic Image.* Princeton University Press, Bollingen/Princeton, 1974, 430.
15. Lifton, R.J. "Medicalized Killing in Auschwitz," *Psychiatry,* vol. 45, no. 4, November 1982, 295.

16. Iyer, P. "A Mysterious Sect Gave Its Name to Political Murder." *Smithsonian,* October, 1986.
17. Deikman, A.J. *The Observing Self: Mysticism and Psychotherapy.* Beacon, Boston, 1982.
18. Nehru, J. *Toward Freedom.* Beacon, Boston, 1958.
19. *New Yorker,* October 13, 1986, 35–37.
20. James, W. See Introduction, n. 2, 326–333.
21. Brinkley, J. "Four Veterans Ending Fast on Policy in Nicaragua," *New York Times,* October 17, 1986.
22. I Cor. 3:18.
23. Dogen. *A Primer of Soto Zen: Translation of Shobogenzo Zuimonki,* R. Masunaga, trans. East-West Center Press, Honolulu, 1971.

10: MEANINGFUL DEATH

1. Ps. 23.
2. Buber, M. *I and Thou,* see Ch. II, n. 7.
3. "Phaedo," in *The Works of Plato.* See Ch. III, n. 12.
4. Yalom, I.D. *Existential Psychotherapy.* Basic Books, New York, 1980, 30.
5. Heidegger, M. *Being and Time,* J. Macquarrie, E. Robinson, trans. Harper & Row, New York, 1962.
6. Lifton, R.J. *The Life of the Self.* See Ch. IV, n. 34, 31.
7. *Dhammapada,* J. Mascaró, trans. See Ch. II, n. 2, 42, 56.
8. Senzaki, N. *Like a Dream, Like a Fantasy,* E. Shimano, ed. Japan Pub., Tokyo, 1978, 15.
9. Matt. 4.17.
10. Koran. See Ch. I, n. 5, III.
11. Eccles. 3.20.
12. Erikson, E. *Gandhi's Truth.* See Ch. I, n. 15, 195.
13. Erikson, E. "Eight Ages of Man." See Ch. IV, n. 23.
14. *Dhammapada.* 57.
15. Zimmer, H. *The King and the Corpse,* J. Campbell, ed. Princeton University Press, Princeton, N.J., 1971, 37.
16. I Cor. 15:55.
17. McNeil, W. *The Rise of the West.* Chicago University Press, Chicago, 1963, 336–353.
18. Koran. 257.

19. Lifton, R.J. 126.
20. Schell, J. "The Fate of the Earth," *New Yorker,* February 1, 8, 15, 1982.
21. Simpson, K. *The Mysteries of Life and Death.* Salamander Books, England, 1979. Pgs. 154–173.
22. Gen. 19:24–28.
23. Freud, S. *Future of an Illusion.* See Ch. II, n. 1, 23, 27, 88.
24. Becker, E. *Denial of Death.* See Ch. VIII, n. 8.
25. McNeil. Ibid. 115–129.
26. Thomas, L. "Death in the Open," in *The Lives of a Cell.* Viking, New York, 1974, 96–99.
27. Yalom, I. 115–129.
28. Thomas, L.
29. Levine, S. *Who Dies?* Doubleday, Anchor, Garden City, N.Y., 1982, 2, 14, 28, 200.
30. Kübler-Ross, E. *On Death and Dying.* Macmillan, New York, 1969.
31. Ibid., 265.
32. Ibid., 138.
33. Buber, M., quoted in *Martin Buber,* R.G. Smith. John Knox, Atlanta, 1975, 14.
34. Thoreau, H.D. *Walden,* Chapter 2, "Where I lived, and what I lived for."
35. Tillich, P. *The Courage to Be.* See Ch. VII, n. 27.
36. Lifton, R.J. 149.
37. Breo, D.L. *American Medical News,* November 14, 1986.
38. Levine, S. 183.
39. Milosz, C. "Unobtainable Earth," quoted in *New Yorker,* June 23, 1986, p. 18.
40. Thomas, D. *Collected Poems.* New Directions, New York, 1957, 128.
41. Yalom, I.D. 75–110.
42. Levine, S. 154–156.
43. Lifton, R.J. 141.
44. Huxley, L.A. *This Timeless Moment.* Celestial Arts, Millbrae, Calif., 1968.
45. Kaplan, A.H., and Rothman, D. "The Dying Psychotherapist," in *American Journal of Psychiatry,* May, 1986, vol. 143, no. 5, pp. 561–572.
46. Tagore, R. *Selected Poems,* see Ch. VIII, n. 36.
47. Tagore, R. Quoted in "American Friends Service Committee in New England," Cambridge, Mass., 1986–1987.

NOTES

48. Kübler-Ross, E. 259.
49. Kübler-Ross, E. 276.
50. Tagore, R. *Selected Poems,* Ibid, 107.
51. Zimmer, H. 44.

CONCLUSION

1. Quoted in: *Aditi: The Living Arts of India,* Smithsonian Institute Press, Washington D.C., 1985, 179.

Index

INDEX

INDEX

INDEX

INDEX

INDEX

Suzuki, D. T., 108, 122
Szaz, Dr. Thomas, 174

Tagore, Rabindranath, 76, 126,
  208–209, 216, 248, 249, 260
Tales of the Hasidim (Buber), 123
Tantrism, 180
Tapas, 220, 221, 223
Theravada Buddhism, 253
This Timeless Moment (Huxley), 254
Thomas, Dylan, 253
Thomas, Lewis, 244–45
Thoreau, Henry David, 64, 66, 249
Tillich, Paul, 129, 157–58, 173, 200;
  study of faith, 198
Timerman, Jacobo, 191
Tolstoy, Leo, 30, 64, 65, 118
Transcendental Meditation, 159, 160
Transference, 36, 83, 207
Trungpa, Chogyam, 129
Tyranny, 31

Unity, sense of, 30; *see also*
  Affirming acceptance
Upanishads, 70, 71, 72
Uruguay, 191

Valmiki, 151, 152, 161
*Varieties of Religious Experience,
  The* (James), 142
Varna, *see* Castes
Vedantic philosophy, 29–30
Vedas, 222, 223; worldview of the,
  154
Vietnam, 229
Vision quest, 67–68, 158, 159–60, 162,
  163
Vivekananda, 91

von Franz, Marie-Louise, 66
Voyeurism, case of, 39–41, 50–56

White, Lynn, 106–107
Whitman, Walt, 120–21, 155
Wholeness, *see* Affirming acceptance
Wilhelm, Richard, 12
Williams, William Carlos, 182–83
Witnessed significance, 5–20, 111, 132;
  case study, 5–7, 15–20; distortions
  of need for, 10–11; explanation of,
  7; grandiose strivings and, 9; mass
  movements to achieve, 9–10;
  positive results from need for,
  11–14, 15
Women, religious fundamentalism
  and orthodoxy and, 27–28
Wonder, 155–56, 158
World Congress of Religions, 91
Worldview (cosmos), 94, 132, 147–71,
  199, 202, 259; case studies, 148–49,
  158–64, 165–66, 169–72; deficient,
  152–53; described, 149–51; dreams
  and, 152; ecstasy and, 154–55, 158;
  sacrifice and, 228–29; sorrow and,
  156–58; therapy and shaping of,
  162; wonder and, 155–56, 158
World Wildlife Fund, 227

Yalom, Irving, 245
Yoga, 217

Zen, 91, 111, 122, 131, 241; poetry,
  196
Zen Mind, Beginner's Mind
  (Shunryu Suzuki Roshi), 131
Zimmer, Heinrich, 11–12, 61–62, 72,
  241, 260

288